CW00381652

NOT QUITE

34 Years in the Diplomatic Service

JOHN CRANE

ISBN:9781983206849

This book is dedicated to Valmai, my wife of over half a century, without whom all this, my career as well as the book, would not have been possible.

In particular, she and Stephanie, my daughter, have, over a long period, read and re-read a number of drafts and redrafts and offered many corrections and suggestions.

Any inaccuracies and errors that still remain are, of course, all my fault.

The cover picture is a cartoon of me taken from a poster by the late Eric Smith inviting members to a farewell drink at the Antigua Club when I left the island in 1986. I am standing in the doorway of the British High Commission Office in St John's.

CONTENTS

Foreword   4

Chapter 1 - London 1962-1964   13

Chapter 2 - Kampala 1964-1967   28

Chapter 3 - London 1967-1970   63

Chapter 4 - MECAS 1970-1972   80

Chapter 5 - Abu Dhabi 1972-1976   99

Chapter 6 - London 1976-1979   126

Chapter 7 - Damascus 1979-1983   140

Chapter 8 - Antigua 1983-1986   179

Chapter 9 - London 1986-1989   229

Chapter 10 - Jerusalem 1989-1993   246

Chapter 11 - Khartoum 1993-1997   282

FOREWORD

Friends and family have often said that I have had an interesting life and asked why don't I 'put it all down on paper'? All right then, I thought, I will. So here you are: my time in Her Majesty's Diplomatic Service.

I'm not quite sure how this book should be categorised. It's certainly not a biography in the normal sense; too restricted in time and lacking much personal detail and comment. A memoir then, I suppose, but not as formal as most.

It was in Khartoum that I came up with the words that I have used as the title of this book. The correct form of address for an ambassador is 'Your Excellency', but a chargé d'affaires is not due the title. Nevertheless, while chargé, I was occasionally addressed as 'Excellency', to which I responded: "Actually, I'm not quite excellent, but I am pretty good."

I first made a start on this project fairly soon after retiring in 1997, but progress was very spasmodic and without much progress until, finally in 2010, I was spurred on by my wife, Val, to sort through all the pictures and papers we had accumulated over our career. Then, after a completed first draft, the project again fell into abeyance for another 6 or 7 years.

You will note that I said 'our career' as she was with me practically the whole time, and her life was pretty well as much at the whim of the Office as was mine. Indeed, often she had the harder time of it when medical and family problems cropped up.

In spite of my reference to 'pictures and papers', this work is in fact mainly based on personal memories, plus two main documentary sources. Firstly, Val's copious diaries and secondly. a number of personal letters between Val and me when we found ourselves apart. and also between us and various family members while we were abroad, which was most of the time. This was helped when, after the deaths of our respective parents, we came across in their effects many of the letters we had written to them in earlier years. And, thanks to the Freedom of Information Act, I have also had the benefit and occasional embarrassment, of having been able to refer to parts of my personal FCO file. In addition, to refresh my memory on some of the historical background and check on one or two dates, I have used the excellent facilities of the Internet.

So, first of all, a bit of preliminary background. The fact that I got a job, and spent most of my working life, in the Foreign Office, as most people still refer to it, surprised a lot of people; including me, when I think about it. I come from a family that had had no graduates in it until my younger brother. and so a degree was not on my horizon, quite apart from the fact that I left school at sixteen. But, as most people who have served in the Diplomatic Service to the end of their working life seem to agree, the job itself was really an education, as well as a very interesting and rewarding career.

I actually started my government service with the Commonwealth Relations Office (CRO) in October 1962. This was my third employment since dropping out of school in 1959 and I stayed on until I was 54, taking early retirement from its successor, the Foreign and Commonwealth Office (FCO), in January 1997. During my time, I reached the high point of my career when, from January 1994 to April 1995, I ran the British Embassy in Khartoum as Chargé d'Affaires. It was by no means a large embassy, but Sudan at the time was the largest country in Africa by area. and that makes it sound pretty important, so I usually find a chance to drop that fact into conversations.

These days, spending over 34 years with one employer would probably be seen as indicating a certain lack of ambition. I am inclined to accept this as fair comment on my character, although in mitigation, they do things differently in the past, and at the time I joined, it was still the general expectation, at least in my family, that you should get a good job and stick with it for life. This was what my father did: he was an employee of Lloyds Bank the whole of his working life, apart from a period of national service during the Second World War. So the fact that this was my third job since leaving school was regarded by my parents as worrying.

Although I stayed with one employer for more than a third of a century I moved around and, apart from a variety of jobs in London, I travelled quite widely in the Middle East and eastern Africa, as well as doing one stint in the West Indies. During my time I effectively changed jobs on average every three years and have, in the course of my career, had a go at pretty well every task in the Diplomatic Service from repetitious clerical chores to dealing with a foreign government.

You will notice that, as my story moves through time and I progress through the ranks, my viewpoint changes. Naturally the perspectives available to a clerk on the one hand, and to an acting head of mission on the other, are very different, even when they may be the same person. Not only does the world look different, but they are treated differently and the work and the people dealt with both become more interesting.

I have met some famous people along the way and I'm conscious of a good deal of what could be regarded as name-dropping in this book, but after all I actually did meet the Queen as well as her husband, her sister, two Archbishops of Canterbury, Douglas Hurd, Desmond Tutu, Michael Hesseltine, James Callaghan, Sarah Ferguson, Terry Waite, et al – and to that extent they are part of my story, and I'm certainly not going to leave them out.

During my time I worked in a number of home departments, two high commissions, three embassies and a consulate general, as well as attending a full-time language-training course. We lived in eleven units of official accommodation overseas, plus living for just over seven months in a hotel in Kampala and about three months in a hostel in Jerusalem. I have worked in some fifteen different countries, counting a number of short official visits from London when on a home posting, and to neighbouring posts while overseas. We also lived at various times in three different houses in the UK, so we had a lot of experience in packing, moving and unpacking over the years covered by the book. As a result, for a while after retirement, it seemed strange that we were now going to stay put.

Over the years I have accumulated a number of mementoes, both physical and abstract. In the first category are old driving licences and identity cards in various languages, as well a visitor's permit to the US Naval Base on Antigua and a number of passports with diplomatic visas and entry and exit stamps. In the second is a far more eclectic collection, but this time of information. This includes some knowledge of the histories of East Africa, the West Indies and the Middle East, a background to Islam and Arab history, a fairly detailed knowledge of British nationality legislation up to 1981 and a broad general understanding of nuclear power and radioactivity, including what happened at Chernobyl. And, of course, a basic knowledge of Arabic, as well as a couple of words of Hebrew and Swahili. None of this is much use to me today, although the knowledge element allows me to pontificate to those whose knowledge of the particular subject is nil (or, at least, less than mine). And I'm often quite useful in the occasional pub quiz.

One aspect of our life overseas was that, in most countries, we could not be anonymous. Apart from usually having to carry a diplomatic identity card, the registration of our car, invariably in a special series for diplomats, meant we were always identifiable in public. In addition, in some countries we were followed, or reported on, when we moved around outside the capital. And in Syria, Jerusalem and Sudan we took it for granted that our phones were tapped by the local security bodies as a matter of course.

And while on the subject of espionage, I should emphasise that diplomats are not spies. The closest I ever came to spying was attending the 'Spy School' in Lebanon, which, as I explain in the chapter on MECAS, wasn't anything of the sort. Oh, and once I was approached by one of the security services with what I think was a view to recruiting me, but I pretended I hadn't understood and they then left me alone.

Over my career, I was subject to an annual performance report. The pattern of the report itself changed over the years, but it was usually along the lines of a general description of the officer, both physically and temperamentally, an evaluation of their work over the period in question, and then a series of markings on certain qualities and aspects of their character. There was also a section confirming that any shortcomings identified had been discussed, objectives for the coming year agreed and other plans for the future made.

In my early years the reports were not shown to the officer. Although reporting officers could do so if they wished, very few did. The officer's wife was also reported on. Female officers who married had to resign, so there were no husbands - and certainly no unmarried partners. Clearly this was not in relation to any work, but as far as general character and background were concerned.

There was also a provision for an estimate of what rank the reportee could be expected to reach before retirement. I don't know how much this last part of the exercise was worth for new recruits, as it required the reporting officer to gaze pretty well forty years into the future based on twelve months observation of a still developing individual. It was massively subjective, and very few reporting officers would allow themselves to foresee their underling reaching a higher rank than their own current one.

My own report in January 1964 opined that I had "...shown considerable improvement during the past few months and become a useful Clerk. More experience [was] needed."

During my later years of service, reports were handed to the officer to read before being discussed and signed off and the wife was no longer mentioned. While this latter point is understandable from the point of view of privacy and so on, it can hardly be argued that the attitude, appearance and behaviour of a wife had no bearing on the work of the embassy and, by extension, the career of her husband. For example, if the wife was known to be habitually drunk by 10.00 a.m. and generally free with her favours, this could hardly have passed without comment and would certainly damage the image of the embassy and of Britain in general. I must say that, during my career, I have never come across any wife who remotely fits this description. However, I have certainly come across instances where a wife's attitude and character had been a distinct benefit or handicap to their husband's career.

Of course, while this system applied, Val was reported on and almost invariably attracted positive comments. I say 'almost' to allow for the mention made of her in my June 1974 report. My reporting officer at the time recorded that he found her "...incredibly and disarmingly absent-minded. A charming and endlessly good-natured person." With which both comments very few people would disagree, I think. She certainly did no harm to my career; in fact in many ways she often took to the representational duties of the job better than I did.

Obviously, this book is not in the same category as the memoirs of a number of retired senior FCO officials: those in the ranks of the 'The Great and the Good'. Although, did I mention that I have met the occasional famous person? I believe I did, but, in truth, I was never much more than a 'spear carrier' on the diplomatic stage and my direct experience of, and influence on, affairs of state was minimal.

So this is a mostly chronological ramble through my memories of these 34-odd years (while I can still find the way), with a record of the bits that I find interesting. I hope you will too.

CHAPTER 1

LONDON 1962 – 1964

Slightly before ten o'clock on the morning of Monday the 15th of October 1962, I walked into 4 Central Buildings, Matthew Parker Street in Westminster (now apparently occupied by the headquarters of the Conservative Party) to report for my first day of employment with Her Majesty's Government as a clerical officer in the Commonwealth Relations Office (CRO). Purely coincidentally, it was the day after my twentieth birthday.

Some four weeks previously, I had received a letter confirming my appointment, and welcoming me to the CRO. This was to be my third job since leaving school in July 1959, some three months before my seventeenth birthday. Like this one, both the others were clerical, first with the P&O shipping company in the City of London, and then with the Eastbourne Waterworks Company in, of course, Eastbourne. I had considered applying for a position in the Foreign Office (FO) several years before as I was attracted to working overseas, but the entrance requirement, even at clerical level, had seemed to me pretty stiff, so I never followed this up.

I then realised that the CRO offered very similar opportunities of overseas travel, but was a

Home Civil Service department and had the slightly less daunting Home Civil Service entry requirements. So, I took the entrance exam for appointment as a clerical officer, putting the CRO as my first choice of department, and was successful. Within three years the CRO and FO were merged anyway, to form the FCO, so I was in, if not through the back door, then a side door, so to speak

On the day of my joining, after my introductory talk, during which I was required to sign the Official Secrets Act, I was put to work in the Pensions Section of the Accountant General's Department, which was also in 4 Central Buildings.

The CRO had been formed from the amalgamation of the Dominions Office, which had dealt with the 'Old Commonwealth' countries, with the India Office, when India had been partitioned and India and Pakistan had achieved independence in 1947. Pensions Section was a hangover from this time, and was basically the bit of the old India Office that dealt with the payment of retirement pensions to former military and civil servants of the Raj or their dependants, of which there were still large numbers in 1962. It had more recently also taken over similar pensions paid to colonial civil servants retiring from Nigeria, but not, oddly enough, other recently independent countries, such as Ghana.

The section was mostly staffed by young junior recent recruits, who were all looking for an overseas posting. The rest were much older hands, who had been around for some time, and whose last thought was of going abroad. The CRO being a Home Civil Service department, there was no commitment to overseas service. However, it did provide the staff for high commissions around the world, (as well as, for historical reasons, the British Embassy in Dublin.) Because this was the early 1960s, these were being opened up all the time as territories gained their independence, and there was a need for increasing numbers of staff overseas.

The way the overseas jobs were allocated was for Personnel Department to circulate a list of forthcoming vacancies and ask for volunteers. The result was that pretty well all we youngsters put our names down for everything at our respective grades every time and then often forgot what we'd asked for. There was a lower age limit of 21, as this was still the age of majority, and to send a younger person overseas could apparently create a legal problem. So, for my first year with the CRO, I was not eligible for an overseas posting.

Apart from the support grades of secretarial, paper-keeping, security and housekeeping, there were three main branches in the Home Civil Service; clerical, executive and administrative. At the bottom were clerical assistants who were recruited from bright boys and girls with fewer than five 'O' levels, next came clerical officers, who came in with five or more 'O' levels and then executive officers, who had at least two 'A' levels. (The Foreign Service had an equivalent structure, but with different grade titles and nothing equating to clerical assistants). It was from these three grades that all of us in the younger group came.

Promotion from the clerical to the executive branch by seniority or by competition (exam) was normal, but promotion to the administrative branch by internal competition, although possible, was quite rare. This last was the graduate entry grade and the one most people think of when the words 'civil servant' or 'diplomat' are mentioned. Normally, recruitment into this grade was by way of an external competition, with the prior qualification of a good degree (usually, but not necessarily, from Oxbridge) or an equivalent entrance exam, this last often taken by retirees from the commissioned ranks of the armed forces.

In times of full employment, there tended to be qualification creep, when those having the minimum entry qualification for the higher grade, but failing to get in, would take a job at a lower one. In 1962 there were already a few graduates in the executive intake, who hadn't got a good enough degree and who came in at this level with a view to trying for quick promotion through the internal competition to the administrative ranks.

National Service having only recently been abolished, almost every male in the department over the age of 23 had done time in the armed forces, the older ones during the last war. Among the most senior members of the section were two men who had been evacuated at Dunkirk. The older of them went even further back. He had joined the cavalry as a boy soldier in about 1913 and claimed to be able to recall the drill with lances. He had seen out the First World War and reached the rank of sergeant major before his discharge in the 1930s, and then was called up again at the start of the Second World War. He struck us all as terribly old and was certainly the oldest person in the room, but he must have been under 65.

The hours of work in Pensions Section were strictly nine to five, with an hour for lunch, Monday to Friday, Saturday morning working having been done away with a few years earlier. Everybody had to sign an attendance book on arrival in the morning, and sharply at nine the most senior executive officer ruled a red line across the page under the last signature. Anybody arriving after that would have to sign under the line indicating their tardy arrival.

It was all very Dickensian, as was the method of payment of the pensions. The calculations were recorded by hand in huge loose-leaf ledgers, each sheet of which was numbered and the issue of which was registered. Once a month, the payments themselves were sent, either as instructions by post to the appropriate bank, or made by hand-written payable orders posted to the pensioner.

Many of the former servants of the Raj had

settled elsewhere overseas and the governments in many other Commonwealth countries and some colonies paid on our instruction and accounted to us periodically. Usually this was simply by a copy of a list of payees and amounts, but I remember that New Zealand was very up to date, and also sent us the punched cards representing the computerised payments under their system. We never knew what to do with these cards. They were much too bulky to file in the ordinary way and, as this was the civil service in the 1960s, to just throw them away went severely against the grain, but I think that is what happened to them eventually.

The man in charge of the section was a bit of a throwback. The signing in process, of course, didn't apply to him and he came in slightly late every morning. We were on the ground floor of the building, and the whole department was in an open-plan design, but he had a partitioned cubicle in one corner, with windows in it at a height of about five and a half feet, so that he had to stand to peer out at his domain, which he did periodically. Balding, rotund, bespectacled and with a moustache, he habitually came to work wearing a bowler hat and carrying an umbrella and brief case, he was a cartoonist's caricature of a civil servant. But he was only a higher executive officer, which, at his age of, I suppose, the mid-fifties, was nothing to be proud of. The word was that he had been promoted to the grade during the war when staff were scarce. This was, of course, now some twenty years ago and he clearly wasn't going to be promoted again.

Apart from signing the Official Secrets Act when I joined, I was issued with my pass. All government buildings had security officers on the doors and there was a system of passes, involving pieces of pasteboard with different coloured patterns, one for each building. In modern terms, these were pitifully inadequate. I think we were required to sign them, but there was no photograph and no security features, as we understand them today, simply a complex coloured pattern printed onto the card. Moreover, if you were entitled to use a canteen in another building, then you were issued with a pass for that building as well. As there were a number of canteens in government buildings around Whitehall, it was perfectly possible to have a considerable collection of these cards. Of course, they were passed around as people wanted to visit various canteens. On top of all this, in most instances, the inspection of the passes by the security guards was very cursory.

In starting the new job, I was determined to avoid the commuting journey from Eastbourne, which I had made when working for the P & O and so, in December, I moved into a flat in Warwick Road, Earl's Court, sharing with Larry Newall-Smith, a friend from Eastbourne. We had two rooms and a kitchen on the second floor, and the use of the bathroom and toilet on the half landing between us and the first floor flat, which was occupied by our landlady. It was to be my home in London for the next eighteen months or so. The flat above us was the top one in the building, and was occupied by the artist Bridget Riley, who had her studio high under the roof. She is now world-famous for her 'op art', which she was clearly producing at this time. We didn't see her often, just occasionally bumping into her on the stairs.

Just after the 1962 Christmas holiday the worst winter for decades started, with temperatures dropping below freezing and heavy snow; conditions which didn't really improve substantially for nearly three months. Our flat was heated by coin-operated gas fires, and these still worked, but even so the flat became barely habitable. Not only did the incoming water pipes freeze, but so did the waste pipe from the kitchen. So, even when we got some water from Larry's aunt next door to do our washing and the washing up, we had to take the waste water down the half flight to the toilet and pour it down the pan. Fortunately, the toilet down pipe was apparently too wide to freeze.

After some months Pensions Section moved from Central Buildings to Palace Chambers on Westminster Bridge Road, immediately opposite Big Ben. It was an old Victorian building and has long since been demolished for the construction of

Portcullis House. The entrance was through a hall with a rather worn and uneven tiled floor from which two lifts operated. On the right was a sort of concertina mesh affair which was operated by a man whose sole duties were to open and shut the doors and operate the lift by pressing buttons. This could easily have been done by the passengers, and often was at the end of the day, when the operator had finished work. But at the time there was a strict government policy of providing employment for the war wounded, although I don't recall him having any visible war wound.

However, on the other side of the entrance hall was another, much smaller lift. It consisted of a little wooden cabin, which could only take three or four people, and through which passed a vertical rope apparently connected to a pulley and counterweight at the top of the building. The rope was pulled one way or the other, and the lift would move the opposite direction. It was easy to identify the war wound of this operator, as he had only one arm. That, of course, was all he needed to do the job and it produced much comment amongst us.

The CRO took over only a couple of floors of Palace Chambers; the rest of the building being occupied by commercial firms. The whole appearance was very down-at-heel and there was a ban in some rooms on any heavy items, for instance filing cabinets full of papers, being placed in the centre of the floor as apparently this was unsafe and might cause collapse to the floor below. The back windows of the building overlooked Westminster Underground station. This was when only the District and Circle line ran through, and there was no roof over the station, just canopies over the platforms, so we could look down on the trains.

At the start of 1964, military insurrections in the newly-independent countries of Kenya, Uganda and Tanganyika, known as the 'East African Mutinies' generated a huge amount of telegraphic traffic for the CRO, and a call went out for clerical volunteers to do overtime in Communications Department. I jumped at the chance of a little (and it was little) extra pay and volunteered. For a few weeks I was working there in the evenings after the end of my normal day, sorting telegrams in and out of dispatch boxes.

At the end of one of these evening sessions I had arranged to meet Valmai Jones on the corner of Whitehall and Downing Street. There were no gates across Downing Street then and, in fact, you could walk the length of it to St James's Park. I had met Valmai about five years earlier while we were both (separately) at school in Eastbourne. She had come up to London a couple of years before as a trainee nurse, and I had been seeing her on and off over the years, both in Eastbourne, and, more recently, in London.

A few months later, I was getting frustrated

with the lack of an overseas posting and actually went as far as answering an advert for a job with the Dexion company, which made adjustable metal storage shelving. I went for an interview somewhere in the northern suburbs of London, and had even been accepted for a job as a sales rep, working in Sussex, when my posting came through. I was offered the position of Assistant Passport Officer in Kampala, Uganda and immediately accepted.

My posting crystallised things in my relationship with Valmai and on Sunday 24th of May I took her out for the day from Brookwood Hospital in Surrey, where she was then working, and proposed to her in the evening. She accepted, and we were married on 18th of July. It had been intended that I travel to post by sea via Mombasa as that was the normal route to East Africa at the time. The date of the marriage meant that we could instead travel by air and still arrive by the due date, but the timing was tight, and we had a number of things to deal with before that.

First of all, there was a medical examination before posting. No allowances would be paid until this had been done. Later in my career, this was varied to apply only to officers and dependants over a certain age; 50, I think. Once medically cleared, we were covered overseas by the Diplomatic Service Medical Scheme (DSMS) which was intended to provide cover comparable to what would be available under the NHS at home. In many parts of the world this meant the Office would pay for private treatment, as the local state provision would be well below British standards. We were expected, though, to make sure we used the NHS to have check ups when we were on leave.

Pay overseas was slightly different from at home. My normal salary was the same, but I was additionally paid allowances. The basic overseas allowance was to permit us to live at the level the Treasury reckoned we would be able to on our basic salary in Orpington, which was selected as a typical residential town within the London commuting area. The extra cost of goods and services, due to our being overseas was calculated as an annual amount and paid monthly.

Whenever there was a post inspection, the inspectors always reviewed this particular allowance and there was invariably a heated discussion about what was or wasn't a reasonable expense. The calculation was based on a 'basket' of items laid down by the Treasury and there could be no negotiations on it. So the argument was based on the availability and cost locally of these items, or what could be considered reasonable substitutes. The inspectors themselves would go around the local shops and markets to check the prices.

But you often got this money up front. Two lump sums were paid when you first went abroad or were posted overseas after a period at home: an 'advance of allowances' and a car loan. This first was intended to allow you to kit yourself out and stock up on goods you would need at post. In effect it was an interest-free cash loan.

The car loan recognised that you would have to buy a car specifically for overseas use. For junior officers this meant that nothing much more than a basic small family car could be bought, whereas more senior officers were allowed to have progressively grander cars. However, it was not possible for junior officers to buy and freight, say, a Rolls Royce and claim the allowance and cost of freighting of Mini; if they were to do that, they would get nothing.

The loan and the advance of allowances were repayable over the first two years of posting. The Office would also pay for the freight to post of a car suitable for your grade and this was paid outright. When I first joined, it was a condition of the loan and freight on a car that it should be British, although this was later relaxed. HM Customs & Excise permitted the use of an export car for a period in the UK before departure.

The effect of all this was that, following the announcement of my posting to Kampala, we suddenly had a fairly large amount of money available to spend. And spend it we did - apart from anything else, of course, we would be setting up home for the first time.

My new job required detailed knowledge of

nationality legislation and immigration procedures, which were all new to me and I had to absorb the basics of these before going to post. So, in the midst of all my other preparations, I left my job with Pensions Section and was attached to the CRO Consular Department for instruction on these subjects. As part of this training, I went to the General Records Office at Somerset House to learn how to register births and deaths of UK citizens, as this was something that was just about to be introduced in Commonwealth countries. I was also sent to the Passport Office, which was then part of the Foreign Office, to be introduced to the mysteries of issuing British passports.

After we returned from our honeymoon in the West Country, we stayed with my parents for a few days before our departure. We were booked to travel to Entebbe, Uganda's international airport, leaving on the 31st of July, but I had got it fixed in my mind that we were to travel on the 1st of August, which was the day we would have arrived and rather stupidly never looked at the tickets again to check. The result was a tetchy phone call from the Office early on the 1st of August, just as we were preparing to leave for the airport, asking why we weren't already in Africa. I was ashamed and embarrassed, nay, mortified; here was the first move of my career and the first serious responsibility of my married life and I'd blown it.

The Office claimed it was not possible to rebook the tickets straight away, but I don't know why as flights then were normally far from full. Anyway, as I had no more leave due to me, I had to return to work in London for another week or so, and we eventually flew out on Sunday the 9th of August. Both our families accompanied us from Eastbourne to Heathrow Airport, even though the flight was due to depart at ten in the evening, and it was just getting dark as we took off. Before that, though, the weather was fine and so, after we checked in in very good time, we all went up on the roof of the sole terminal building to watch the aircraft come and go, as you did then.

Val's parents had given her a little posy of flowers as parting gift and she clutched these the whole time we were whiling away the minutes. When we two eventually went down again and through the departure gate, the rest of the family all went back up on the roof to see us go. My mother later told me they all waved like mad at us as we walked across the tarmac to the plane., but our thoughts and sights were set on the future and neither of us looked back.

CHAPTER 2

KAMPALA 1964 – 1967

Our flight to Entebbe was overnight, but it did involve two stops, first at Frankfurt and then at Benghazi. This last must have been only for refuelling, I think, as I don't remember anybody joining or leaving the flight in Libya. Benghazi Airport was a quiet place while we were there; no other planes were around and the only activity, apart from the refuelling of our BOAC Comet, was a Libyan army sergeant riding past in the dark on a bicycle. As was usual in 1964, the plane was far from full.

These are not very prominent memories. One novelty of the journey remains firmly in mind, though. In the Benghazi Airport transit lounge, we saw tea bags for the first time. They had not been introduced in Britain yet; at least we had never seen them. Val was unhappy to see a piece of cardboard on a bit of string dangling over the edge of her cup of tea and didn't know what to do with it. She left it there to start with, but eventually took it out, by which time she found the tea undrinkable. The intrusion into tradition represented by this novelty rankled with her, but in Uganda, she was glad to discover, the old ways still held sway and she resisted the use of tea bags for some years

28

afterwards.

So, early the following morning, Monday the 10th of August, we arrived in Uganda at Entebbe airport. It was only just over a year after Kenya, the final part of the old British East Africa, had reached Independence and within a few months we would be seeing the celebrations of the second anniversary of Uganda's Independence. The East African Mutinies had been put down at the start of the year and the area was politically pretty quiet, at least on the surface.

Most of the federal mechanisms introduced to East Africa by Britain since the 1920s were still in place. There were common postal, railway, monetary and air transport systems and the border between Uganda and Kenya was marked by a police sergeant standing in the middle of the road checking vehicles. The East African shilling was the common currency throughout Kenya, Uganda and Tanganyika and was at par with the British shilling. As a result, British postal orders could be bought in East African post offices and cashed in UK at face value, a currency control loophole that was not stopped for a little while. Further south in Africa, none of the other British territories had yet quite gained independence, although the count down had started in most and Southern Rhodesia was soon to be in revolt.

Uganda had been a protectorate rather than a colony and the white population had always been comparatively small, but there were still several hundred in the country. Although a couple of training or specialist officers in the army or police remained, most of the Europeans in government positions were leaving at about the time we arrived; and when we eventually moved into our bungalow, we took over the cat of a departing Brit who was leaving his post as an under secretary in the Uganda Government.

Uganda had come to Independence with a constitution that seemed a good idea at the time. The various traditional rulers of the tribal areas that made up the country were to take turns at being non-executive president. The vice president was the next ruler in line for the presidency. The first to get the title of President had been the Kabaka of Buganda, the area in which Kampala was. Something similar had also been instigated at Independence in Malaya, where, in the new federation, the sultans of the various constituent parts took turns at being king. It worked there - and still does. In Uganda it hardly lasted three years.

The Kabaka ruled the Baganda tribe, whose language was Luganda and had its own legislature, the Lukiko, which had a sort of county council responsibility for Buganda. The scope for confusion between the positions held by one person of tribal leader and titular president of the country of which the tribal area formed part were, in retrospect anyway, great and we were to see the overthrow of this system and the introduction of a new republic during our time there.

Meanwhile, back at the airport....

Before being able to actually get off the plane we had to suffer the indignity of being sprayed with insecticide by a Ugandan official with a hand operated pump. This was apparently to kill off any dangerous bugs we might be introducing to Africa from Europe. At the door of the plane, when we got there, the first impression I remember was that somebody had left the heating up too high. It was early in the morning, but the day was hot and bright and quite humid. Entebbe stands on the edge of Lake Victoria, so the air was moist as well as warm and smelled - different.

In contrast with our first attempt to get to post, when we had failed to arrive, this time it was the post's turn to fail; there was nobody from the High Commission to greet us and see us through the arrival procedures. Actually, the plane was early, I think. Anyway, unaided, we passed through immigration and customs. At the latter, Val was forced to give up her little bunch of flowers which she had cared for since our departure from London. They were a bit sad by now, but they were her link with England on her trip into the unknown and she had been going to keep them for as long as possible. She felt the otherwise insignificant bureaucratic niggle quite sharply.

With complete and, it should be said, probably naïve faith that there would eventually be somebody along to meet us, we turned down all offers of taxis into Kampala and sat on a bench outside the rather modest terminal building with our suitcases beside us and waited. This trust was rewarded when my new boss, Al Harrington, eventually arrived, very flustered, to take us into Kampala. He was thirty-one, but looked older and seemed to me at the time to be quite a senior person in both senses. It was because of his cries of overwork that my new job had been created. However, a couple of years after my arrival, when his successor went on leave for nearly two months, I was to run the Passport Section single-handed and caught up on a backlog in the processing of passports to boot.

Al took us to Kampala, a half-hour drive away, in his own car. I can't now remember why he used his own car, as normally new arrivals at post have an office car laid on; maybe he was not able to get one so early in the day or had forgotten to order it the day before. I noted that the road we travelled on the way into town was tarmac and had a good surface, but was no wider than an English country road, although generally without the bends. It was also without hedges, so on this journey we got our first view of typical African rural life, with its simple huts and houses, small plots of agriculture and the pervasive impression left by the rich, red, fertile soil. This is known as murram and is common throughout much of Africa.

The Harringtons very kindly offered us lunch, but first we checked into the Grand Hotel, Kampala, where we were to be staying initially. This was the best hotel in town at the time and had, until just before Independence, been called the Imperial Hotel. The wind of change having gusted round the owner, an Asian named Kassim-Lakha, the name was changed to a version more in tune with the times. The expression 'politically correct' was not known then, but that's what it was. However, the faint image of the old name could still easily be made out on the glass lamp bowls at the entrance and the replacement of the cutlery and crockery had proved too expensive, so there were plenty of reminders of the Imperial past. In another sense, this was also still in evidence in the person of the staff manageress; an elderly British lady who bossed the African personnel as she presumably always had. The hotel manager, too, was British: a tall, languid and effete man who fawned on Kassim-Lakha when the latter visited from (I think) Nairobi.

In this establishment, we were given an en suite room in the new wing on the ground floor. It was perfectly adequate as hotel rooms go, but a bit small for what turned out to be our peculiar circumstances, as this was to be our home for the next seven months and three days, while waiting for our permanent residence to be made ready for occupation. I have always suspected that this was a record of some sort in the Diplomatic Service. There was a reference to the delay made on my file in 1965 with the comment that "…. this does not seem to have left any sourness." Not an entirely accurate reflection of our attitude.

The delay was a result of a stupid oversight in the Administration Section of the High Commission. As I was filling a new post, there was no predecessor's accommodation for us to take over, which is the normal arrangement. A small semi-detached bungalow had been identified for us, though, and this should have been ready a month or so after we arrived. But there had been no thorough structural survey when it was bought and when one was carried out, it was discovered that the roof needed re-tiling. This naturally increased the cost and there was no money for this until the next financial year. So we could not move in until then and eventually had access to our first home of our marriage shortly after the following Easter. I strongly suspect that the cost of accommodating us in the hotel was a lot more than the cost of re-tiling the roof.

A week after we arrived, another couple on their first posting joined us in the hotel; Mike Abrams and his new wife, Chris. Mike was also a clerical officer and was to work in a new position in the Administration Section and so was also arriving without a predecessor. The Abramses had been allocated the semi-detached bungalow next to ours, so had a similar long wait in the hotel. Inevitably we were lumped together in everybody's minds and invited together to the various welcoming entertainments given by our new colleagues. Fortunately, we got on well and tended to go around together anyway as we did have a lot in common; both of the same grade, about the same age and both newly married.

During our early few weeks while we were in the hotel, Val had the first of a number of medical misfortunes of our married life when she suffered a miscarriage. This threw a very poor light on how weak the Office was in those days in matters of welfare. It was known in the High Commission what had happened, in fact the wife of the Second Secretary (Administration) happened to be with Val at the time. She personally was very supportive and helpful, but I can remember no formal reaction from the High Commission; no sympathetic calls, flowers or even suggestions of a medical check-up. And, something that rankled at the time, no suggestion that we should be better looked after than in the hotel. Moreover, as I have since discovered, nothing of this was noted on my personal file.

At the time of our arrival, the High Commission in Kampala was housed on three sites. First there was a two-storey building that had been a small hotel, which contained the bulk of the office, then a shop-fronted property on the main road where the

Information Section lived, and lastly, the first floor of a bank building down the hill from the other two where I laboured in the Passport Section. Later we all moved into a new purpose-built building, which included all these parts.

As I have mentioned, my position at work was Assistant Passport Officer, my boss of course being the Passport Officer. In addition to the main job of passport issuing, we also dealt with immigration, which was predominantly issuing entry certificates. In 1964 an entry certificate was the rubber stamp needed by a citizen of another Commonwealth country to enter the UK. It was only a few years since Commonwealth citizens hadn't needed even this. The reasoning was that, as notional British subjects, they were free to come and go in the mother country. This was fine until they started to come in large numbers and then not go again.

One of the main requirements for the issue of a visitor's entry certificate was evidence that the applicant was coming back. At the most basic, this would involve the production of an air ticket with a confirmed date of return, but it was quite easy to cash in the return half and simply stay in the UK. I came up with a cunning plan to avoid this. I would stamp the return coupon of the ticket with the High Commission official date stamp and write the words 'Not to be refunded without reference to this office' across it. In fact, this had no legal force, but it did make some of them think. And on one occasion we had a visit from a worried traveller who wanted to cancel the whole ticket, but was being stopped by an overcautious airline clerk.

Some foreigners required visas to enter the UK and we dealt with those too, using a different rubber stamp, but we issued very few in Kampala. We also issued visas on behalf of colonial administrations, of which there were still a fair number. These usually had to be referred back to the relevant capital for authority, although some we could issue off our own bat, subject to conditions listed in a reference book. Among these were visas for Chinese diplomatic couriers travelling to soon-to-be independent territories such as Nyasaland (now Malawi) and Northern Rhodesia (now Zambia) where Chinese embassies were being set up. These, of course, all had to be referred.

We issued quite a lot of these visas and, as I was the contact the Chinese had for this, Val and I received an invitation to the next National Day celebration at the Chinese Embassy. The Cultural Revolution was in full swing at the time and relations between the UK and China were pretty frosty so, the High Commissioner, who must also have received an invitation, sent his deputy. But nobody in the High Commission had considered that a clerk from the Passport Section might be invited and, for my part, I was completely naïve about political protocol and hadn't mentioned the invitation to anybody else. So, Val and I politely greeted the Deputy High Commissioner and his wife when we met them and regarded it as rather rude when they left early as a diplomatic snub. We stayed on and were much photographed looking at pictures of Chinese achievements. Strictly, this was a diplomatic *faux pas*, but, as far as I recall, nobody ever mentioned it to me.

The main task of the Passport Office, of course, was the issue of British passports, a good ninety percent of which were to Asians of Indian or Pakistani descent or, in many cases, birth. Almost all of these had no connection with the United Kingdom and their grounds for citizenship were to be found in the inner workings of the British Nationality Act 1948 and the various Independence Acts of the African territories where many had been born. As I mentioned earlier, I had been on a nationality course in London and the application of what I had been taught I found much to my liking and I was soon an expert on the intricacies of this legislation and have regarded myself as one ever since, as many bored interlocutors could attest.

Many applicants could not be issued with British passports, as they had lost UK citizenship when they became citizens of one or other of the newly independent countries. And some holders of British passports issued in these countries were no longer entitled to them. These we withdrew and cancelled. This naturally produced some very unhappy people. It was now that I became aware of the pressures that could be brought to bear as a result of the common assumption in some societies that everything must have its price. We had to be aware that friendly approaches and unsolicited gifts came with an expected quid pro quo. And sometimes the attitude was blunt. I remember a Sikh shouting in the Passport Office waiting room that he would pay £50 for a British passport - a tidy sum in 1965.

There was also a rule that we should not accept passport applications from agents. For practical reasons this rule was only partially observed. It was far easier to deal with an honest agent, who knew the rules well and would sift out impossible cases rather than go through the bother of considering them all ourselves. We had two or three agents we dealt with and a number of others we didn't.

Part of my duties was to check details of passports reported lost in other parts of the world that had been issued in Kampala. As far as the ones we had issued since Independence were concerned, this was a straightforward comparison with our files, but the records of those issued by the pre-Independence Protectorate authorities were Uganda Government documents. The records relating to these were kept at the Ugandan Immigration Office, which was a few hundred yards away from the High Commission. Each week I would send off the list of the passport files I would like to check to the person in charge of the records, a gentleman of Goan origin.

He very kindly allowed me space and time in the Immigration Office to go through the application records and compare the descriptions and photographs. The process was greatly assisted by the fact that the person in overall charge of the Ugandan Passport Office was a taciturn Scot who was finishing off his time under his Colonial Office terms of service for pension purposes. After a time the gradual process of Africanisation meant that both the Scot and the Goan were replaced by Ugandan Africans who were either unable or unwilling to provide the same level of co-operation. But this was towards the end of my time and the future checking was a problem my successor inherited.

Apart from us two UK-based officers in the Passport Section, the staff consisted of a number of locally engaged staff, all ladies who were the wives and, in one case, daughter, of various Brits living and working in Kampala. Apart from the daughter, they were all older than I was and some easily old enough to be my mother and, in one case, my grandmother. Not only was I young, but also tended to take myself very seriously and they greeted my arrival with some amusement. I was the butt of some fairly amiable banter and leg pulling, but I knew my job and I like to think that they came to respect me, even if only because I had such a nice wife. When we eventually left three years later, the staff being substantially the same, the farewell was quite emotional.

In Kampala I was introduced to the very civilised FCO system of the provision of British newspapers and periodicals for the benefit of staff overseas. The total number of UK-based staff in a mission was used to calculate a number of periodicals, both daily and weekly, which would be supplied by London for circulation. Within these limits, the choice of the actual publications was left to the mission to decide from a list of possibles.

Thus, I became for a time a regular reader of The Times. Regular, but often two or more weeks in arrears, as the papers were circulated in seniority order and I was well down the distribution list, although I think one of the security guards was below me. Senior staff were never all that prompt in passing the paper on. Both The Times and The Telegraph at that time had airmail editions, which were printed on very thin paper to keep postage costs down. They were very flimsy and so my copy of The Times was considerably crumpled and often torn by the time it reached me.

Another thing that we were introduced to for the first time while in Kampala was the daily requirement to take a malaria prophylactic pill. This necessity cropped up from time to time in our subsequent posts when these were also in malarial areas. Not all members of staff were scrupulously observant in taking their pills, but as far as I recall there were no cases of malaria among staff in any of my posts. The pills we took were called Paludrine, but unfortunately the US diplomatic medical authorities recommended and supplied for their overseas staff another drug called Chloroquine, which was taken weekly. The difference caused some discussion about the relative benefits of the two drugs by those with contacts in the American Embassy. The main attraction of Chloroquine, of course, was that it was not taken daily. Naturally both national medical authorities were aware of the other's views, but firmly stuck to their own and refused to supply any malarial prophylactic other than their own recommendation.

Personal communications were something that improved tremendously over my time. Today, we all take for granted telephonic and televisual contact with our loved ones in any part of the world, but in 1964 many junior staff overseas didn't even have a telephone and the regular method of contact was by post. We could use the diplomatic bag for this, with mail being fed into the postal system when the bags arrived in London from overseas and the Office acting as a collection and sorting point for mail going out to post. Parcels up to a certain size limit were also permitted. The arrival of the bag with this personal mail was always the high point of the week throughout my time overseas. When we sent our mail to London, it had to carry the correct postage to enter the Royal Mail system and so we all had to have with us at post a supply of British postage stamps.

When we first arrived in Kampala, we had no personal transport. Our car had not been delivered and junior staff were not allowed to hire official vehicles, as was later the case. In fact, it had not been very long since junior staff were not permitted to bring a car out to post at all. When our Morris Minor arrived, at about the same time as the Abramses' Ford Anglia, we were able to get about much more. So, for Christmas 1964 the four of us, plus two bachelors in the High Commission in another car, went off to the Queen Elizabeth Game Park in the west of the country.

On the way to the park, I managed to turn our little car on its side by putting two wheels through a deep puddle while driving quite briskly on a dirt road. I was in the lead and those behind later reported that they saw a sheet of water shoot into the air after we passed from sight round a corner. The car had to be sent back to Kampala to be mended and for the rest of the holiday we shared the Abramses' car. The delay while the accident was sorted out meant that we arrived at the game park entrance after dark, when we shouldn't strictly have been allowed in, but we were.

I remember that the repairs to the car were

eventually completed on 30th January 1965 as a delay in picking the car up meant we were late for the memorial service for Sir Winston Churchill which was held in the local Anglican cathedral that day.

I had bought a second hand cine camera shortly before this visit and we still have some rather scratchy film of the trip. Apart from this, I don't have any specific memories of the holiday, but the timing of subsequent events suggest that our son, David, was conceived during this time as he was born on 25th September the following year and was reckoned to have been a couple of weeks late.

In almost every posting we had, we took the opportunity to visit neighbouring areas. In Uganda this was a trip to Nairobi in Kenya in Easter 1965. At this point, we were still living in the hotel and Val was four months pregnant. Naturally we drove from Kampala to Nairobi, but the trip was rather arduous for our little Morris Minor. The car itself performed adequately, but it had no air-conditioning and we kept the windows at least partly open the whole time. The road for much of the way was dirt, not tarmac and, as a result, whenever a lorry came past in the opposite direction a huge cloud of red dust would billow across the road and we had to wind the windows up. So often did we have to do this that by the end of our journey the window started to stick and we could no longer easily move it up or down.

The trip itself was fairly uneventful, but leaving early in the morning from Kampala and driving almost due east meant that the sun shone in my eyes early on the outward journey. And, conversely, returning from Nairobi to Kampala this time heading due west, the sun again shone in my eyes as we were nearing the end of our trip.

Soon after our return from Nairobi we at last moved into the newly re-roofed bungalow. Having had to wait so long for this, together with the fact that it was our first home and was completely redecorated, helped our eventual appreciation of the accommodation no end and we were quite happy with it. It also gave us our first chance to unpack our wedding gifts and the various items we had chosen and ordered some eight months before. These had reached Kampala a few weeks after our arrival, but as we were in the hotel they had then been put in store in a warehouse, known locally as a 'godown'. We had sometimes gone there to take out such items as clothing, which was needed before moving into the house. The Abramses, being in exactly the same situation, we four often made the trip to the godown a sort of outing after work to unpack clothes from our little store.

Our bungalow was very small, with only two bedrooms and an entrance hall that gave directly onto the area which served as lounge and dining room. There was a small kitchen at one end of the central area and one bathroom-cum-toilet at the other. Beyond the kitchen, across a passage which ran across the width of the building from the front to the back garden, were the servants' quarters. These were a bare room with a shower/toilet attached.

To start with, there was no garage: this lack had to be dealt with, but that did not require us to wait any longer to move in. In front of the house was a small garden, but large enough to allow the garage to be built there eventually. Behind the house was a comfortably large garden with poinsettia, roses, bougainvillea and a large stand of bamboo in the corner. It also had a couple of avocado pear trees, which produced the occasional fruit.

As I have mentioned, in common with other junior staff, we had no telephone as this was considered to be above our grade, unless the job obviously implied the likelihood of out of hours contact, such as for communication or security staff. As a result, should a message need to be delivered to us, this was done by the personal appearance of a messenger, usually a High Commission driver.

After we moved into our house, I took up again a task I had started in England a year or two previously. This was to teach Val to drive. In Eastbourne, before we were married, I had allowed her to practice on my old pre-war Ford. Not much progress had been achieved, to be honest, but I did manage to have this attractive girl to myself for an hour or so from time to time. After marriage, we decided that she would have to make a more determined effort. Unsurprisingly, this caused some friction between us and eventually Val took lessons with a local driving school run by an Italian. In spite of the fact that one of her instructors couldn't speak English, she eventually passed the local test and obtained her Ugandan driving licence.

Apart from the seismic change in our lives represented by marriage and migration, we were also thrown into the deep end of African expatriate life. There we were, both 21 years old when we arrived, neither of us ever having been abroad before, apart from a short school exchange trip to France by Val and both having very limited social experience by the standards of the world we now found ourselves in. Suddenly we were expected to cope with a 'household' of a full time house servant, soon to be joined by an ayah, or child's nanny, plus part time gardener and shared night watchman as well dealing with the niceties of being entertained and entertaining in return. Inevitably it was a steep learning curve and we committed a number of *faux pas* along the way.

We were both gauche and naive and, whereas Val was always perceived as 'nice', I tended to come over as a bit brash. This was the 1960s and these things were noticed and noted, although actually not on my record, as I've since seen.

Nevertheless, we are amazed today to see from Val's diaries how quickly we settled into the pattern of social entertainment. Although, at my then grade, none of this was 'part of the job', as it was to become at every subsequent post, it did mean that we hardly had a day when we weren't going out or having people round.

In later years the Office eventually recognised this problem for young officers going on first posting and a 'Going Abroad Course' for them was introduced, as well as a similar 'Wives' Course', later 'Spouses' Course' and presumably now 'Partners' Course'. But there was nothing remotely like that in 1964 in the CRO and we just had to pick things up as we went along.

My position in the High Commission hierarchy was at the bottom of the heap of the mainstream grades. As I have already noted, the secretaries, communicators and security officers were also low down, but they were in different branches. The effect of this stratification was sometimes quite brutal. For example, when Princess Margaret and Lord Snowdon paid an official visit in 1965, junior grades were not included in the introduction line. We had to be there, of course, but we were only allowed to watch from the sidelines. This contrasted with my position in 1983 when the Princess visited St Kitts and I was to have a short chat with her on the tarmac of Golden Rock Airport.

Similarly, when the British Council had a copy

of Olivier's film *Othello* to show in 1966, clerical officers and their wives were not included in the invitation to the High Commission staff. This play is one of my favourite Shakespearean works, so I asked that we be allowed to watch. The request was met with slight surprise that the minions could be interested in such a cultural event and we were rather grudgingly allowed in the hall, provided we sat at the back behind the clattering projector.

And, of course, there was the annual Queen's Birthday Party, for which nothing had prepared us. In the UK we are slightly odd in not having a National Day, at least not one we celebrate at home. Overseas in the diplomatic world, though, all countries have national days. Usually this commemorates an event such as Independence, establishment of republic, revolution, unification and so on. But we don't have any of these anniversaries that we care to recall, so ours is decreed to be the Queen's Official Birthday in June, which is marked in London by the Trooping the Colour parade. On the appointed day, British diplomatic missions in countries where the Queen is not Head of State give the Queen's Birthday Party, or QBP, as it is always known. In Commonwealth countries where Her Majesty is still Head of State, the local Governor General does these honours and the British High Commissioner goes as a guest.

Over the course of my career I attended QBPs some 24 times, including two a year in Jerusalem while I was there as Consul and three given by the Governor General in Antigua at which we were guests.

This sequence started in 1965 in Kampala. At this first QBP, we were very little more than an adjunct to the waiters and knew hardly anybody there beyond the High Commission staff, as the outside friends we knew were too junior in their own organisations to have been invited. Later years saw us moving through stages of actually knowing people who were invited, on to suggesting names for inclusion on the guest list and then introducing 'my' guests to the Head of Post.

As far as my career in the FCO was concerned, the process culminated in 1994 in Khartoum, where, as Head of Post myself, I actually hosted the QBP and vetted the list submitted by my staff. However, in 1999 and 2000 in Jerusalem, when I was in my post-retirement job as Administrative Director of the British School of Archaeology in Jerusalem, I was present at two QBPs at the Consulate General purely as a guest and a senior member of the local British community. So I could just socialise and not 'work'.

In 1965, though, we were almost literally thrown in at the deep end. It was emphasised that we were not there to enjoy ourselves, but that this was part of the job. To endorse this, the senior staff were very insistent that we juniors should 'circulate' and would move us around when we were standing alone or talking among ourselves: we had to move on and 'entertain' the guests. One over-enthusiastic senior wife physically pushed Val, at the time over six months pregnant, into one rather surprised group of guests. This may have increased the entertainment of the guests; it certainly didn't add to ours. But circulate is what staff are supposed to do at QBPs and some thirty years later in 1994, as Head of Post, I was to write an office circular to my staff exhorting them in very similar general terms.

When I arrived in Kampala the High Commissioner was Sir David Hunt. Shortly before he left in 1965 it became common knowledge that his marriage was breaking up and that his wife had had an affair with another man. This information caused some considerable frustration amongst the ladies of the Passport Section who considered themselves well informed of the local gossip and had heard nothing of this. Sir David was succeeded by Roland Hunt. The same surname caused some confusion locally, as one High Commissioner's wife was Lady Hunt while his successor's was Mrs. Hunt. Roland Hunt however fell foul of President, Milton Obote and was transferred early in 1967.

In Kampala I decided that I would take advantage of the French and German cultural centres, the Alliance Francaise and the Goethe Institut, to brush up my languages. There was no qualification to work towards, but it did serve to keep my eye in, so to speak. The German teacher was Frau Hills, a Valkyrie-scale woman married to Denis Hills who later caused problems for the British Government during the Idi Amin era. I never met him and I rather think that, although they presumably came to Uganda together, he and his wife were effectively separated by the time I took the German course.

The birth of our first child, David Rhys John, on Saturday the 25th of September 1965 produced a step-change in our life. However, with the lack of our own phone, I had to make a trip to the High Commission Office and book an international call through the switchboard to pass on to our parents the news of his birth. His arrival was not straightforward, as he was a breach birth, and Val had to have a caesarean delivery.

As I have already mentioned, we had to recruit an ayah, or local nanny. When I say, 'had to', I mean it was what people did at that time in that place. We chose an old woman, who was strongly recommended, but spoke hardly any English. She taught Val a lot about looking after small babies, but as David grew and became more active, she was clearly too old to cope and after a short time we replaced her with a younger woman, who remained with us until we left.

Soon after we arrived at post, Val had got a job

in the High Commission as a clerk in the registry, which she held until she had to leave for David's birth. Later, after we got the ayah, she got another job for a time as a copy typist at Makerere University. She used her new driving skills to get to work there, while I cadged a lift to the office from colleagues.

One day, when she came out from work at the university, she noticed that car had a puncture. Now, in spite of her many and impressive positive qualities, my spouse has always had an antipathy towards anything mechanical and on this occasion couldn't even remember where the spare wheel was in the car. So she simply looked, and indeed was, helpless until a kind male came to her rescue. The ploy was so successful that she used it again nearly thirty years later in the middle of the Jerusalem rush hour – although on that occasion, she had to prompt assistance from a reluctant passer-by. It has always amazed me that with such a wife, we went on to produce a daughter who obtained a BSc in engineering.

In Kampala, we were introduced to the game of badminton. This was first in the garden of John and Elsie McQuiggan. John was the burly head of the local British Information Services office, effectively the PR section of the High Commission, and he and Elsie took the trouble to be accommodating to us newly arrived juniors. We later graduated from their garden to a weekly game in a local church hall. This had ceiling fans installed along its length at a height of about six and half feet, which made overarm shots a bit hazardous. Although we were no experts, we rather took to the game and continued to enjoy badminton in a number of places until the end of the millennium.

The Passport Section of the British High Commission in Kampala was one of a number of such sections in British High Commissions throughout east and central Africa. They had a lot in common, including a large number of locally engaged British female staff, and the requirement to issue large numbers of the British passports to people from outside the British Isles. Another thing that they had in common, apparently, was a high proportion of stamp collectors. Both I and my then boss, Trefor Llewelyn, were in this category as well as a number of our locally engaged staff.

I cannot now remember how, but it became known that the various passport sections in the British high commissions in Uganda, Kenya, Tanganyika (later Tanzania), Zambia, Malawi and Rhodesia were all of a similar mind and a regular trade in the issues of new stamps sprang up between the various offices. I no longer actively collect stamps, but I still have the collection I made at this time, which includes a fairly good selection of these issues. I strongly suspect that the mint ones which were passed between the offices through the diplomatic bag contravened some international agreement.

On the 15th of December 1965 we left Kampala for our first mid tour leave and Christmas at home with our families. We were, of course, also bringing back our first child, who was also my parents' first grandchild. This caused great excitement and, as had been the case when we left in 1964, a family delegation from Eastbourne was present at the airport. As we did for many years after when we returned to the UK, we brought back with us a bottle of spirits and large carton of cigarettes for each pair of parents and were very careful to spread our time equally between them during our time in UK.

We left for post again on the 15th of February 1966. As with the first time we travelled to Uganda, there was a hitch with the flight. I had been issued in Kampala with an open dated return ticket and had booked the return flight at a travel agency in Eastbourne. When we got to Gatwick Airport to return to post, we discovered that the date for the return flight had been filled in wrongly and the plane actually left the following day. The fault clearly wasn't ours, so we were given two options; we could be put up in a local hotel overnight, and travel the next day, or be transported to Heathrow to catch a flight from there later in the evening. We opted to keep travelling and go to Heathrow to catch the East

African Airways Comet. Wrong decision.

The plane developed a fault at our first stop, which was Rome, where we had to overnight and we actually arrived in Entebbe only about two hours before the plane we had decided not to wait for. The journey was one of the worst flights we have ever experienced. David, by now five months old, did not travel well and required constant attention, so we had little rest. On top of this, there was the question of nappies. On returning to post we had bought a full supply of nappies for the second half of our tour. Of course, these were not the modern disposable ones, but the old fashioned washable ones.

To avoid the risk of exceeding our baggage weight allowance, these had been spread in the bottom of the carrycot the baby was travelling in as this was not weighed. So he was perched on a thick pile of material and lying only just below the edge of the cot. The good news was that this meant that we had access to an adequate supply of nappies for the extended journey. On the other hand, once used, they obviously couldn't go back into the cot and we arrived in Uganda with large plastic bag bulging with noisome nappies, to the amazement and amusement of all.

During the second half of our posting, the High Commission moved into the new, purpose-built office in the centre of town, so that all the parts of the mission were housed together. This made it easier for me to be temporarily transferred to the Admin Section to cover for Mike Abrams's absence on his mid-tour leave. While I was doing this job, it was noticed that the grass sown in an area in the central and mostly shaded, area of the new building was not growing properly. Bill Francis, the Second Secretary (Administration) told me that it probably needed rolling.

Now, the area in question was some four feet above the paving and behind a retaining wall and I suspect in retrospect that he was not being serious, but I took it literally and regarded it as a challenge. I managed to borrow a roller from the Rugby Club and devised a system of small ramps from some Dexion racking we had waiting to be installed. So, with the muscle power of the highly amused local staff, I managed to get the roller up over the wall and, later, back down again. During this operation, my efforts were a focus of attention because, as the whole High Commission was built round the central area, pretty well everybody had a good view of the work.

I recall two comments; one from the Military Attaché, who was suitably impressed by my efforts, reminiscent as they were of the sort of test potential officer cadets were put through. The other was more a complaint from John McQuiggan, who bewailed the fact that the racking earmarked for his section was being mistreated. However, I don't remember there being any obvious change to the pattern of grass growth.

A revolution broke out during 1966, with Milton Obote, the elected Prime Minister deciding that the Independence constitution was ripe for replacement and that he should be the executive head of state. As with so much in African politics, tribe was at the root of it. The President, Sir Edward Frederick Mutesa (known in the popular British press as 'King Freddie'), as I mentioned, was also the Kabaka, or king of Buganda and thus was leader of the Baganda tribe. During the protectorate, we British had relied heavily on the Baganda in various aspects of our rule in Uganda. After Independence, it irked Obote that they should still have the top job.

He took a similar view a few years later, shortly after we had left, when the senior military officer in the army, Brigadier Opoloto, again from the Baganda, was passed over for appointment as army commander in favour of one Idi Amin. As so often, it seemed to be a good idea at the time.

During the disturbances, a night-time curfew was declared, which applied to High Commission staff along with everybody else. This only affected us inasmuch as we had to be home by, I think 7.30 in the evening, but there was one aspect of office life where it had rather more effect. Once a week, the diplomatic mail arrived and somebody had to go to the airport in Entebbe to collect it. As the plane arrived early in the morning, before the curfew round Kampala was lifted, the 'meeters' had to travel to Entebbe early the previous evening and stay overnight at the local Speke Hotel. The UK-based security guards were responsible for the collection duties, but there always had to be an escort as well and there was a roster of junior staff to fill this role. So, every now and again, one of us juniors had the company of a crusty old retired warrant officer, as most of them were, for a couple of hours to and from the airport and, during the curfew period, an overnight stay at the hotel.

Some of the security guards had had very interesting lives in the armed services. One had been in the Army, risen to sergeant major and then joined the Navy and risen to petty officer, which was pretty unusual. Another had been in the Navy and was captured by the Japanese while trying to flee from Singapore when that colony had fallen. He didn't speak of his experiences as a prisoner of war, but had the odd mannerism of always covering his beer glass with something in between swigs. The senior security guard, though, was retired from the Colonial Police Service and had held commissioned rank. He rather resented being lumped together with the ex-warrant officers.

The security guards were comparatively well off, being in receipt of at least one and sometimes two pensions from their previous lives, on top of their salary. They also had a good union, which had ensured that they received shift allowance and overtime pay even while overseas. This did not go down too well with us junior staff, who were often required to work similar hours with no such financial recognition. There were no 'conditioned hours' applicable to mainstream officers, and while overseas we were available for duty 24/7, as the modern rather graphic expression has it.

In 1967 the Uganda Government had a bit of a dilemma in how to react to the Six-Day War in the Middle East. While they were instinctively inclined to support the Arabs, they had close military ties with the Israelis, who were actually training their air force at the time. (This, of course, came in useful for the Israelis when the Entebbe Raid was undertaken in 1976). As a result of this difficulty, the main daily paper, the Uganda Argus, memorably produced an edition during the fighting in which the front page was split down the middle, with a different story of the progress of the battle on either side, each with its own banner headline, the one giving the version according to the Israelis and the other that according to the Arabs. The readers were left to make up their own minds about the actual facts

At the start of my career I had determined to get on as fast as I could and so sat the Executive (subsequently Diplomatic Service Grade 9) Limited Competition in 1964, 1965 and again in 1966, when I finally passed. As a result of this eventual success coming at the end of my time in Kampala, I was posted home on promotion to Grade 9. While the promotion was good, the home posting was not. We had been counting on at least one more overseas posting, which was the normal pattern at the time, and had made no provision, socially or financially, for the situation we found ourselves in. We suddenly had to decide where to live and buy a house in England.

I appealed against the home posting, citing the case of Mike Abrams, who had also been promoted, but had been posted overseas again. To no avail; he had been promoted because of his seven or eight years' seniority as he had joined the Civil Service from school at 16. It was different in my case I was told, but better for my career in the longer term. So I returned to a London posting.

It was still possible to opt to travel home by sea, but with the blocking of the Suez Canal during the Arab/Israeli War earlier in 1967, this would now entail a trip right round Africa from Mombasa after a train trip to the coast. With a small child, and following our experiences flying back from leave, this did not appeal to us, so we flew home on 13th of October, the day before my 25th birthday.

The Abramses finished their tour shortly after us, but had no small child, so chose what was effectively a sea cruise to finish their time in Africa,. However, for spending money on the trip, Mike needed travellers' cheques and, given the choice between US dollars and Sterling pounds, he patriotically chose the British currency. A week or so into their journey, the pound was devalued by the Wilson government and they had a very tight time of things for their trip home. The pound in the pockets of people in Britain may not have been affected, as Harold Wilson famously stated, but the one in poor Mike's pocket certainly had.

CHAPTER 3

LONDON 1967-1970

As I said, we came back for a home posting very unwillingly, and had to set about looking for a home within commuting distance from London. At first, we toyed with the idea of finding somewhere in the London area and I actually stayed up in London with my old friend Larry for a month or so ostensibly looking for a place, but our hearts weren't in it and eventually, Val found us a small chalet bungalow near Eastbourne on the outskirts of Polegate.

We had no furniture, but managed to get together a motley collection of hand-me-downs and second hand items, which sufficed for the three years we were back. However, on the positive side, we were right on the edge of the countryside: there was only one house between us and the open fields and we could (and did) often walk down the nearby country lane, with first a pram and then a pram and a tricycle as our family increased. On the other hand, though, being on the outskirts of the town and as we had no car, Val had to walk about a mile to get to the shops and the playgroup to which she took David.

The drink drive laws had been introduced shortly before our return, and this meant that there were restrictions on the earlier pattern of our evening outings. Initially this was circumvented to a certain extent with Val's help. The Ugandan driving test was not recognised as valid for the long term in this country, and she eventually passed the British driving test and obtained a UK licence. But with her Ugandan driving licence she was legally entitled to drive in the UK for six months after the date of her return to the country. During this period we would sometimes go out for a drink at the weekend with Val acting as the abstemious chauffeur (or should that be chauffeuse?) of our friend's car, with one of our mothers kindly baby-sitting.

We did look around for a second-hand car for transport, but after buying a real turkey and getting rid of it, we recognised that we weren't realistically going to be able to afford one, and so then relied on public transport for family movements. However, I was offered a cheap second-hand scooter which I used for short trips such as popping into town of a Saturday morning.

My promotion to Grade 9 took effect on the 12th of December 1967, the day I started my home posting and returned to the daily commute to London. On a normal day, I would leave the house in the morning just before seven and get back in the evening at about half past seven. This meant that in the winter I wouldn't see my home in the daylight and throughout the year would hardly see my children at all except at the weekends.

Shortly before I came home, the CRO and FO had merged to form the FCO and the administration of the two Offices was taken over for a time by a third body called the Diplomatic Service Administration Office (DSAO). I was allocated to General Section of Establishment & Organisation Department in the DSAO and worked initially in the Treasury Building, across King Charles Street from the main FCO buildings. Our building gloried in the formal title of Government Office, Great George Street or GOGGS. (Great George Street being the road on the other side of the building.)

Later the department name was changed to Personnel Policy Department of the FCO and we moved to the Curtis Green Building on the Embankment. This is the white building next to the red brick Norman Shaw Building, which is better known as the old New Scotland Yard, just down from Westminster Bridge. Both these buildings have now been taken over for parliamentary offices. In our new building, the section was lucky enough to be put in a room on the second floor with a good view across the Embankment and the Thames to what was then still County Hall.

In this section I was part of a team that ruled on the entitlement of staff to the cost of travel and freight of personal effects which they could claim on the way to and from post and on their leave entitlements. At the time, policy in the Office was that we should defend to the last the principle of 'surface travel'. This, in effect, meant most staff and, in particular, senior staff wanted to go by sea to the far reaches of the globe. However, at the time regular passenger sailings were being axed as the rest of the population was opting to travel by air. Stubborn adherence to this policy was throwing up all sorts of oddities. For instance, passenger sailings to Australia and New Zealand were becoming very few and far between as the liners were being redirected to the burgeoning cruise trade. But, oddly enough, you could still get to Hong Kong this way. So, the 'approved route' as it was called to the Antipodes was by sea to Hong Kong and then onwards by air.

In another example, there were no longer passenger sailings to many places in Africa and the Middle East from the UK. But some Italian lines were still sailing there, so the 'approved route' was by train across Europe to Trieste, for example, and then on by sea. This, in turn, caused difficulties. Junior staff were entitled only to second class rail travel and to get to an Italian port by rail involved an overnight sleeper train. Second class in these trains involved sharing a sleeping compartment. Was it fair to ask a young female officer to share her sleeping accommodation with a stranger? Should she not be allowed to travel first class to get sole use of the berth? If so, what about equality with male officers?

Eventually, the whole thing became self-evidently ridiculous and the Office had to come to a deal with the Treasury that air travel became the 'approved route', and all costs were based on this. However, there was a concession which allowed all staff to travel business, or club class if the journey was more than four hours. Of course this change affected the time allowed for travel, which was similarly based on the 'approved route'. It was decided that a day for recovery from the flight should be allowed in addition to the actual travelling time on transfer for long journeys, but, even with that concession, travelling time shrank from a month or two in some cases to no more than three or four days at the most.

The agreement that all staff could travel on long journeys by club class came at the expense of the previous rule that heads of mission could go first class when travelling by air. One ambassador tried to appeal against this change, on what were known as 'representational grounds', by claiming that his host government expected to see the British Ambassador arrive travelling first class. This was put to the Treasury, who (I suspect with their tongues in their cheeks) came back with the suggestion that on arrival at post, he wait until most of the passengers had left the plane and then walk through the aircraft, exiting through the first-class doorway. This would satisfy both economy and prestige.

Prince William of Gloucester had decided in 1965 that he would like to join the Diplomatic

Service. Naturally, it was intended that he would enter the Administrative Grade, but he was unable to pass the required entrance competition, even though he was given more than one go at it. While he was attempting to do this, though, he was employed on a temporary contract basis and served for a time in Lagos and then in Tokyo.

The Prince was very keen on flying and took himself to post in his own aircraft. This caused us a considerable headache in trying to calculate how much of his expenses could be claimed back. The normal way was to make the calculation of allowable costs within the cost of the approved route, but nobody had ever flown themselves to post before. What should be allowable? For instance, although the question of travel time was quite straight forward, should he be allowed to claim the cost of the commercial airfare or the notional cost of driving a car and be paid mileage? And when he transferred direct from Lagos to Tokyo what road route could possibly be used as notional basis for the mileage calculation? As I recall it, the Prince himself was not much concerned about the money, but it was an interesting mental exercise for the rest of us. I don't remember what the solution was.

Eventually, having yet again failed to qualify for entry to the Administrative Grade, the prince left the Diplomatic Service in 1970. Two years later he tragically died in a light aircraft crash in Britain.

Other imaginative journeys home caused some problems. There was the case of an officer and his wife who decided to drive back from, I think, Pakistan. (Interesting that in the 1960s it was possible to do so.) On the face of it, this was simply a matter of calculating the mileage that could be paid for running a car over that distance. But the officer insisted that he be allowed to claim also for oil change and service for the car as the distance exceeded the service interval for his model. This particular claim was resisted stoutly even though the total amount was well under what would have been paid for two airfares. The grounds for refusal were that the mileage allowance covered more than just the price of fuel; it also included elements for depreciation and service costs, so these couldn't be claimed again.

Apart from giving advice on travel and baggage entitlements, the section to a certain extent was required to police the claims and actions of officers in this area. In later years, of course, the whole system was completely simplified by giving one company the world-wide contract for moving personal affects throughout the Diplomatic Service and by having a travel agent 'implanted' into the office to deal with personal travel, by air or any other way. However, in the late sixties there were rules that had to be followed, as there were those who wished to take unfair advantage of them.

I can recall a couple of cases. There was the officer who shipped his personal effects back from South East Asia. The cost was much higher than expected and, when the figures of weight and volume were produced to support his claim, it was noticed that, whereas the volume was well within his entitlement, the weight was considerably over. Normally officers were allowed to claim within whichever limit, volume or weight, was most advantageous to them, but on this occasion, someone was sent to check. What they found was that this individual had instructed the packers to make his wooden lift van out of solid teak planks. His idea, of course, was that on arrival no one would ask for the packing materials back and he would have a quantity of valuable wood at his disposal. However, the 'rules' said that the packing materials actually belonged to the Office, who, after all, had paid for them. Usually these had such small value as to make recovery pointless, but on this occasion they were reclaimed and he obtained no benefit. Presumably his personal file was suitably noted.

Another occasion was when an ambassador in the Persian Gulf recruited a female servant from the Far East and claimed the cost of her fare, as ambassadors' servants' travel costs were also paid. His Excellency was transferred home a short time later and claimed the travel costs of the servant to the UK on the grounds that it was no more than the cost of returning her to her country of origin. Further checks, however, revealed that the girl in question was to be his future daughter-in-law and he had come up with this wheeze of paying the girl's travel costs from her home to the UK at the expense of the British taxpayer. On this occasion the ambassador concerned argued quite strongly that he be allowed to do this. However, one of the basic principles laid down by the Treasury was that officers should not gain any personal advantage from the rules and his case was eventually rejected.

At this time there was a concession from HM Customs & Excise that ambassadors coming home on retirement could import the 'remnants of their cellar' duty free, provided it was for their 'personal consumption'. Unsurprisingly, a number of retiring ambassadors discovered that they were in possession of a large cellar of wines at the time of their retirement, and this concession was eventually withdrawn. However, this was still in the future and one retiring ambassador had had the misfortune of having his wooden lift van broken into and the wines he was bringing back stolen. HM Customs & Excise decided that he would have to pay duty on the missing bottles, which were, of course declared on the packing list, on the grounds that the concession was for wines for his personal consumption and, as they had been stolen, obviously he was unable to consume them. On the other hand, being the owner, he was liable for duty even if he was not actually in possession of them any longer.

While clearly being according to the letter of the law, this ruling seemed extremely harsh and he asked for our help in getting it overturned. It fell to me to take up his case and I recall having a long and acrimonious, but eventually fruitless, telephone conversation with somebody in the Customs. I pointed out that, as the wines had been stolen, the retiree was hardly in possession of them any more and the thief who had brought them into the country should surely be liable for any import duty, even if we didn't know who it was. However, my interlocutor refused absolutely to give way on the point and the money had to be paid.

We also adjudicated on leave entitlements. These usually concerned interpretation of some fairly complex rules governing leave earned at home or abroad (the rates were different) and whether leave could be carried forward and, if so, how much and for how long. The 'killer' regulation allowing us to rule that leave would have to be forfeit in some circumstances was a long-standing Civil Service principle laying down that leave was 'a privilege and not a right'. Not surprisingly this never went down well.

Again, there was an interesting case. At the time, the Supreme Restitution Court in Germany was still in operation. This was set up in 1945 to sort out recompense for property stolen by the German state during the Nazi period. The British judge and, I think, one court clerk were, like the British warders forming part of the international team guarding Rudolf Hess at Spandau Prison, on the FCO payroll. As such they were theoretically subject to Diplomatic Service Regulations, including the provisions on leave. However, the judge was each year due more leave than he could take because of the pattern of sitting of the Court. I don't know if he had been doing the job since the end of the War, but I do recall that he had accumulated something like three years of leave and had no prospect of being able to take it until he retired. Of course in practice this meant that he would remain on the FCO books for three years after he eventually stopped work. Common sense would suggest that he should be paid a lump sum in compensation, but that, too, was frowned on by the Treasury as a matter of principle and I don't know what eventually did happen in his case.

Dental treatment decisions on what would and wouldn't be compatible with the NHS were also adjudicated in General Section. US-trained dentists were always a source of friction, as their standards tended to include cosmetic work, which was not necessarily covered by the NHS. One ambassador in South America produced an estimate for dental treatment so high, that, as it was pointed out to him with some emphasis, it would be cheaper for him to travel by air first-class return to the UK for the equivalent free (as it was then) treatment under the

NHS.

At this time, the Office was starting to offer places on various courses for junior staff. One of these was an economics course, which I managed to get on at the third time of asking. It was a very useful course on the background to economics, but the benefits were somewhat marred by the fact that I never did a job where the knowledge was put to use. It was also a bit odd that I was put on exactly the same course, with the same lecturer, as part of the so-called Mid Career Development Course (MCDC) some fifteen years later.

I was also selected to go on a Civil Service Junior Management Course for executive officers and equivalent grades at the Civil Service College at Sunningdale. This was a four-week residential course. My colleagues on the course were from various other government departments and it was immediately clear that, for them, attendance was a marker of selection for greater things; indeed, one or two had already been told they would be promoted on rejoining their departments. For FCO staff, on the other hand, it was just part of the general career pattern, with no particular expectation of rapid advancement. Again, I was to return to the College as part of the MCDC, by which time it had been vastly enlarged and I couldn't relate the layout to my memory of the first visit.

During this home posting I decided that, having passed the Executive Grade Competition, I would now have a go at the Administrative Branch Competition and started a private correspondence course to prepare myself for the written part of this. I also decided that I would grow a beard; why I can no longer remember, but I think it was probably in order to gain an extra an extra ten minutes or so in bed in the morning.

Meanwhile, there was the birth of our second son, Alun James Michael, on the 5th of November 1968. Val was confined in the old St Mary's Hospital, which had once been the Eastbourne Workhouse and, before that, a barracks, Unsurprisingly, the facilities were far from ideal and she actually shared the delivery room with four other mothers. On the other hand, unlike with David, there were no complications this time and the birth was normal. It was still not possible to tell the sex of the baby in advance and in view of the date I briefly entertained the possibility of the names Guy or Catherine, but received no encouragement from Val in this.

Then, towards the end of my home posting in 1969, there occurred the event which marked a significant fork in my career. I had decided to take the Language Aptitude Test, which was open to all. This consisted of sitting in the FCO language laboratory with a number of others, listening to a tape of a series of short aural tests through earphones. Abilities probed were such things as vocabulary retention, tonal recognition, grammatical construction and so on. Tonal recognition was in a Chinese dialect and the language used for the rest was one that in those days nobody was likely to have any prior knowledge of; Urdu or Pushtu, I think. The responses to the tests were written down in an answer booklet. At one point, when instructed to turn over the page for a fresh segment of the test, I found that my booklet had a printing error and that two sheets were blank. I waved urgently at the invigilator who came over, saw the problem and went to get me a replacement booklet. But meanwhile, as I was one of many taking the test, the tape continued to run. Afterwards, the invigilator told me that an allowance would be made to my marks to compensate for the hitch.

As I knew him personally, I suspect he was generous in compensating my score for the printing error. When the results came out, I was told that my score was on the borderline of the two percentile scores that indicated an aptitude for either Slavic or Semitic languages and I was given a choice between them. Although there are more languages than one in each of these categories, in practice this choice was between Russian and Arabic.

I asked what the practical differences were as regards the courses. The Russian language training, I was told, involved a three months' residential course at the Army Language School at Beaconsfield, while the Arabic one was based at the FCO's language school, the Middle East Centre for Arab Studies (MECAS) at Shemlan, a little way outside Beirut in Lebanon. At Beaconsfield I would be at home only at weekends, while time at MECAS would count as a short overseas posting and meant that I would be on overseas allowances and accompanied by my family. There was no contest and I opted for Arabic.

So, if there had been no printing error in that booklet, I believe that in all probability I would have got a more realistic score placing me clearly in the Slavic aptitude sector: it certainly turned out that I had no particular gift for Arabic. This, in turn, would have resulted in my being put on a Russian course and my subsequent career, and indeed my life, would have taken a very different path. Not quite the butterfly's wing beat causing a storm, but illustrative of the same general principle.

Just as I took the language test, my home posting was coming to an end and, although I didn't know it, I had been selected for the position of Passport Officer in the High Commission in Kingston, Jamaica and had been accepted by the post. This was now cancelled and my posting to MECAS for Arabic language training confirmed.

Although to a great extent this was treated as a regular posting, in Lebanon, MECAS students were not on the Embassy staff and so had no diplomatic status. This meant that we had to obtain residence permits to stay in the country longer than a tourist and our cars remained a temporary import on British plates and with an international vehicle registration document, known as a *carnet de passage en douane.*

We now got ready for our first overseas post with two small boys. I was paid a transfer grant and car loan and ordered a new car, a Hillman Minx. We had a number of other hoops to jump through. The whole family had to have the usual medical clearance for the posting, I had to obtain my *carnet* for the car and Val and I had to get international driving licences. We got all these documents from the AA, which I joined so as to get a detailed route across Europe from Calais to Genoa, where we were to join the Mediterranean ferry to Beirut. No clicking on the Internet for the best route to follow, let alone a GPS to guide you. And, of course, we both had to apply to the bank in order to purchase our £50-worth of foreign currency, which was duly noted in our passports. Some things are so much easier these days.

As we were driving to post, naturally this time I took delivery of the car in the UK and sold the scooter to my brother. So we had the novel luxury of driving a new vehicle while still at home. It was a novel experience in another sense, as the car was a left-hand drive version and took a little getting used to. The left-hand drive also caused some surprises to other drivers as it was a British registered car and looked at first glance just like any other Hillman Minx on the road, except that it had a thin red border to the number plate to show that duty had not been paid.

Something we had to decide on now was what to do about our house. There were two possibilities; to sell it again, or to keep it and rent it out while we were away. We decided to sell, although on future occasions we were to opt for letting. We failed to find a buyer before we left,

and had to leave it in the hands of my father, who put a fair amount of effort into dealing with our affairs. He did this very willingly and certainly never complained or even commented, but I must admit to being very conscious that we were considerably in his debt. In due course, though, I made retribution by having my parents with us for residential holidays in Abu Dhabi and Syria.

So, packed into our new car with two new sons, we left the UK for our second posting.

CHAPTER 4

MECAS 1970 - 1972

Our route to Beirut was via the English
Channel, across Europe to the Mediterranean and
then by sea. We stayed the night before crossing the
Channel at a motel just outside Newhaven to be
ready for the early departure of the ferry for Dieppe
on the morning of the 14th of September 1970. It
was quite a stormy day and I should have had more
sense than to have a cooked breakfast on the boat
before we sailed. This meal proved to be, shall we
say, an ill-advised and very short-term investment.
The worst part was seeing another ferry leaving
Dieppe as we came in towards the harbour; until
then I hadn't realised just how much we were
pitching. I didn't feel really better until well into the
evening and was not able to do justice to the lunch
we stopped for on the way.

This was the first time I had driven on the right,
but I had no problems. We drove down through
France, where there were not yet many autoroutes,
staying at a couple of hotels picked at random on the
way. At one town we made the classic mistake of
wondering why there seemed to be nobody around
in the evening at the Hotel de Ville, but fortunately
there was a real hotel on the other side of the town
square. At another hotel, the guests at dinner

included a middle-aged English couple who were clearly annoyed that other Brits had discovered their bit of France. At least, that is what I deduced from their refusal to acknowledge us in any way. But it might have been because we had two small children with us, even though they were well-behaved.

This trip was also the first time I had had to use my basic French with people who didn't speak any English and, apart from some confusion about whether I was ordering fruit or chips for dessert at one point, we managed on that front, too.

Our route took us through France, across a sliver of Switzerland and on through the Mont Blanc Tunnel reaching Genoa the day before our sailing. This was, however, after a detour through the adjacent mountains, having taken a wrong turning at an autostrada junction. We stayed the night in a small hotel quite close to the port area called the Hotel Morpheo. The following morning the car proved embarrassingly hard to start in the hotel's underground car park, but we eventually made our way to the correct part of the port to board the ferry for Beirut, via Marseilles, Barcelona and Naples – a bit of a cruise, really. The ferry was not roll-on roll-off; cars were hoisted on and off by sling. We had a four-berth cabin with upper and lower bunks for the boys. David fell out of the top bunk one evening, but suffered no injuries.

It was an outside cabin, with a porthole not that far above the water line and just beside my bunk.

One night, with this porthole open, I was woken by a douche of cold water that had slopped in when the sea had become a bit choppy. Val tells me that in my half-awake state I sat up and accused her of throwing water over me. Apart from that, looking after two young children on a ship which was really not equipped for them, meant that the voyage was not as relaxing as it might have been.

As I mentioned earlier, MECAS stood for the 'Middle East Centre for Arab Studies'. 'Arab', note, not 'Arabic'; in addition to the language, we were given our first introduction to Islam, its relationship with the various forms of Christianity in the Middle East and the intractable problem of the Palestine/Israel question as well as a brief history of the Arabs.

MECAS had been set up during the Second World War, originally in Jerusalem, to teach British military staff Arabic and a background of Arab culture. After the end of the British Mandate in Palestine, it had moved to Shemlan, where it remained until the civil war in Lebanon forced its complete closure in the late 1970s. Over the years, the military element had waned and, when I was there, although there were still four or five British Army personnel on the course, it was run by the FCO and most of the students were from the Diplomatic Service and the British Council. We did, however, also have amongst our number some foreign diplomats from Germany, Switzerland and Australia, as well as a number from the commercial sector: mainly oil companies and banks, and also a couple of private American students.

Up until a few years before I went there, as far as the FCO was concerned, the course had been the preserve of the Administrative grades. Recently, however, the language aptitude test had been introduced, which was aimed at identifying any officer with the latent ability to speak 'hard' foreign languages. But there was still effectively a divide between the graduates and the school leavers. The former had comparatively recently spent three of four years in full time Oxbridge university study, whereas most of the rest of us had never studied at this level, and had not been in any educational establishment over the last six or more years. With some honourable exceptions, the result was that we were in effect a two-tier student body and, for many of the lower tier, it would prove a wasted investment. For example, I was the only Executive Branch officer of my year remaining in the Diplomatic Service five years later, and I was far from the best of them.

The building housing MECAS at the time had been designed as a hotel, but not, I think, ever actually used as one. The downstairs rooms were all used as classrooms and the upper ones as single accommodation. All married couples and families lived in rented accommodation. The staff were mainly Palestinian, who in some cases had followed the school in its move from Jerusalem a quarter of a century earlier. The others were Lebanese.

The Centre was a major element in the economy of Shemlan and the surrounding area, as many local families profited from the student population who mainly shopped and rented flats in and around the village. The effect was that the Centre was quite institutionalised. For instance the conversational dialogues distributed as part of the teaching aids were so well known amongst the villagers that, if a student practising his or her Arabic with a villager deviated from the text, they would be corrected verbatim.

It had become a belief in the area and in the Arab world in general, come to that, that there must be something behind the establishment of a school to teach Arabic to foreigners: it could not just be what it seemed. And so the Centre was known colloquially as the Spy School, *'madrasat al jawasees'*. When a squash court was constructed on the roof of the building, local inhabitants took individual students on one side and ask about 'the secret apparatus' being installed.

This in itself was a useful introduction to the Arab compulsion not to take things at their face value and to see a 'plot' in everything done by the West. Unfortunately, most Arabs seemed to choose to believe in their own fabrication, and it was to prove a hurdle to employment for some of the students from commercial companies, as their time studying at MECAS could be cited as a reason for their unacceptability for any particular job in the Arab world.

As far as we diplomats were concerned, it seems also to have been accepted that any former student would be a spy, but many Arab regimes believed that of most Western diplomats anyway. As I noticed throughout my career, as soon as it was known that I was a 'graduate' of MECAS, there was a lot of head nodding and nose tapping to show that my audience knew all about what this really meant. It became really tiresome.

Arabic is spoken from the Atlantic to the Tigris and from the eastern Mediterranean to the upper reaches of the Nile, so inevitably there are many dialects. At MECAS, it could not be hoped to cover them all, and it had been decided to teach students to understand the newspaper and radio version of the language, which is fairly standard across the Arabic-speaking world, and to speak a broadly based, but necessarily Levantine, dialect. We were also taught to write the script.

The result, as some wag has recorded, was that a MECAS graduate could go anywhere in the Arab world, confident in the knowledge that he could always carry out a conversation with any other MECAS graduate. In fact, it wasn't as bad as that; you could usually make yourself understood, but more so with an educated Arab than with a peasant. The latter often thought you were talking English, even when you were using your finely honed linguistic skills. There were always, however, the gifted among the students. One such was so fluent at the end of the course that he was told during a conversation with an Arab that he was tall for a Lebanese. However, when he had arrived at MECAS, he could already speak fluently a number of European languages as well as, allegedly, Azerbaijani.

From Shemlan our elder son, David, attended the International School in Beirut, which involved an hour's trip by taxi each way each day. Alun, on the other hand, although only three years old, we sent to the kindergarten at Suq al Gharb, a village nearby. This was a Lebanese school with no English instruction and so he started his education in the Arabic language. He would bring back a copybook with the Arabic letters which he had filled in with coloured crayons and always obtained a score of something like 96%. I am not sure if this experience had any effect on his education one way or the other; certainly today he doesn't have any memory of it.

The climate in the Lebanese mountains was a bit of a surprise. Spring was a joy, with wild flowers in bloom that, in Britain, we normally expect to see only in cultivated gardens. The summers were, of course, hot, but we were high enough to be away from the worst of the Mediterranean humidity. However, the winters were surprisingly severe, with snow and frost on many days and heavy rainstorms which cut off the electricity supply and sometimes the water as well, when the supply pipes were washed away.

We settled in a flat in a small block a couple of hundred yards down the road from the Centre. It was built into the hill so that, while we had a small first floor balcony at the front, we also had a small back garden. Opposite our building, over the road and across an open space, was a small coffee house; 'The Coffee House of the Rock' which was appropriately perched on the edge of a cliff overlooking the valley below. In the middle of the waste ground between us was an old oil drum where the owner of the coffee house threw most of his rubbish for weekly collection. The rest, in accordance with local tradition, was simply pitched over the edge of the cliff: it was long way down and nobody could see it from up there.

The drum was a magnet for the numerous stray cats of the neighbourhood, which would climb in and scavenge through the food scraps. Occasionally, a dog would be attracted by this feline concentration and make a lunge into the drum. The effect was always dramatic. Cats seemed to explode out of the top of the drum like a novel Chinese firework, hitting the ground several feet away in all directions, and fleeing for their lives. I never saw one caught, though. Come to think of it, how often does a dog ever catch a cat?

The cat population was feral and always fighting and mating amongst themselves, although many would beg for titbits at our kitchen door. This was Val's fault, of course, as she was always putting food out for them. Over the months we spent in Shemlan we adopted two kittens, one from the continuous production line which operated in the village and which died fairly soon for unknown reasons, and a replacement provided by friends, which flourished and which we took with us to Abu Dhabi when we left Lebanon.

The local feline community included a huge scarred ginger tom, which could have stood as a model for Terry Pratchett's Greebo. He was vile in appearance and temper, with shredded ears and patchy coat and was foremost among the beggars at the kitchen door. One day, he appeared with a gash across his face which cut right across his left eye.

We watched him every day and, as time passed, this wound clearly became infected. Val could not let this pass, but we couldn't realistically catch him to do anything, so she hit on the idea of simply lacing his food with antibiotics. These were quite easy to buy locally and so the scraps we put out for all the cats were heavily seasoned with ground up broad-spectrum antibiotic for a week or so. And this did the trick: after a while the gash healed, the eye turned a light pink and fell out and our now one-eyed hero lived to fight and no doubt love for many more days. He was still going strong when we left. The other cats which also ate the same food were presumably very healthy for a period, too.

During the warm summer months we used to go down to the Mediterranean coast below the mountain to visit the beach or a swimming pool. On the beach, Val was initially dismayed to find that Alun was regularly abducted by the local ladies and passed round amongst them to coos of admiration. He was a sturdy youngster with very fair hair and bright blue eyes, a combination which appeared to be irresistible to the Lebanese. After a time, we got used these brief kidnappings, as he was always returned safely to us with many compliments and, for his part, he obviously loved it.

Among the foreign diplomats present on the course, were two Pakistanis, both married. One was a Pathan from Western Pakistan and the other a Bengali from the East of the country, as it was at the time. While we were on the course, there was the conflict that led to the secession of East Pakistan to form Bangladesh. We were on good terms with both these students and the Bangladeshi couple actually lived in the flat below us. The events back home caused our neighbour considerable distress. He was very concerned lest the Pakistani authorities take some action against him and asked if we could guarantee him some sort of safe haven in Britain. We did make some enquiries, but things never became as bad as he feared and he went on to have a successful career in the Bangladesh Foreign Service.

As they were living below us, we could always smell their meals cooking. These often seemed to be curries, of which I have always been very fond. We mentioned this to him once and he invited us to come and try their food. We gladly accepted and were looking forward to a spicy curry when, to our dismay, we were served a fairly bland stew. Our neighbours explained that they were well aware that British food was not spicy and they did want to offend us in any way. It was a rather disappointing cultural misunderstanding.

On another occasion he came up to tell me that he had, for the first time in his life, tried alcohol. He was clearly slightly tipsy and was quite reassured to be told that this was normal and that he was not going to have a severe negative medical reaction. I never remembered to ask him afterwards if he had much of a hangover, but as far as I know he never repeated the experiment.

The large majority of the students at MECAS being university graduates, and some being very recently out of university, from time to time social life tended to echo undergraduate high jinks. Apart from the MECAS Ball every year, there were occasional outings, such as the hiring of the first passenger train to run from Beirut to Tyre for about 20 years, and a game of donkey baseball.

This last was arranged by a private American student and the idea was to play baseball in the normal way, but to travel between the bases on the back of a donkey. The necessary animal had been hired for the afternoon, but it became highly unco-operative after the first few circuits and, by the middle of the game, was refusing to move at all. I can't remember the details now, but I suspect the game deteriorated into farce as it was only too easy to get the ball to a base while the batter was failing in his attempts to get the donkey to shift.

Part of the course was for students to be placed with Arab families in other parts of Lebanon, or even Syria, when political conditions allowed. There they would live for a week or so and supposedly absorb some Arabic from their social environment. There was a parable told underlining the problem we all found when trying to exercise our Arabic: that our interlocutors were even more interested in exercising their English. The story was that an English student, with rather poor Arabic, was sent to live in a remote village, where no one spoke any English at all, in order to acquire the necessary linguistic skills. After three months, his teacher went to reclaim him and on the outskirts of the village asked in Arabic where the Englishman was, to be answered by a local in English that he was "down there, mate, in the fish and chip shop."

In my first year, as part of this scheme I was sent with three or four other students to a small vineyard village called Wadi al'Araish just beyond the town of Zahle, at the head of a valley off the Bekaa. The village is Christian and the young man of the house was an active member of the Falange, the military wing of the extreme right Maronite party. It was generally assumed in Lebanon that all westerners were Christians and therefore would inevitably support the Christian factions.

The family house was fairly typically middle class Lebanese and I shared a bedroom with one of the sons of the house who was, I think, a teacher. They obviously went out of their way to look after me and the food was adequate, if somewhat unexpected. The bathroom facilities however were in the Middle Eastern, rather than European, style; the toilet being the hole in the ground variety and situated next to the shower head, all water and waste going down the same hole.

There was a story that, in an earlier year, one of the students from America had been introduced to a similar household. He had a fast car and found the arrangement so incommodious that every morning he would drive back to Shemlan from the village where he was staying in order to shower, use the toilet and have breakfast. Then he would return later in the morning to his puzzled hosts. What they made of this I can only guess, but it does not seem very polite.

Once three of us students were sent off for a short break to a small monastery in the valley of the Nahr al Kalb (Dog River). This was really quite comfortable and I, having drawn the long straw, actually had a bathroom en suite. Sitting on the roof of a Lebanese Christian religious establishment with the resident priest and two of my fellow students, one a Japanese, drinking wine in a Lebanese summer evening and discussing politics and religion was really a very pleasant experience.

In January 1971 I took the Administrative Grades Limited Competition written exam and, in contrast with my performance when taking the executive exam earlier when I only passed on my third attempt, I sailed comfortably through first time with a score of 316, a clear 46 points over the pass mark. Although I don't recall being told so in 1971, my file has a note that this put me 'well within the top 14% of DS Limited Competition Candidates' and that my analysis of statistics was 'one of the best answers given by any candidate'. As a result, I was invited to London later in the year for interview as the next step in the selection process. The timing proved a bit of a stumbling block, with the first date offered clashing with the Intermediate Arabic exam, and then the Civil Service Selection Board being on leave for the summer. Eventually, a date was set in

September.

I decided that if I were to go to the interview I would have more gravitas if I were clean-shaven. So I shaved off my beard again. The evening I did that, we were out to dinner when, after the meal and about three hours after we arrived, one of the other guests suddenly noticed and announced that I had shaved my beard. So, clearly, I didn't look much different with or without one.

I took the Intermediate Arabic exam at the end of the summer term in 1971 and, crushingly, was the only FCO student to fail. This caused some discussion between the FCO and MECAS, one argument being that I should leave MECAS, the other that I should stay and take the higher course, at the end of which I would surely pass at least the intermediate exam at the second attempt. This would ensure that the effort expended in educating me would not go to waste. In the event, I stayed and did indeed pass the intermediate exam as expected. I have since seen from my file that I had been pencilled in for a position in the embassy in Sana'a if I were to leave at that point., but Val was then pregnant with Stephanie and the medical facilities at Sana'a were poor so this was a factor in the decision that I should stay on.

After being informed in late August that I had failed the Intermediate Arabic exam, I was then told in mid-September that I had also failed the Administrative Competition. Having shone in the written part of the competition, which was effectively a substitute for a degree qualification, I had done disastrously in the interviews. One favourable comment in the final report was the rather patronising remark; "Perhaps the basic brainpower is there and he has never been trained to develop or apply it fully. It is a pity he did not go to university."

Not the high point of my career. Nevertheless, the family was thriving and our daughter, Stephanie, was born in the Trad Clinic, a private hospital, in Beirut on the 3rd of November 1971.

Her arrival had been slightly complicated, although not in a medical sense. After Val had started to experience contractions, Hilary, the wife of Ivan Callan, one of my fellow FCO students, had generously offered to baby-sit David and Alun while I ran Val down the mountain from Shemlan to the clinic. However, the nurse declared that Val's arrival was premature and sent us back up the hill again. The following evening, again Val had contractions and again Hilary kindly sat in the house while I drove my wife down the hill. The opinion of the nurse was exactly the same, but this time she relented and allowed Val to remain in the clinic while I went back up alone to Shemlan.

This was a Friday. On the Saturday morning I phoned the clinic from the school to ask how she was and was told that "they were both" fine. This was extremely annoying, as we had intended that I should be present at the birth. Val later told me that Stephanie really was on the way at the time of the second visit and, in spite of the nurse calling on her to "stop, stop!", our daughter insisted on arriving in her own time not long after I left the clinic. As in Kampala, we had no phone in the flat and so there was no way for me to be told at the time.

This was during the second part of the course and, in the lead up to the confinement, I should have been away on a language break again, staying at an Arab house and immersing myself in Arabic for a second time. But, in the circumstances, it was recognised that this would hardly be the right thing to do, so instead I attended a local secondary school on a daily basis. Sitting at the back of a class of 13 year-old Arab boys listening to their history lessons was not necessarily a terribly good study method. The teachers tended to want to talk to me in French and the children tended not to talk to me at all. Not only that, but one of them stole the GB sticker off the back of my car.

My performance at MECAS can best be illustrated by the last occasion that I bought a chicken at the little shop that we patronised at the bottom of the hill, just beyond Beirut Airport. It was after the end of the course and I had been a customer at the shop on and off for most of the previous 14 months. After the transaction, I was congratulated on my command of Arabic – but in English.

By the end of my time at MECAS, the posting to Sana'a had long been filled and I had been selected for the Vice Consul/Administration Officer (VC/AO) post in Abu Dhabi. This meant I had to attend a number of consular courses in London over the next few weeks. Before my departure to my new post, though, there had been an inspection of the Abu Dhabi Embassy, which, among other things, had created a new post of Third Secretary (Political) and it was decided that I would fill that position instead. However this would mean another person would have to do the VC/AO's job and it would not be possible to find this replacement for a month or two, during which time I would act as VC/AO. So my extra consular training was not wasted.

While I was at MECAS, Abu Dhabi had been a non car-owning post because of the poor state of the roads, in other words, the Office would not pay for a car to be sent there. But I already had a car in Lebanon and had to export it from that country, as it was only a temporary import. In the event, I sold it fairly cheaply to a MECAS colleague who was being posted to Saudi Arabia.

With MECAS finished, we flew back to England on the 12th of February 1972, this time as a family of five. Meanwhile, following Stephanie's birth, Val had been experiencing pains in her ear, and while we were back in Eastbourne, she went into hospital for a check-up. A tumour in her skull behind her ear was diagnosed and an operation was scheduled. But I had to go out to Abu Dhabi, so initially I went alone, with Val to follow with the children when possible.

CHAPTER 5

ABU DHABI 1972 – 1976

I arrived in Abu Dhabi on the 20th of May 1972. This followed a three-week stop in Lebanon to brush up my Arabic at MECAS after a three and a half month stay in the UK, which had included the required consular training. The rest of the family didn't follow me for some time because of Val's medical problem. Even though the tumour had been dealt with, it was to be some four months before she was given the all clear and she and the children came out.

Part of the trouble was that the surgeon, who had performed the operation, was so pleased with the outcome that he was loath to let his patient go. The technique was tricky and he was justly proud of the result. In the end, Colin Oliver, our friend who was then working at the pathological laboratory in the hospital and who had seen the results of Val's tests, passed on the word that there was really no reason why she couldn't travel. So she took this up with the surgeon and, eventually, the green light for her travel was given.

But there was one more snag; no notification was sent about her travel. This meant that, when the family arrived late one evening, I was not expecting them. Fortunately, I was at home when there was a phone call from an employee of the travel agency the Embassy used who knew me and who, very fortuitously, was on duty at the airport. I grabbed the necessary papers and shot out to the airport.

The year before I arrived, Abu Dhabi had become one of the United Arab Emirates (UAE), which had previously been known as the Trucial Oman Coast and had been under British protection. Originally, all the emirates, from Bahrain to Ras al Khaima, were supposed to form this federation, but both Bahrain and Qatar decided they could go it alone. For a time, one or two of the others toyed with the idea of following suit, but they were really too small and, more to the point, lacked any large oil reserves.

The rulers of these statelets had been in their positions for many years, which meant that most of them had been born camel herders or fishermen. The exception was Shaikh Rashid of Dubai, whose emirate had been successfully involved in trade long before oil was discovered in huge quantities in neighbouring Abu Dhabi. Dubai was therefore much more sophisticated, an edge which the emirate seems to have hung on to. Shaikh Zaid of Abu Dhabi was very much a late comer. Not only was Abu Dhabi regarded by Dubai as slightly beneath them, but Zaid himself had not been born to be ruler; that had been his elder brother, Shakbut. But, with the arrival of riches from oil, it was realised by the British authorities that Shakbut was not prepared to spend the money for the betterment of his people, so a small coup was manufactured and Zaid was placed in charge.

Zaid, in contrast to his brother, was certainly a spender; the infrastructural development started under him was massive for that time. Anything built then has since been completely dwarfed by more recent projects. When we arrived the road between Dubai and Abu Dhabi was just being finished and the first generation of tower blocks was still under construction. The road to Al Ain, the settlement in the interior of Abu Dhabi and bordering on Oman on the edge of the Empty Quarter, had been finished the year before. However, there was still no road north to Qatar and to drive there was a real adventure, even with a Land Rover, although one or two saloon cars had made it.

The problem was the area known as the Subkhat Matti, which was a lake when there was rain, but which for the rest of the time, which was most of the year, consisted of an area of loose sand. This was so soft, it had to be driven over at some speed to avoid bogging down. To be caught there by rain was an end to the journey until the sand dried again, even for trucks.

Although there are some rocky outcrops, Abu Dhabi is geologically basically a large sand bar and the shape of the island was continually being changed as dredgers pumped sand from the sea bed onto the shore, making new land.

Before Independence the various emirates were administered by officers known as British Agents, under the overall supervision of the British Resident in Bahrain. The whole arrangement existed under the terms of a 'Treaty of Maritime Peace in Perpetuity' between Britain and the various rulers which had been signed in 1853. However, as with so many other things as time passes, perpetuity was not what it had been and came to an end in 1971, when the treaty was terminated.

The British Agents in Abu Dhabi and Dubai had offices known, naturally enough, as Agencies. The Abu Dhabi Agency had now become an Embassy and the Agent, Jim Treadwell, became Ambassador. This really rankled with the Agent in Dubai, Bertie Saunders, who became a Consul General, but refused to regard his office as subordinate to Abu Dhabi. His attitude was bolstered by the fact that, although Abu Dhabi was the richest and largest of the emirates, the rulers had not finally agreed on a number of things about their federation and one of them was where the capital should be. As a result, Abu Dhabi was formally only the 'provisional capital' of the UAE.

Although, as usual in an embassy, there was a Head of Chancery as number two under the Ambassador in Abu Dhabi, the Consul General in Dubai was regarded as the deputy to the Ambassador within the UAE as a whole and, when the latter was away, the former came down from Dubai to sit in the ambassadorial office in Abu Dhabi as Chargé d'Affaires. All very unusual.

As I have mentioned, when I had first been posted, my job was to have been VC/AO, but, as I've already mentioned, before I got to post, the inspectors had visited and created a new position of Third Secretary (Political), which I was selected to fill, So I took over from the outgoing VC/AO and then moved over to political work when the new VC/AO arrived. However, a post can get by without a political officer far more easily than it can without an administration officer and I was often called back to admin work, for instance, when the incumbent caught hepatitis quite badly and also whenever he went on leave.

Shortly after I arrived, the Ambassador, Jim Treadwell, was transferred and a new Ambassador, Don McCarthy, was appointed. As is usual for a new Ambassador, a short time after his arrival, he presented his credentials to the head of state, Shaikh Zaid, in a ceremony at the official palace. It was normal that an Ambassador would take with him two or three members of his staff on these occasions and I was included in the accompanying group.

This was the first time I had attended a presentation of credentials but after Abu Dhabi I was present at the ceremonies of three other Ambassadors; Patrick Wright and Ivor Lucas both in

Damascus and Alan Goulty in Khartoum. The form of the ceremony was always similar. The Ambassador would hand over his Letters of Credence signed by the Queen and make a small speech in Arabic referring to the good relations which so happily existed between the two countries, whether this was strictly true or not. There was nothing much for the supporting staff to do except make up the numbers and stand there looking suitably serious.

On these occasions, the host government would provide the transport and on both occasions in Damascus I had to point out to the driver of the official car that the Union Flag was upside down. Each time, they readily complied by turning it round the right way, but obviously could see no difference and were simply humouring me.

My main job in Abu Dhabi as Third Secretary was one grade higher than it had been in Kampala and carried representational responsibilities. This meant that I had diplomatic status and was expected to entertain on an official basis both local officials and, if necessary, British visitors. It also meant I had diplomatic plates on my car. Diplomatic status also meant I received an extra 'representational allowance' to cover the increased cost of these duties.

This allowance was accountable and so a record had to be kept of all the food prepared, drink consumed and the wages of any supplementary staff hired for the occasion, such as waiters and barmen. The practical effect of this was that at the end of a party, dinner or other function, after the guests had gone and while the debris was being cleared away, we went round and counted up the various empty bottles or cans etc. in order to calculate the actual cost of the drinks. Of course, the costs of the food and staff were clear.

The climate in the Gulf is extreme in the summer, with the temperature, measured in Fahrenheit and humidity both around 100. So, during the summer months practically all vehicles and buildings were air-conditioned, with the exception of the middle and lower range cars of the day. Which brings me to a sore point. As I have mentioned, when we left MECAS, Abu Dhabi was not a car-owning post. But, while I was at home waiting to come out to Abu Dhabi, the rules were changed and we were allowed to take a car. But I had already sold mine in Lebanon and now I hadn't the money to buy a similar new one, so I bought a smaller one, a Hillman Imp. This was a sort of reply to the Mini, but with a rear-mounted aluminium engine.

There was no suggestion from the salesman that it wouldn't do for Abu Dhabi, but it was completely unsuitable. With a rear engine and a cooling system depending on a fan passing air over a radiator positioned in the middle of the vehicle, it was just the car not to take to an area with very high ambient temperatures. It was also a tad small for a family of five including three growing children. On long journeys, we had to drive with an eye on the temperature gauge, which was thoughtfully provided. On one trip we had to obtain water from a house we were passing and on another we sacrificed our orange squash to the radiator in order to keep the wretched thing going.

Such trips as we made while posted to Abu Dhabi did not take us outside the UAE, but we did manage to penetrate as far north as Ras el Khaimah and as far east as Al Ein. Heading north beyond Dubai the emirates were still completely undeveloped and I can recall that when we visited Sharjah, we were able to walk through the coastal suq which only a year or two later was completely demolished in order to build a more fashionable waterside Corniche. On this particular trip we called at one of the small shops in the suq to buy some simple rubber flip-flops for Alun who had managed to lose his. By the time we reach the end of the road we realised that he had walked out of them and was again barefoot.

One of the pleasures of the post was the Embassy dhow. This was a small, locally-made boat with a simple Lister diesel engine and had been purchased for the Embassy from the proceeds of the sale of liquor licences when it had been the British

Political Agency and responsible for such things. While a fee had to be charged for this service, there was no mechanism for crediting the income to the British Government. So it was agreed that the money should be placed in a recreation fund for staff and this had purchased the dhow.

Something else which the Agency used to do and which the Embassy no longer did was to issue certificates of manumission. Slavery had effectively continued in the area well into the 1950s and it had been the law that any slave who could reach and touch the flagpole of the Agency would be manumitted, that is, regarded as free and granted a certificate to that effect. I remember a stock of these certificates still in the registry of the Embassy, but somebody later took them as souvenirs.

The dhow was our transport to the neighbouring island of Sadiyat where there were few inhabitants and one almost continuous beach. In Muslim countries, Friday is the day of rest and Sunday is just another working day. British Embassies in these countries follow this pattern. So on a Friday those who had booked the vessel, plus their guests, drove down to the Beach Club at the end of the main island of Abu Dhabi, where the boat was kept and pulled it in from its offshore mooring. They then hoisted on board the picnic requirements, followed by the women and children, cranked up the engine and puttered off to a boozy afternoon. The main problem was lack of shade; there was none on shore, so we had to provide our own and often retreated to the dhow, which was rigged with an awning.

While in Abu Dhabi I decided I would take up scuba diving. The local oil companies had a number of qualified divers working for them and one of these agreed to give lessons to some of us in the Embassy. These were initially based in the Embassy swimming pool and I was one of three males from the Embassy who decided to take the course. It was the BSAC (British Sub Aqua Club) qualification which is more demanding than the equivalent American qualification from PADI (Professional Association of Diving Instructors). To start with we had to swim two lengths of the swimming pool with a weight belt on and then later dive to the bottom of the pool, where the full set of scuba equipment was waiting. We had to collect this and put it all on in one dive, getting hold of the breathing apparatus first followed by the weights, the mask and then lastly the flippers.

Having passed this section of the test we went out for a sea dive from the dhow. As I recall, this only happened once and was quite a traumatic event for me. We sailed a short distance and anchored out of the way of any shipping, but in a deepish channel and there was a fair tide running. The instructor and two divers went down and one person remained on the boat. A plastic rope was paid out into the current as a grab line and this floated downstream.

At this time I had just an ordinary plain glass face-mask. Later, in Antigua, I invested in a two-lens face mask which was prepared to my prescription and was a great help when diving. But in Abu Dhabi my short-sightedness was a bit of a handicap.

So down we went. The visibility was quite good and, after a swim of some 15 minutes or so, the instructor decided we should return to the boat. The accepted underwater signal for 'I am ascending' is to raise the thumb, which is usually the symbol for 'I'm OK'. The sign for 'I'm OK', on the other hand, being the forming a circle between the finger and thumb of the right hand. Along with many others, I did not find this intuitive, even though, of course, it had been covered in the training we had received. Naturally, the instructor made sure we were both looking at him and raised his thumb. I was fine and so without thinking I simply raised my thumb back and kept on swimming. The instructor did not look round again to make sure I was following and by the time I realised I was alone I could no longer see the others.

The current was running quite fast by now and, although I could see the hull of the dhow from below, to keep station with it took a lot of effort. Now, the one thing you can't do in a scuba set is pant, nor can you do it through a snorkel, which we all had as well and I was becoming breathless through my efforts to fight the current, so I had to surface. I came up well within earshot of those on the dhow, all of whom were now back on board. But, although they told me that I was next to the rope lifeline, I couldn't see it and was being washed further away all the time. In the end, as I was clearly tiring, they told me to float and they would come and collect me. So off I floated on the tide while, in the increasing distance, I could just about make out the activity as my friends raised the anchor, started the engine and sailed after me.

While just floating and waiting for the rescue I was able to regain my breath and, in the event, I didn't have to ditch the scuba equipment and weights, which had been a possibility. This must have been a great relief to the instructor, who had borrowed them from his employers. Although the outcome could have been serious or, I suppose, fatal, I have never made much of it and can't remember what the version of events was that I related to Val.

Soon after this our instructor was transferred by his employers and no one took his place, so I had to wait several years until my posting to Antigua to actually qualified as a scuba diver and then with the simpler American PADI system.

My duties in Abu Dhabi included acting as a contact point for the British Council. For most of my time the Council did not have an office in Abu Dhabi, but covered it with a resident officer up the coast in Dubai. Earlier in my tour, I think in 1973, the new Chairman of the British Council, Baron Ballantrae, the former Brigadier Sir Bernard Fergusson, came out on a visit. I assume he must have called on the Ambassador, but as the Dubai representative of the British Council, Doug Pickett, was a friend of mine from MECAS days, we were taken out for a meal with the lord and his lady.

He was a strikingly tall man with an old fashioned military moustache and a monocle. He is one of the very few people I have ever met to wear a monocle as a normal item and he had the rather odd habit of polishing it between his thumb and forefinger. No cloth or handkerchief, just his digits. As a result it was easy to see that the glass was quite smeared, but this clearly didn't bother him.

A few years earlier, the Sheikh of Abu Dhabi had presented the then Political Agent with a plot of land in Al Ein. As was the case with the all generous gifts in the Middle East, it was recognised that it would be extremely rude to refuse it and therefore some thought had to be given to how it should be used. Eventually, the Office agreed that a small bungalow could be built on the site, which would be generally available to Embassy staff for recreation. The drive to Al Ein was on a black top road, although the minor roads leading to the bungalow were rough tracks. It was often used by staff and when my parents came to visit we took them out there for a stay of two or three days.

Al Ein at that time still retained many of its traditional features and it was possible to walk through the date palms irrigated by a system of small channels, known as '*qanawat*'. A short way outside the town, there were hills which were effectively made up of millions and millions of sea fossils. We always took the children there when we went to Al Ain and to one particularly well-stocked valley, which was easy to access, providing we used the Embassy Land Rover. We rather unimaginatively called this 'Fossil Valley' and I still have a number of the fossilised seashells we picked up there.

Most of the admin work I was required to do during the regular incumbent's absences was the normal run-of-the-mill stuff, but on one occasion I did manage to save the FCO a considerable amount of money.

A new Embassy building was being constructed and two resident construction supervisors were posted to us. One of them was not only married, but also had three children and, as there was no Embassy accommodation available, they were initially placed in a hotel. Even after a flat had been identified for them, furniture had to be ordered from the UK and, as the Suez Canal was still blocked, this would take some two months to come out by sea round Africa. During the whole of this period the family would have to stay in the hotel.

I did some calculations and discovered that it would cost some £3,000 to accommodate the family in the hotel for this period, whereas for about £2,000 I could buy sufficient furniture on the market locally to equip the flat, saving Her Majesty's Government the difference. And, of course, the family in question would have a home of their own that much sooner. When I put this scheme to the authorities in London they were very doubtful. Would the locally bought furniture fit with the style that they were supplying, and how long would it last? This was complete nonsense, because we could have thrown the whole lot away as soon as the new furniture arrived and still been in pocket, but I reassured them and was given the go-ahead.

The exchange of diplomatic bags every week was the norm in Abu Dhabi, as it had been in Kampala. However, in Abu Dhabi there were no security officers and the registry staff did the courier runs to the airport, with other UK based staff taking turns as escorts. A diplomatic courier, grandly known as a Queen's Messenger (QM), flew down the Gulf on a local service which hopped between the various posts from Dubai to Kuwait.

On one occasion, I was the escort to a registry clerk, Jeremy Larner. As there had been some delay in the flight, before leaving for the airport, we were waiting to hear from Dubai that the plane carrying the QM was on its way. Eventually, we received a call from our colleagues up the Gulf saying that the plane with the QM had taken off. That was a bit late for us, as the flight time from Dubai to Abu Dhabi was less than the drive time from our Embassy to Abu Dhabi Airport, so we shot off.

When we got to Abu Dhabi Airport, the plane had not only landed, but had its engines running in preparation to take off again. This was a plane with steps built in to the door which extended out and down. As we arrived and rushed across the tarmac, the steps were already being retracted. The stewardess on the door clearly thought we were passengers nearly missing our flight, and lowered them again. We shot up the steps and found the QM handily seated next to the door.

At this point the stewardess realised her mistake and asked us to leave, as the plane was about to take off. We had only just started the handover process, which involved checking bag numbers and signing for them, so we had to stay. This did not please the crew as the plane had time to make up and we were told that if didn't get off immediately, the captain would take off with us on board.

This would never do, so I told Jeremy to go just outside the door and stand on the steps. This meant that they couldn't be retracted and so the plane couldn't take off. The captain must have been apoplectic, but he had to stay in the cockpit as he had completed his take off checks. Eventually, we finished our tasks, expressed our apologies for the inconvenience and scampered off down the steps, which were immediately retracted. We smartly removed ourselves from the vicinity of the aircraft as it swung round with its jet exhausts fairly clearly aimed at us.

Just before I arrived in Abu Dhabi, there had been an attempt to sell the Harrier 'jump jet' to the local air force. At the time, the Abu Dhabi Air Force flew Hawker Hunters, which, even then, were a bit long in the tooth. The demonstration of the speed at which the Harrier could become airborne compared to the Hunter was extremely impressive. From the call of 'scramble', the Harrier was in the air and making its first pass over the airfield by the time the Hunter had taxied to the end of the runway in order to take off. However, in spite of this rapid response performance, the French could offer them the delta-winged Mirage, which was far sexier to look at and travelled faster. Whether or not it was a suitable aircraft for the needs of Abu Dhabi was not really considered.

However, probably the defining problem with the Harrier, as far as sales to Abu Dhabi were concerned, was a demonstration of the plane when it was flown in front of Sheikh Zaid. It had been intended that it should fly slowly towards the Ruler at a few metres height in hover mode and 'bow' by dipping its nose in front of him. A miscalculation by the pilot meant that, as the plane moved towards the dais, it overshot slightly and had to reverse. It could easily do that, of course, but this was in the desert and, apart from blasting sand over the Sheikh and his entourage, in reversing the plane moved into its own dust cloud, which was quite extensive and the pilot lost sight of the ground. As a result, he cut the engines too soon and landed heavily, punching both the wheels through the wings in the process. The demonstration was not a success and the plane had to be air-freighted out for repair. Needless to say, the Abu Dhabi Air Force bought Mirages.

During our time, there was an attempt to sell hovercraft to Abu Dhabi. They were ideal for travel over shallow water and even mangrove swamps that were impenetrable to any other vehicle. There had been sales of these air cushion vehicles to Saudi Arabia some years before and it was felt that a similar effort would also be successful in Abu Dhabi.

While the visit was taking place, we, as a family, were invited to go on a flight. It was quite memorable, as this was the military, not passenger, version and we were simply sitting in the open air on the cargo area in the front of the vehicle. As advertised, it passed effortlessly over the shallow water and low mangrove swamps, which grew around the coasts of Abu Dhabi, and was equally at home skimming over the water and the sand.

However, there was an irrational fear amongst the local military that, if the air cushion skirt were punctured, the vehicle would crash and sink. A demonstration was given where a number of rifle shots were deliberately fired through the skirt to no ill effect. As with the Harrier, though, the air displacement over a sandy desert meant that people in the immediate area tended to be sand blasted. Again, there were no sales.

During one of my periods as acting Vice Consul, I had to deal with the case of a forged British passport held by a South African girl who was illegally in the UAE. She had been sharing a flat with another girl in London when she had fallen for an oil engineer who was later posted to an oilfield in Abu Dhabi.

At the time, South Africa was applying apartheid and was a pariah state as far as much of the world was concerned.. As a result, South African citizens could not travel to the UAE, so the girl stole her flatmate's British passport.

British passports of the time had a hand-written personal description on the second page, which was either written at the time of issue, or had a sheet stuck on which had been written up by the holder in advance. This one had such a sheet and the South African girl had steamed this off and written her own details on the blank page underneath. Photos in British passports were not laminated in those days either and she had also steamed off the original photograph and substituted a photograph of herself printed on fairly thin paper, which effectively took up the impression of the embossment. She thus had the other girl's name on the cover and on page one and her details and photo on the other pages. She then persuaded the boyfriend to arrange for her to be sponsored for a UAE visa by his employing company.

Unfortunately, there was a falling out after they got to Abu Dhabi and, during a drunken episode, he pushed her out of a moving vehicle on the road to the airport. As a result, she was temporarily hospitalised and the story came out. Fortunately, she had brought her own South African passport with her and this established her true identity and nationality. Unfortunately, though, the boyfriend had written obscenities in red felt tip pen on this passport.

The boyfriend was British, but the company he worked for was American and the local manager came to the Embassy claiming that the British Government should pay for the girl's return to the UK as she had entered on a British passport. I took a robust line, pointing out that she had travelled out on a forged British passport, was in fact a South African citizen, and actually had a South African passport. To make the point, I withdrew the British passport and cancelled it. I guess that the manager was in some way responsible for the fact that the company had been persuaded to sponsor the entry of the girl and he was furious. What, he asked, if he announced that the South African passport was also a forgery. In that case, I replied, she would be a potentially stateless person and become the responsibility of the UAE Government, as she was present in their territory.

All the while the subject of all this discussion remained in hospital, although there was some doubt as to whether she was really ill enough to warrant this. Nevertheless, it was convenient all round that she stay there, as it neatly dodged the question of who was responsible for her accommodation.

In the end I agreed to ask the FCO to contact the South African authorities through their Embassy in London, who very unwillingly agreed to repatriate her from Abu Dhabi as far as London.

To make sure she actually left the country, I went to the airport, where she arrived by ambulance from the hospital, and was entertained with a view of her waving to all and sundry while being carried to the plane on a stretcher wearing a large wide-brimmed hat, having produced her obscenely defaced South African passport at immigration on departure.

I subsequently received a plaintive letter from Consular Department in London reporting that their contact in the South African Embassy in London had bemoaned spending most of their emergency budget getting the girl back to London. No mention of thanks for making the actual arrangements for the girl, though.

Abu Dhabi had an increasing population of

Christians both European and Indian, but there was no area allocated for Christian burials. Eventually, Shaikh Zaid was persuaded to donate a piece of land off the island of Abu Dhabi as a designated Christian burial ground. The area seemed to have been chosen at random on a map as, when it was investigated, it was found that a large portion of it was in fact solid rock. There was a small sandy area, but this tended to be appropriated by the Christian Indian community for burial of small children. This practice was an unrecorded use and caused considerable concern to the local Anglican Archdeacon, who was primarily responsible for the cemetery.

On one occasion when we did have to bury a British Christian, the nature of the ground caused serious problems. The deceased was a harbour pilot, who had fallen from a boarding ladder as he reached the deck of a tanker which was in ballast and thus riding very high in the water. The distance was several metres and the impact on the water killed him.

We registered his death at the Embassy and were also involved in the arrangements for the burial. However, when the company that employed him made its preliminary investigation of the graveyard, it discovered the problem caused by the rock and so a pneumatic drill had to be brought down from Dubai in order to create the grave. In the event, this was done in advance and did not detract from the service, although the stark illustration of the difficulty prompted the preparation of three graves in advance for future use while the drill was to hand.

Shortly before Christmas 1974, we saw a sign in the local supermarket asking for volunteers to form a choir for Christmas to sing at the local Anglican church. Val and I decided it would be rather nice to participate in the singing of Christmas carols and meet more people, so we both volunteered. However, our idea of what this was to entail was somewhat at variance with what was intended. The group had envisaged a serious organised choir, with distinct vocal parts, descants and so on. The various individual singers were allocated categories. I was a tenor apparently. We were encouraged to practice our parts and were issued with cassette tapes to help with this. Although we declared our limited ability, our dismay at the implied level of ability went unrecognised and we were not allowed to withdraw. Nevertheless, we were not asked to participate in following years.

The local British community school had a slightly idiosyncratic headmistress who was determinedly against the idea of a parent teacher association and forbade any of her teachers to join one. As there were a number of parents who were also strong minded, this resulted in the establishment of a purely parent association of which I ended up as chairman. It was a rather odd situation as the money raised by the association was not really required by the school, which was basically funded by the local oil companies and had all the money it really required. We therefore had the embarrassing task each year of deciding how to spend the money we had raised. Almost everything we suggested would have been provided by the oil companies, but it was a vehicle for social activity.

In theory, the UAE observed the Muslim prohibition on alcohol. In practice, there were many exceptions. For instance, all expatriates had a liquor licence and the local branch of Gray MacKenzie was authorised to sell a very generous monthly quota to them. On top of this, the large hotels were also allowed to serve the stuff to foreigners. There were a couple of small restaurants where a rather transparent charade was carried out of serving wine brought in by customers out of a teapot, but there really didn't seem to be much point.

Many of the locals, though, were generally observant in this area, and thus had pretty well zero tolerance of the effects of alcohol. This was brought home on one occasion when the Royal Navy frigate, HMS Ariadne, was visiting and the Ambassador gave a cocktail party for the officers in his residence. As usual, the Embassy staff were helping host the function and there were a few others invited.

In Abu Dhabi all local men tended to dress in the long white gown know as a dishdasha, which made it hard to gauge the status of the wearer. So it was not easy to identify the stranger who was amongst the guests, but he certainly seemed to be enjoying himself, as Val pointed out to me with some concern. I asked him in Arabic which ministry he was from. The Ministry of Education, he replied. Odd, nobody recalled anyone from there being on the invitation list.

Then the penny dropped; the officers had been brought from the harbour in a school bus, provided by the Ministry of Education. The man was the driver, who had wandered in with everybody else. No wonder he was enjoying himself; he had almost certainly never had alcohol in his life before. I immediately told the serving staff that he should have nothing more to drink, but it was too late. At the end of the party he did actually manage to get the officers back to their ship in the port, as we could see the following day from the tyre tracks leading straight across the roundabout by the entrance to the port and the skid marks beside the ship's gangplank.

Having sold our first house when we left for MECAS, we realised during our posting to Abu Dhabi that we had better get back on to the housing ladder. So, during our four weeks leave period in 1974, we managed to buy a small semi-detached house in a different area of Polegate from where we had been before. We were fortunate in that the sellers were emigrating and therefore were not in a chain and, of course, neither were we.

Our intention was to let to this house out while we were overseas and use it as a base when we returned. Unfortunately the law at that time allowed sitting tenants absolute priority on the question of tenure and when we came back from Abu Dhabi we had to stay with Val's parents for a week or two until our tenants could find somewhere else to go. They were not being awkward, but having been unable to find alternative accommodation, they were legally entitled to remain in our house thus making us, rather than them, technically homeless.

The normal period of posting to Abu Dhabi was three times 12 months. However, I had anticipated been brought back for a further UK posting and therefore volunteered for a fourth year. Thus, at the end of my time, I was by far the longest serving member of UK-based staff.

My reports towards the end of my time had qualified me for accelerated promotion, but this would only take effect the next time I moved. As I had already asked to remain at post, ironically this meant I had delayed my own promotion.

We left post on the 17th of July, 1976 for, as I had feared, another home posting. This time, though, I was not to be posted to an FCO department, but had been selected for a nominally postgraduate course at the Polytechnic of Central London leading to a Diploma in Management Studies (DMS), which would last the best part of a year.

CHAPTER 6

LONDON 1976 – 1979

We arrived back in England in the middle of the 1976 heat wave and when we got home the temperature was very little different from that in the Gulf. This should have meant that we weren't too uncomfortable, but in England we had no air-conditioning and we were expecting a relatively cool British summer, so it was quite bothersome while it lasted. In particular the commuting I was required to do in this weather was dire, as the trains also had no air-conditioning. There would be a through draught from open windows once the train was moving, but sitting in a carriage waiting for the 'off' in Victoria Station could be a sweaty misery.

It was during this home posting that we started to move the children into boarding school. Because state education in the UK was always free, as soon as children started school overseas, any fees were refunded, provided the education was as close as possible to the British standard. This was generally alright for kindergarten and infant levels., but for higher levels, boarding education in UK was paid for because, in many parts of the world where we might serve, there would be no English language school available, let alone any providing education to a British syllabus. This applied to officers of all grades as well as, in the interest of continuity, to periods of home duty.

However, one of the cock-eyed Treasury regulations was that, even if you were on a home posting and the school was sufficiently close by, you could not send your child there as a day pupil. The point of principle was that if you could send the child as a day pupil, you should do so at the local state school and so didn't qualify for the education allowance. (No mention of continuity there, then.) As a result, everybody in this situation kept their children at their local boarding school and saw them at the weekend while the Government footed a larger bill.

We sent David to boarding school in 1976 on our return from Abu Dhabi, Alun the following year and Stephanie in September 1979, just before we went out to Damascus. She was only eight and Val was deeply unhappy about this, more so than with the boys, but they were all in our home town and had four grandparents and an aunt and uncle living locally, so they were hardly cut off from the family. Moreover, Val wrote to them religiously every week, whether they replied or not - often not, in the case of the boys. Much later, we sent Robert to boarding school when we went to Khartoum in 1993.

For the second time I was returning to London on promotion, this time to Grade 7E, a second secretary grade. The day of my promotion was Monday the 27th of September, the day I had to return to the daily commute. This was the start of the course and I was technically a student. I was even officially enrolled in the National Union of Students, as this was a condition of the course.

This course was entitled a 'Postgraduate Course in Management Studies' and at the end of it I was awarded a Diploma in Management Studies, so I'm actually entitled to put the letters 'DMS' after my name, not that I've ever felt inclined to do so. The course was held in the Polytechnic of Central London building in Baker Street. The place is now part of the University of Westminster, so I can almost say I went to university after all. There were no private British students on my full-time version of the course; they were on the evening version and we never saw them. I was one of two civil servants; the other one, oddly enough, was Andy Kidd who had been in the year above me at Eastbourne Grammar School and whom I had not seen again up to then, or since, if it comes to that. There were a few foreign students and the rest were a selection of the unemployed who were being paid for from a government scheme called, I think, TOPS, which stood for something like Training Opportunities.

The final part of the course was the preparation of a project in the field of management, which, in my case, had to be relevant to the FCO. After looking at the suggestions put forward by the few departments that responded to a request for them, I decided to accept the challenge offered by Finance Department to review the financial recording system used by the FCO and recommend improvements. This involved working with Finance Department and, much more interestingly, looking at the systems used by other, similar organisations, mainly other foreign services. So I visited the admin sections of the UN office and of the US and German embassies in London to collect copies of their forms and talk to their accountants.

I produced three copies of the final report; one for the Polytechnic, one for the FCO and one which I still have. I doubt that the result had much effect on the later operations of the accounting procedures of the FCO, as the technological advances which have actually been adopted were unforeseeable in 1977.

At the end of my course, in spite of my newly acquired qualification, there was no post immediately available for me and I was somewhat supernumerary. So I was asked to undertake a review of historical staffing levels of all overseas posts since the merger of the FO and CRO, as there was no comprehensive record of these. I was promised the help of a clerk, but this was forthcoming only for a short period; staff levels were, as always, tight and the job was not exactly an attractive one, as it involved trawling through old files dealing with staffing and inspection records. In the event I did nearly all of it myself, which was pretty boring stuff.

For small posts, the exercise was quite straight forward, but in larger posts it was surprisingly quite tricky trying to identify, for instance, those in diplomatic missions who were not FCO employed, but were staff of other government bodies. In Washington, to take the extreme example, a huge number of the Embassy staff were not and never had been on the FCO payroll. The Ministry of Defence and Treasury in particular have dozens of staff as do many other home departments.

And then there were both MI5 and MI6. Being concerned mainly with domestic security, MI5 has relatively few overseas staff, but MI6, dealing with external security, naturally has many. The policy is always that their presence is neither confirmed nor denied in any particular place, so their numbers were obscure, as was the aim, of course. With this in mind, I asked them, through my Head of Department, for a list of the numbers of their people in posts over the years so that I could deduct this from those at post to get the figure for FCO staff. When this came, I only needed to check the given figures against my personal knowledge of the posts I had been in to see that they were, for the most part, a complete fabrication.

Anyway, I did eventually produce my figures, which I think have formed the basis for various statistical exercises since. This is not because of any necessarily intrinsic high quality in my work, but more because nobody else is likely to have had the time or inclination to go through the whole exercise again in order to check or replace my figures.

After this, I was offered a job in Manpower Section of Personnel Policy Department, where I had been based during my project research, and I accepted. I already knew the head of the department, so the appointment interview was pretty much a formality. As I have come across so often in the Service from time to time, though, there was an annoyingly patronising element to the meeting.

After the date of my joining had been agreed, the Head of Department, writing the date in his diary, commented that I would be arriving on that date "d.v." I smiled politely, but didn't say anything. "*Deo volante*" he expanded and, when I still didn't respond immediately, assuming I was puzzled by the erudite Latin expression, translated for me - "God willing." I forbore from explaining I knew full well what d.v. stood for and meant and that the pause in my response was due to my considering whether it would be rude for me to embarrass him by responding with the Arabic equivalent; "*in sha'allah*", which I was pretty sure wouldn't be familiar to him.

The actual job was to monitor the current establishment numbers of staff in posts at home and overseas. Apart from dealing with various claims for increases in numbers, we also provided briefs for the inspectors who reviewed the operation of overseas

131

posts and FCO home departments. We then applied their staffing recommendations as and when these were accepted. This required us to read through inspection reports in full. At that time inspections took place about every three years on average and I remember gaining the strong impression that over two cycles of inspections, what one inspector recommended as a change at one time, his successor might well change back again.

At that time both the Passport Office and the India Office Library and Records were under the FCO and were subject to the inspection cycle. So I treasure two nuggets of information from reading the inspection report on the India Office Library and Records - that it held the death registration details of Napoleon Bonaparte and had a 'working model' of the Black Hole of Calcutta.

The second item is perhaps understandable, if a little bizarre, but why should they have records of Napoleon? Well, it seems that at the time of his death, Saint Helena was administered as part of the Bombay Presidency, so the records fell under Indian jurisdiction.

These records have since been digitised and all the India Office Records data are now held by the British Library. If you want, you can see Napoleon's death record on their website at 'St Helena Baptisms, Marriages and Burials, Archive reference N-6-2, page 211.'

I think it was in 1978 that the Government, as periodically happens, was looking for savings. The cry invariably goes up that the FCO is an obvious waste of money and is thus always targeted. The fact that the whole diplomatic expenditure on salaries and property is less than that of any one of several large British municipalities never receives a sympathetic hearing. Anyway, on this occasion the minister of state responsible for staff decided that a straightforward way of reducing costs was to cut staff numbers by simply suspending recruitment – completely. This was to include all Diplomatic Service employees, both at home and abroad, and both UK-based and locally employed. This sounded good in theory, but in practice, around the world in over 150 different posts there were many thousands of local staff. All these, we were told, would be also subject to this restriction.

With such a huge and disparate work force, it was always going to be the case that large numbers each month would be leaving, retiring or being sacked for various misdemeanours. Never mind, was the ruling, no recruitment was to take place for any reason.

The screams of rage soon started to roll in. One head of mission in a small post who was forbidden to replace a cleaner asked if the Office expected him to clean the toilets himself. And I took a call from Mike Abrams, now in the administration section of the Embassy in Brazil to explain to him that if they sacked their driver for deliberately driving over flower beds to impress the local ladies, then they would have to drive the car themselves as they couldn't replace him.

As the complaints built up, a submission was made to the minister pointing out these and similar consequences and it was agreed that a limited number of staff could be recruited world-wide, subject to ministerial agreement on each occasion.

Well, that didn't last long, either; the power of agreement was devolved from the minister to an under secretary and fairly soon after that it all faded away. But I think I remember that the first 'derogation' from the rule was made in favour of the Ambassador to Ireland, who wanted to recruit a butler, a position paid for by the Office and therefore subject to the ban.

On the 19th of October 1978, having completed my two-year probation in Grade 7E, I was issued with my Diplomatic Commission. Commissions were not issued to lower grades and this marked a milestone in my career. This was the first of three occasions in which Her Majesty recorded her view that she regarded me as 'Trusty and Well-beloved'. The other two were when I was issued with consular commissions, first as Consul for Jerusalem, and then as Consul General for Sudan. In those two latter occasions she additionally assured the world that she 'reposed especial trust and confidence in [my] discretion and faithfulness.' Which was all very nice, but when I actually met her in 1983, she didn't seem to recognise me.

On the 3rd of May 1979, the day of the general election that saw Margaret Thatcher brought to power, I was asked to be the FCO representative on a Civil Service Department recruitment board for clerical officers. This was purely for Home Civil Service positions and none of these would be candidates for the FCO, but apparently we usually supplied one person for the board. Given the events of the day, we were allowed to ask the candidates about politics, but not how they had voted.

The general standard was not very high I noted with dismay, casting my mind back some 17 years when I had been interviewed by just such a selection board. The impressive ones had already got other, better jobs in view. In this category, I remember one young man from East London and a girl whose family had travelled quite widely. Others were unlikely to go far. These included the married woman returning to work after some years and the girl who claimed she was studying politics, but whose comment on the election was to regurgitate a Labour Party election slogan as her own opinion.

Also during 1979 I took over the administration of another cost-cutting exercise that had been introduced the previous year. This was the concept of a simplified administration system for some smaller posts, intended to cut the amount of work and thus, and most importantly, the number of staff required to do it. Originally these posts were to be called 'mini missions', but the ministerial view was that this sounded too cheap and so they were formally, and unimaginatively, called 'small missions'. The idea having been introduced, the next step was go round the world finding posts small enough to be reduced in this way. This had been started by the time I took it over and my work involved replying to various inquiries about how the system should actually work in practice.

During my time in London I had been persistently badgering Personnel Department for another overseas posting on the grounds that I'd only had two since I joined the office in 1962. I have seen from my file that they weren't particularly sympathetic with this view, but when my posting did come it was to the Arab world which meant that I would again receive a language allowance. In 1979 I was told that I would be going to Damascus to take on the position of Second Secretary (Commercial) for a posting of three years. After that they would look again at my promotion prospects.

In May that year, after my posting to Damascus had been announced, I was selected to be part of the scheme, introduced at the request of the Israeli government, to expose FCO Arabists, who were, of course, assumed to be biased towards the Arabs, to the 'reality' of the situation in Israel. So, from the 20th to the 27th of May, I was paired with a young new entrant second secretary who was on his way to post in Saudi Arabia after language training. We were taken around Israel and the Occupied Territories, first by the Embassy in Tel Aviv, and later by the Consulate General in Jerusalem.

At this time Israel was still occupying the Sinai Peninsula in Egypt and the Embassy had responsibility for this area as well as Gaza. For that reason, they had a first secretary Arabist on their staff. Later, after the settlement between Egypt and Israel and the Israeli withdrawal from Sinai, responsibility for Gaza was shifted to the Jerusalem Consulate General and the Embassy lost their Arabist.

Most of what I saw, of course, I was to see again in much greater detail after my posting to Jerusalem some 10 years later. But one of the things that was not there when I returned to the area was the Israeli settlement town of Yamit on the coast of the Sinai Peninsula beyond Gaza and in Egyptian territory. The Israelis had constructed a complete small seaside town, together with a war memorial on the outskirts recording the names of their troops who had died there in a tank battle during the Israeli advance into Egypt. Later, as part of the settlement with Egypt, Israel withdrew from the area and as is their normal practice with surrendered territory, completely razed the town, ensuring there was nothing left for the benefit of the returning Egyptians.

Two things stick in my memory from the visit, apart from the fact that it was extremely hot. One was the walking tour of the Old City of Jerusalem that the Consul General, Michael Hannam, took us on. He was an expert on the history of the area and this was his retirement post, I think, so the outing had a lecture-like quality. The other was that the locally engaged (Israeli) staff from the Tel Aviv Embassy were pumping Israeli propaganda at us the whole time they were driving us from Tel Aviv to the Golan Heights and back.

Shortly after I returned from that tour, we had to get on with pre-posting preparations once more, ordering clothes, tax free equipment and a car for our new post and arranging for the packers to call. This time the car I decided to go for was a Hillman Avenger estate, a decision I really didn't regret. As with our posting to MECAS, we took delivery of the car in England as we were again planning to drive much of the way.

I had planned our route across Europe to Brindisi in southern Italy, where we would take a ferry to Igonomitsa in Greece, then across Greece to Volos for another ferry to Latakia in Syria.

As with our trip to Italy on the way to Lebanon

in 1970, we had to make detailed preparations for the trip, although this time we were without accompanying children as they were all in boarding school.

CHAPTER 7

DAMASCUS 1979 - 1982

We set off on the 5th of October, 1979 and our planned route worked quite well until Volos. Apart, that is, from missing our way completely in Brindisi, going the wrong way down a road and ending up looking at (and being looked at with interest from) a large open-air market in what was probably the central piazza. A large and exasperated *caribiniero* was on duty there. He took one look at our British registration, bent down to my window and said; "All a-right – where a-you a-wanna go?" (Yes, really; just like that). He then efficiently directed us back to the straight and narrow, so to speak.

The ferry trip to Greece was overnight and, although we had a cabin, there were many who were travelling as deck passengers and the ablution facilities were, shall we say, over-stretched in the morning. After a short stop at Corfu, the ferry arrived, still fairly early in the morning, at Igonomitsa. We had been told that petrol was cheaper in Greece than Italy, so we had run our fuel reserves down and the first thing we did after driving off the ferry was to fill up at a petrol station which was conveniently pretty well on the quayside. We were somewhat perturbed to note that the attendant (no self-service) filled our tank while holding a lighted cigarette in his spare hand with which he gesticulated while talking to his by-standing friends.

We drove across Greece without mishap and arrived at Volos on the eastern side. We already had bookings on the ferry from there to Latakia in Syria on a newly inaugurated ferry service brought in to provide a link for transcontinental truckers from Europe to Saudi Arabia. Turkey had recently introduced a massive road tax on foreign heavy commercial vehicles passing through the country in order to cash in on the increasing transit traffic from Europe to the Gulf. The result of this huge increase in the cost of transiting the country was to shift most of this traffic through Greece where ferry operators gratefully supplied an alternative sea route round Turkey to Syria.

Our ferry was brand spanking new and did take private vehicles, but it was primarily for trucks and, when we went to the shipping office, we were told that there was no room for cars on the sailing we thought we had booked on. And, what was more, there was no guarantee that there would be space on the next one in two days' time, either.

We were not the only disappointed travellers. There was a young Jordanian on his way home and a young married couple from Tunisia who were on their way to perform the Hajj. The Jordanian was very solicitous and after we had all found rooms in a rather second rate hotel near the port area, he rather fussed round us. The hotel had on its glass front door

141

stickers of a large number of credit card companies, but when I tried to pay with my card, I was met with amazement that I should think this indicated that these cards were actually accepted as payment. Surely I understood that these were just part of the décor of any decent Greek hotel at the time - they had no other function.

The Jordanian now got the idea that we were stuck for cash and generously offered to pay our bill. We cleared up this misunderstanding and remained friendly with him for the rest of the journey. He also later discovered that 14th of October, the day we were due to dock in Syria, was my birthday and insisted on giving me a birthday present; a large and rather brash representation of Achilles in a chariot, which he had bought as gift for a member of his family.

Eventually, we all got on board on the second sailing. The accommodation on the ferry consisted of four-berth cabins, each with en suite facilities and most of the passengers were therefore having to share, but I paid an extra $50 to buy out the other two places and we had a cabin to ourselves.

Naturally, the majority of passengers were truckers, some with female companions and the ship was geared to them and their tastes, literally, in the case of food. Huge portions of cholesterol-saturated food at every meal was the unvarying menu. And, of course, no entertainment, apart from cards and, we believed, pornographic films shown very late at night.

During the voyage, when we were on deck with the Jordanian and the Moroccan couple, I had the rather odd experience of translating from Arabic to Arabic as neither could understand the other's accent, whereas, I, with my slow and laboured version of the language, could just about manage both. Many years later I was to be asked to translate from English to English by an Italian colleague in Khartoum who couldn't make head or tail of the announcements of a master of ceremonies with a Chinese musical troupe, who was speaking in heavily accented English.

We eventually arrived in Latakia, but it was quite late by the time all the trucks had got off as there was some problem with the ramp between the ship and the quayside and many of the larger trucks couldn't clear it without 'grounding'. It was so late in fact that it was not really feasible to drive to Damascus that night. Our Jordanian friend, who had been met at the port by his family from Amman, generously insisted that we shared a seaside 'villa' in the town they had rented overnight.

We left early the next day and arrived in Damascus in mid-morning. This was before the days of GPS systems and computer designed routes and when we reached the city, the directions we had been given were slightly less than adequate. We gave up eventually and asked the way. An impressively friendly man in a Volkswagen beetle not only knew the way to the British Embassy, but also insisted that we follow him as he drove there. He then said goodbye and we never saw him again. This was our introduction to the generally typical friendly attitude of the Syrians.

My predecessor had a fairly large flat in the Mezzeh area some way outside the centre of Damascus and a few miles from the Embassy. He was divorced and had lived as a bachelor and with no female influence, so the flat was furnished with as motley a collection of Office furniture as I had seen during my career. As was usual, we took this over in the first place. Later, when we moved to another, more central flat just down the road from the Embassy, this furniture came with us and it was over a year before I managed to get at least some of it replaced. When I did, the new dining suite which I had chosen was followed some months later by a second, identical dining suite, the order having been processed twice. So one of the secretaries benefited from an unexpected furniture upgrade.

The position of Commercial Secretary was not a satisfying one. Syria had a Soviet-style socialist government and a strict dirigiste regime as far as overseas trade and foreign currency were concerned. Virtually all industry and all the banks had been nationalised many years before, leaving only very small concerns in the private sector. The nationalisation had included all the employees of these companies too, producing a huge public sector. Inefficiency, bureaucracy and corruption were massive and in this environment international trade was hardly easy.

However, the job did have the benefit of offering the chance to travel to other parts of the country on a fairly regular basis and, as a result, I was the most widely travelled officer in the Embassy. I regularly visited Aleppo and, to a lesser extent, the ports of Latakia and Tartous, as well as Homs and Hama, all of which housed rather more than their share of private enterprise.

These trips meant that I frequently had small tasks to perform on behalf of other parts of the Embassy. The most regular of these was a request from the Defence Attaché to note military movements around the country. Usually this involved counting the number of tanks on a convoy of transporters as we drove down the main roads, but would also include such things as any concentrations of military personnel visible from the road.

On a couple of occasions, I was also required to act in a consular capacity by visiting the prisons in Latakia and Tartous. The case of imprisonment in Latakia was a really unfortunate one. A couple of young British honeymooners were on a camping trip in northern Syria, when they were befriended by a man who said he could ensure that they could earn a lot of money for very little effort. He persuaded them to take some drugs packed into a gas cylinder of the type which they carried on their camper. He said that they would get their reward if they would take this across the border into Turkey. To make sure that things went smoothly, he gave them the exact date and crossing point at which they should carry out this operation.

Meanwhile, he went to the Syrian customs officials and told them of the plan, collecting a suitable reward for his information. The young couple were stopped, searched and the drugs were discovered. There was no doubt that they were guilty, but the court allowed the bride to go free, while her husband was incarcerated in Latakia jail.

It was a long way for thc vice consul to travel for one visit, so I was asked to drop into the jail the next time I was in Latakia and check that our prisoner was OK. I had no problem in arranging this and, although there was always an official present while I spoke to him, the prisoner seemed clean and healthy and had no complaints that I can recall.

The second prison visit was in Tartous and was also to a British national who was accused of smuggling. In this case, it was a truck driver who had arrived in Syria by ferry through Latakia with drugs hidden in his vehicle. I don't know if he was also the victim of a similar sting, but again there seemed little doubt of his guilt and, again, when I interviewed him, admittedly in the presence of the prison governor, he seemed to be in good condition and had no complaints.

It was interesting that, on both these visits, the message I had attempted to send in advance had not reached the prison authorities, but, as a British Embassy official, I was allowed access to the prison on request.

It is normal international practice that the national authorities confiscate any vehicle used in smuggling, and this was applied in both these cases. However, in the case of the truck, the Syrians decided to extend the principle additionally to the ferry the truck arrived on the grounds that it, too, was a vehicle involved in the smuggling. I later had a visit from a lawyer sent out from Britain to try to deal with the resulting impounding of the ship. I can't remember the outcome, but I do recall that my advice was for him to find a good local lawyer and negotiate a price for the release of the vessel as to haggle over the legality of the action would take so long that the resulting loss of earnings from the ferry would surely be more.

With all the children at boarding school, Val was able to accompany me on these trips outside Damascus, which often involved evening entertainment with merchants' families. As ever, her equable and open character was always a huge plus in this social world. In addition, on trips to Aleppo, we usually stopped on the way at the archaeological site of Ebla, which lay right beside the main road.

We were always greeted by the children of the local village shouting '*Ciao, ciao*', as the archaeological team carrying out the work was Italian and the locals assumed that all Europeans spoke Italian. But, to our slight frustration, we were never there at the same time as the archaeologists. However, many years later, when I was running the British School of Archaeology in Jerusalem, we were able to read their report, which was in the library there.

In general, we took full advantage of our time in Syria to visit as many archaeological sites as possible – and there are a lot. We enjoy being amateur archaeologists and this was a real pleasure for us, as the sites are pretty well all explored and recorded, but there were practically no tourists and, on the few occasions when we didn't have the place to ourselves, we felt quite hard done by.

On trips outside Damascus, we took it for granted that we would be followed; this tended to make the merchants I visited a little nervous and sometimes reluctant to meet me, but, on the whole, we just 'lived with it.'

On one occasion when we were in Aleppo, we had come back to the hotel late one night and then left pretty early the next morning to do a bit of sightseeing at Saint Simeon's, the ruin of the cathedral built to mark the spot where the saint supposedly lived on top of a pillar for many years. Our shadow had not managed to keep up with this brisk schedule and missed our departure. On our return, we were implored by the hotel manager not to do this again as it caused him trouble. We didn't want this to happen so, afterwards, we checked that our follower was in position before setting out.

We once had a short conversation with him and discovered that he was doing his national service with a security department. At Val's suggestion and to make his life easier, we even agreed to tell him in advance where we were going each day.

Private visits we made in the region while we were based in Damascus included both Turkey and Jordan, and on both occasions we timed the visits to coincide with the children's holidays. The first time we went on a camping trip in Turkey which I think the children enjoyed, although I found it slightly tiresome. The camping sites were very primitive, as were the one or two hotels we stayed in on our way to and from the final destination. The crossing of the border from Syria to Turkey, however, was quite interesting.

After leaving the Syrian checkpoint, the road wound through a valley before coming to the Turkish checkpoint and, for most of the distance, this road was out of sight of both checkpoints. The riverbed below the road was strewn with the remains of hundreds of rusting car wrecks and Val commented on the poor quality of the driving in the area. Later we were told that this was the way of disposing of a vehicle which would otherwise be liable for Syrian import tax. To avoid this, you simply drove the vehicle out of Syria, recorded its export and then pushed it off the road, getting a lift back in a friend's car.

I found driving in Turkey considerably more dangerous than in Syria. Whereas, in Syria, the drivers would effectively give way if the road conditions forced them to, Turks, especially the truck drivers, seemed intent on killing you if you were in the way.

Our trip south to Jordan in summer 1982 was more enjoyable, but not without its drawbacks. We first stayed in Amman in a boarding house for a night and then went on to the famous historical site of Petra, the 'rose red city half as old as time'. In those days the site was comparatively undeveloped. Entry was completely uncontrolled and there were no gestures towards tourism apart from a few cold drink sellers in the ruins and the basic government guest-house built into the cliff outside the Siq, the cleft in the rock leading to the ruins.

We spent a hot and tiring day walking around the whole site during which Val was extremely upset by the tendency of our three children to clamber on everything in sight. At one point, we were walking through the ruins when we heard their voices calling and looked up to see them standing on a roof some 30 feet above us.

When we returned to the government guest

house at the end of the day, we discovered to our dismay that there had been an interruption in the water supply and each guest was rationed to just one litre bottle of water for washing for the evening. The following day we were pleased to leave once again for Amman where we were at least able to have a decent shower.

It was during this holiday that I received a ticket for speeding. This was politely given to me by a Jordanian police patrol using a radar speed scanner. Rather weakly, I pointed out that I was a diplomat, to which they correctly replied that my diplomatic status was limited to Syria and did not apply in Jordan.

While I was in Damascus there was a move to fix the route for Concorde to fly from London to Australia. The original idea was that, after leaving London, it should refuel at Bahrain, Bombay and Singapore. The first section of the leg from UK to Bahrain would be over Western Europe and so supersonic flight would not be possible, but as soon as it cleared the European coast it was to go supersonic across the Mediterranean and the Middle Eastern deserts and then on to Bahrain.

However, the Syrians needed to give their permission for supersonic transit and they used this as a bargaining chip on the question of Syrian Airways access to Heathrow. In the end, the whole thing fell through. However, I remember hearing that, if the plane had had to cut down to subsonic speed again as it crossed the Syrian coast, this would increase the fuel consumption by something like forty tonnes per flight.

The ostensible basis of the Syrian objection to supersonic flight across their territory was that it frightened the livestock in the rural area along the coast. One of the first secretaries at the Embassy went out to the area under the flight path at a time when the plane overflew to check this. When he came back, he confirmed the volume of the supersonic bang with some emphasis.

On another occasion, a British aircraft enthusiast wanted to re-enact a 1930s flight from Britain to Australia with the actual renovated plane, which was mainly wooden. As a result, it did not show on radar and, as far as the Syrians were concerned, it suddenly appeared in their skies unannounced. I don't know if the pilot failed to register his flight plan, but the Syrians were extremely annoyed about this and we had to work hard to persuade them that this was not an attempt at a spying mission.

In 1980 Syria was experiencing a series of insurrections as the Muslim Brotherhood battled the ruling Alawite regime. Although this did not have a direct effect on us, we were in Damascus during, I think, the November of that year on the occasion of one of the early car bombs. A truck was driven through the gates of the Ministry of Defence and towards the steps of the building, where it was detonated. As this type of attack was virtually unknown at the time, after the truck drove through the entrance, the guards at the gate ran up to arrest the driver and were killed by the explosion. The front of the building itself was damaged, but the people around the truck were blown to pieces and body parts were found several hundred yards away.

In retrospect, we do seem to have often been in areas of excitement during our time in Syria. On another occasion, during the summer holidays, we made one of our periodic visits to Aleppo with the children. While we were in our favourite stopping place, the Baron Hotel, there was some gunfire in the street outside and we had to persuade the children to come into the building and not peer over the edge of the balcony to see what the excitement was.

At this time, the Aleppo citadel, which is a conical mound in the centre of the city, was occupied by the Syrian army and closed to visitors. We were walking around the low boundary wall of the site when Stephanie dropped her favourite doll over the wall. We were peering over to see if we could get it back, when to our concern one of the soldiers patrolling the area started to walk purposefully down towards us from his sentry point. We were quite apprehensive; however he was a friendly fellow and simply picked the doll up and, with a smile, handed it back to Stephanie over the wall

Although there was a rather limited choice of food and drink in Syria, we were able to drive into Lebanon and do our shopping in the town of Shtoura, some ten miles from the border. Apart from the range of British and American products on offer, there was another service offered by the shop. There was strict foreign currency control in Syria and, of course, as diplomats, we were forbidden to break the local law by purchasing Syrian currency at the very advantageous black-market rate.

However, in Lebanon we had no diplomatic status and were simply private citizens. So, when the shop presented the bill at the checkout, we were able to pay with a Sterling cheque drawn on a British bank. Before finalising the deal, though, we would be asked if we wanted to include in the payment an amount to cover the purchase of some Syrian cash. So we got the equivalent of the black market rate and didn't break any laws. The system was so efficient that a cheque handed over had usually been cleared through our UK bank within three days, even though this was a period when the civil war in Lebanon on the far side of the mountain from Shtoura was still rumbling on.

We regularly visited the local glass factory in Damascus. This was a fairly basic, and probably dangerous, place where visitors were allowed to wander round between the kilns and watch the glass blowers at work. It produced a number of fairly basic items, including mugs and candlesticks as well as simple model animals. The predominant colours of glass were green and brown and this was because they tended to recycle Seven Up and Coca-Cola bottles respectively. The quality of the workmanship as well as the glass was very poor and it often cracked and was very seldom symmetrical, but it was interesting to collect a number of these quaint products and we still have few.

As we had in Abu Dhabi, we invited my parents out to stay with us in Damascus. This was, I think, in November 1980, as they were with us for the Remembrance Day ceremony at the Mezzeh Commonwealth War Cemetery that year. They had a very good time in Syria, I believe. My father even joined in the weekly billiards club arranged among the diplomatic and UN community, which I didn't go to. We took them with us to Aleppo and Latakia on one trip and to a number of the ancient sites on the way. Unfortunately, my mother picked up a Middle Eastern 'bug' which rather put a damper on her enjoyment and which she really didn't shake off for some three months after she got home.

During this visit, my parents experienced a side of the Val's character that is not often on display. She had taken them on a trip within Damascus and on the way back, in the general melee which passed for the flow of traffic, was run into by another car. She had earlier been told that, if this happened, the first thing to do was to get hold of the culprit's identity card in order to make sure that he didn't get away. This she did by getting out of the car in the middle of the traffic jam and simply demanding it, to the amazement of both my father and mother, who had always regarded her as a quiet, homely sort of girl. The young man driving the other car was completely intimidated and did as she demanded. Having obtained the poor man's identity card, she ordered him to follow her back to the British Embassy, which he had to do.

The first thing I knew about this was when the receptionist called me to say my wife was downstairs and she had had an accident with the car. My first thought was that she had had a bump on the roundabout near the embassy. I was very surprised to find her in an irate mood, with a very chastened young Syrian in tow. She insisted that I held his identity card and the poor man had very little choice, but to agree. He later pleaded that he should be allowed to keep the identity card, but we could have his driving licence instead. We did this as surety for the cost of the repair of the damage to our car and, in the fullness of time, he did indeed pay, and we returned his driving licence.

There was a postscript to this event. Some weeks later I also had a slight bump with a taxi at the very roundabout close to the Embassy where I thought Val had had her accident. Both the other driver and I stopped and got out while we looked at the damage. I said to him that we should pull over to the side of the road as our cars were blocking the traffic. He agreed and I got into my car and pulled over, while he got into his car and drove off and I never saw him again. Val has never ever let me forget the contrast between these two events.

Among the outings we had with my parents was a visit to Quneitra in the south of the country. It was on the edge of the Israeli-occupied Golan Heights and was in a strictly controlled area. The town of Quneitra had initially been captured by the Israelis in 1967, but later handed back in 1974 under a subsequent agreement. Before they pulled out, though, the Israelis had systematically destroyed as much of it as they could. As I have mentioned earlier, they had done something very similar when they pulled out of Yamit in the Sinai, but that was a town they had actually built; Quneitra was a town which had always been Syrian.

We found a fluent English-speaking young Syrian army officer keen to give us a tour. He took us up to the road south of Quneitra running across the no-man's land between the Syrian and Israeli forces. This was demarcated on the Syrian side by a Syrian sentry, with an Israeli counterpart visible a few hundred metres away. Exactly half way between them was a United Nations Disengagement Observer Force (UNDOF) observation post. Our guide clearly wanted to show off a bit as we were taken some way past the Syrian post and continued walking out towards the UNDOF position. All three sentries were watching us closely. Soon the Israeli sentry could be seen to unsling his rifle and the UN soldier started to move uncomfortably. Our guide took a few more steps and then turned us around and took us back. A different tourist experience.

As I have mentioned in relation to the ferries, while we were in Damascus, it was a time when many intercontinental trucks passed through Syria on the way from Europe to Saudi Arabia and the Gulf. The main route ran the length of the country and passed through a number of small towns on its way. The citizens of one of these, between Aleppo and Homs, became very frustrated with the increasing frequency of heavy trucks driving down their main road at high speed. They tried to get the government do something about it, but the authorities had been slow in responding, and so the local town council decided to act unilaterally.

Few of the residents of the town were actually drivers, but they had seen the sort of thing that they thought they needed to install: a speed hump. As the action was not officially sanctioned, the work was carried out after dark. One night, then, having obtained a supply of tarmac, the village elders arranged construction of their DIY traffic calming measure across the width of the road in the middle of the town. As they lacked any expertise at all, the hump was simply a ridge of tarmac with no grading on either side and constructed to be considerably higher than was normal.

Early the following morning, while it was still dark, the first truck of the day came roaring down the road and hit this unmarked black obstacle. As intended, this did indeed cause it to lose speed, but it also lost its front axle. In the hullabaloo that followed, the powers that be decided that after all that they would indeed install their own, official traffic calming measures.

For our mid-tour leave from Damascus in March 1981, we decided we would take the car back with us, partly for the trip and partly for the benefit of having the use of it when we were at home. The original plan was to drive to Latakia and catch a ferry to Italy, driving up from there to the UK. When we got to Latakia on the 13th, however, we discovered that the ferry was already 18 hours late and I considered it unlikely that it would make up this time and might be even more delayed by the time it arrived back in Europe. This was a problem, as we needed to be back in Eastbourne in time to meet the children at the end of term. We therefore decided, there and then, to drive from Latakia to Eastbourne. Fortunately we did not need any visas and the car had green card insurance, valid throughout Europe, including Turkey, so we notified the Embassy by phone and set off early the following morning.

We drove into Turkey at a small crossing point in the hills above Latakia. This was a border area, of course and the Turks were slightly nervous about activity near their borders, so a fairly short distance into the country we had to stop at a military checkpoint. I say checkpoint, but it was just two bored soldiers, one an officer, who made a show of searching the car and our luggage. I thought that we would be saying farewell to the drink we were carrying home as gifts, but this was all politely replaced. They were not very thorough, though and never thought to look behind the panels in the rear of our estate car, where we had packed shoes to free up space in the bags. So we could in fact have been smuggling a wide range of things.

After the checkpoint, we continued on our way and drove the rest of the day, reaching Ankara at about 7.00 p.m. It was dark and raining. We had no idea where to go and pulled in to the first hotel that looked reasonable. We stayed the night there, had a meal, and left in the morning before dawn. During the next day, we drove through the rest of Turkey, crossing the Bosphorus Bridge (no toll payment going north) and eventually passing through the border into Greece.

The border crossing on the Turkish side was

rather intimidating. Reaching the crossing area, you had to drive through a gate into an enclosed compound which housed the immigration and customs offices and, having negotiated customs clearance, you drove up to the exit gate on the far side of the compound. This was overlooked by a watchtower manned by armed soldiers who would not come down to check your documents. So I had to clamber up and present the passports for the stamp. The guards spoke no English and I spoke no Turkish, but I gathered that they were unhappy with the entry stamps that had been given at the small crossing point from Syria, but they made no more about it and I receive my exit stamp. I then climbed back down the ladder and got in the car, and the gate was opened, allowing us out of Turkey.

After crossing the short distance of no man's land, we entered Greece where the guards were dressed in a traditional Greek military uniform with the tasselled head-dresses and white skirts and were considerably more friendly than the drab camouflage uniformed guards on the Turkish side.

We drove through Anatolia nearly as far as Salonika before finding a hotel beside the road and stopping for the night. The following morning we were up early again and drove through the rest of Greece crossing into what was still Yugoslavia late in the morning. In contrast with the crossing from Turkey the day before, this crossing consisted of the more usual covered border tunnel arrangement. The

Greek officials were again particularly friendly and helpful.

While driving through Yugoslavia, we received two traffic tickets; one for exceeding sixty kilometres per hour while passing over a bridge, which in fact was little more than a culvert. As we approached the police checkpoint on this, the cars coming in the opposite direction were flashing their lights, clearly as warning to fellow road users. I ignored this, blithely dismissing it as drivers recognising friends in the oncoming traffic.

The other ticket was for crossing a solid white line on a bend. On this occasion we were flagged down by severe-looking Yugoslav police with long leather coats who were clearly cmbarrassed to discover that, although the car had Syrian number plates, it contained British passengers. Nevertheless, having stopped me, they proceeded to fine me on the spot. The fine was 80 Yugoslav dinars I remember, although I did not and still do not, know how much that was worth.

I don't think we passed through any large cities, certainly not Belgrade, and we eventually stopped in a small and rather scruffy hotel in the north of Yugoslavia for the night of the 16th. The following morning, we continued on into Austria, through some impressive scenery, and noted with some dismay that there was still snow in the area. We pulled off the road at a little town called Assach where the local bar had rooms and we were made very comfortable for the night, and where the locals were keen to practice their English. In the morning we had to clear snow from the car before we got going, but it was fairly wet snow and presented no real problem.

The whole journey was marked by a continuous improvement in the roads and, from Assach up to the Belgian coast, there was the luxury of driving on motorways. At the Austrian/German border Val said she needed the toilet and I said that as we were clearly going through the Austrian checkpoint, when we came to the German side we would pull over. However, my belief that the two officials who were checking us through the border were Austrian customs and immigration respectively was wrong. In fact, one was Austrian and the other German as this was a joint checkpoint, which we realised as we drove on and found no second check. Fortunately before too long there was an exit slip road which led to a small German town where Val was able to find relief, we had a break and I changed some money.

As the roads were now considerably better we decided to make a 'dash' for the Channel and continued driving through the day, reaching the Belgian coast at about 9.30 p.m. We hadn't booked on a ferry, but at that time of night there was no difficulty in getting a ticket. We arrived in Dover (or was it Folkestone?) at around about midnight and drove from there to Eastbourne arriving at about 2.00 a.m. on the 18th.

163

This had been 5 days of continuous driving for me, every day rising at dawn and stopping at dusk. I was extremely tired and it was several days before I could get out of the habit of rising with the sun.

To be fair, Val had offered to take her turn at driving, first in Turkey and then again in Germany, but I felt she was far too cautious and we had to get on. She loves to tell a story of our 'frank discussions' about this in which she alleges I claimed she was deliberately aiming at all the potholes in the Turkish highway. Well, it certainly felt that way. As for her driving on the autobahns, I felt we were at risk of being overtaken by energetic cyclists and even healthy horses. But we did indeed get back in time to greet the children at the end of their term.

As usual, we split our time between our respective parents. Leave over, we departed from Eastbourne on the 3rd of June to drive back to Damascus. After we left our house, we drove via my parents' place to say goodbye, and the last sight I ever had of my father was in my rear view mirror while he and my mother waved to us as we turned the corner at the end of their road.

Our return route through Europe this time took us past the First World War graveyards in northern France and down through Germany and Austria into Italy, and so to Venice. Although it hadn't been a problem coming through Europe a couple of months before, on this return journey it was a snag that the car had Arabic number plates. At two border crossing points, from France into Germany at Strasbourg and from Austria into Italy at a small crossing point in the Tyrolean Alps, I was stopped and my papers checked because of this.

At the crossing into Germany, the *Grenzschutz* officer actually took my passport away to check it at the back of his cubicle. At the Italian crossing, we were in a long line of vehicles passing through a *Caribinieri* control where a very cursory check of documents took place. The cars were nose to tail, and the number plate was not immediately visible. Moreover, as I was driving a British car and had a British passport no one took much notice. However, after we drove away from the checkpoint, and the Arabic number plate became visible, we were pursued down the road by a *Caribinieri* officer waving his pistol and shouting at us to stop. He was eventually reassured and we continued on our way to Venice. There we joined a Turkish ship sailing to Izmir

Many of our fellow passengers were clearly used to this trip and consisted largely of Germans going to soak up the Anatolian sun. Although we didn't have time to make a tour of Venice, our departure was actually down the Grand Canal, so we did get a chance to have a look at some of the sights along the way. On board we also had the opportunity to change currency; so I was able to swap a large wad of rather grubby Italian notes with big numbers for another, larger wad of much grubbier Turkish notes with even bigger numbers.

On arrival at Izmir, I was confronted by a Turkish customs official who announced that he was intending to search all our luggage. We had a lot of this and I was reluctant to comply. I noticed that our German fellow passengers were not having this trouble, so I adopted my more pompous tone and pointed out that I was a diplomat, indicating my Syrian diplomatic registration plate, which conveniently had an impressive broad red band across it. This had a gratifyingly immediate effect on the customs official and we then passed through the formalities pretty promptly.

As dusk was falling on the second day about half way on our journey from Izmir towards the Syrian border crossing point at Bab al Hawa, the cable connecting the accelerator pedal to the carburettor snapped. Fortunately our car had a manual choke and I used this as a hand throttle to get to a truckers' café, which was conveniently just over the next hill. Although I spoke no word of Turkish, by opening the bonnet and pointing, I was able to get across the nature of my problem to an extremely beefy and extremely friendly Turkish truck driver, who provided a working repair with a length of copper cable. He would accept no payment, but we did offer him our profuse thanks.

A short distance further on we came to a small town and pulled in at a hotel for the night. There was a military night curfew in operation in Turkey at that time and, in addition, the electricity supply was unreliable and the street lights were out. The hotel was comfortable enough, but matters were really not made easier by an amiable Turk, who spoke some German, insisting on taking us under his wing and ordering dinner on our behalf. As a result, we did not get the meal we thought we were getting, but it was good enough.

At the end of the following day, we arrived at the main crossing point from Turkey into Syria at Bab al Hawa just as it was getting dark again and we re-entered Syria in the early evening. It was too late to try and drive to Damascus, so we cut across to Aleppo and stayed overnight at the Baron Hotel, where the only free room was the bridal suite.

The next day we started off early, but as we were driving through the southern suburbs of Aleppo, the Turkish copper wire failed and I had to find a Syrian workshop where the wire was replaced with something approaching the original cable.

In July 1981, just after the children had come out for their holidays, we went off for one of our trips to the north where, as usual, I incorporated business with pleasure. We travelled up to Aleppo on Saturday 18th July and stopped off just outside Hama at a picnic spot next to one of the huge irrigation *nourias* for a snack. While there I had a strong conviction that somebody was missing. This impression was so intense that I had to look around and check that the family were all there, which of course they were. I thought no more about it then, but subsequent events made it oddly prescient.

We continued on, reaching Aleppo in the afternoon and booked into the Baron Hotel. I did my official calls over the next couple of days and then we moved on to Latakia.

On July the 22nd, the day after we had arrived at the Meridien Hotel in Latakia, as usual I had arranged a number of calls on merchants in the area. After we had finished breakfast, I was in the reception foyer heading for the entrance when I was told there was a call for me from the Embassy. I took it on a wall phone next to reception. The Head of Chancery, Mark Marshall, was on the line. He started by telling me that there had been a telegram with bad news for me.

My first thought was that my cousin, Janet, had died as she was very ill and we were expecting her to go any day, but it was odd that this would be the subject of a telegram as she wasn't immediate family. Then he said he was sorry, but my father had died the day before and a compassionate journey home had been authorised.

This came as a massive shock. At 69, my father was not a young man, of course, but he was a fairly healthy one and there had been no warning of this one, fatal heart attack. It was clear from the attitude of the hotel staff that they had been told my news by somebody who had been eavesdropping on the call: they were immediately sympathetic, even the ones who had been unable to hear me at the counter when I said I would have to check out immediately. We left for Damascus again within the hour, getting back in the early afternoon.

Annoyingly, the Embassy Admin Section hadn't tried to get me on a flight that evening, preferring to wait until I returned, so I lost a day in getting home. When I got there, I found my distraught mother being comforted by her sister who had immediately come down from Cardiff. Although my brother-in-law had registered the death, the arrangements for the funeral fell to me as did the initial tidying up of my father's papers. This all attended to, I flew back to post on the 2nd of August. As my father had only recently been with us in Damascus and had met most of our friends and colleagues, we received many visits and messages of condolence.

In late 1981 the Ambassador, Patrick Wright, decided that he and his wife, Virginia, should pay a visit to Aleppo. As Val and I were the only people in the Embassy who regularly went there and so knew some of the local people, it was decided that we should accompany them.

On the way Patrick wanted to visit the Ayubi Mosque in Hama and it was agreed that we should drive ahead and meet them at the roundabout on the outskirts of that town. The following year, the mosque and Hama were both badly damaged in the insurrection by the Muslim Brotherhood which was based in Hama. At the time, however, we were taken on a tour of the mosque by the resident expert. As this was a formal visit by the British Ambassador, it entailed accompaniment by the local Governor and an escort by the Syrian Security Service; the '*Mukhabarat*'. The reason for this was that even at that time, Hama was regarded as a hotbed of potential insurrection.

We left our car at the roundabout on the main road where we had met up with the ambassadorial Austin Princess and got in with Patrick and Virginia. I think we all felt slightly uncomfortable to be whisked through a rather sullen town accompanied by a security convoy.

After our visit to the mosque, we collected our car and drove on in a small convoy of two to Aleppo. As I have mentioned, on our trips we habitually stopped at the archaeological site of Ebla and we made a short stop there with the Wrights. In Aleppo we stayed, as always, at the Baron Hotel. During the visit, there was a reception arranged at the hotel for the notables of Aleppo to meet the Ambassador, but the highlight of the visit as far as representational duties were concerned was attendance at a performance of *The Merchant of Venice* in the local theatre. The performance had been arranged by the British Council as part of its cultural remit. The play always goes down very well with Arabs, including, as it does, a baddy who is a Jew.

The British Council had entrusted distribution of tickets for this event to the English Faculty of Aleppo University, but, rather than ensuring that these went to those students who were actually studying English literature, they were regarded as a perk and many were allocated to friends and relatives of those in authority. As a result, there was considerable unhappiness among the student body about their restricted access to the performance and there was a small demonstration outside the theatre when we arrived.

During the early part of the performance a press photographer was busy taking flash photographs from just below the front of the stage. This was clearly disturbing the actors and one of them came out of character and said severely to the photographer "Will you please go and sit down." This caused some surprise in the audience and considerable dismay to the photographer himself who scuttled off.

At the interval there was some confusion about what was going to happen to the official visiting party. The plan was apparently that we would all go and sit in the director's office and have a cup of coffee. However, as we got up to leave the auditorium, this detail had not got through to those in charge and, as we didn't know where it was, we all walked past the director's office and out of the theatre. This caused consternation as, naturally, nobody was expecting us to leave until the end of the play and there was some scurrying of drivers getting into cars and so on. The error was quickly and apologetically pointed out and we were turned round and taken back into the theatre and to the director's office.

It was wintertime and there was very little central heating in the theatre. The director's office, though, was warmed by an oil stove situated in one corner. This gave out a considerable amount of heat, but only in its immediate vicinity. Those who were on the far side of the room were virtually frozen, while those of us sitting next to the heater (which included me) were nearly cooked.

On the Saturday of our visit, we took Patrick and Virginia to visit one of our favourite archaeological sites at Cyrrhus, some way to the north of Aleppo. In fact it is almost in Turkey and the minaret of the mosque in the village visible a kilometre or so away was actually over the border. This Alexandrian city had been partially excavated, but not in the recent past. It was sufficiently remote to be fairly quiet and sufficiently large to be quite interesting.

In February 1982 the long running conflict between the Alawite regime and the Islamist Muslim Brotherhood burst into flame with the failed insurrection in Hama. Although most details are now available, at the time there were very few we knew for sure, as travel to the town was impossible. But even so, it was known to be a very bloody affair, with the Syrian Army shelling much of the inhabited area to ruins. The regime tried to hush it all up, but, as the main transcontinental road to Saudi Arabia ran through the outskirts of Hama, this was quite difficult. In the event the buildings next to this main road were repaired and painted and traffic allowed to pass, but not to stop.

The following month Val and I, together with a couple of friends, were returning from a visit to the Hejaz Railway sidings in the outskirts of Damascus. The Hejaz railway was the narrow-gauge line linking Damascus and Mecca, a section of which was blown up in what is now Saudi Arabia by Lawrence of Arabia in the First World War. The sidings still contained some carriages of the Turkish Sultan's royal train.

We had finished our tour and were heading towards a restaurant near our flat, when a Mercedes came down a side street at a fair pace. We were crossing this road and somebody shouted a warning to Val who was in the middle of the group. The car was coming from our right, but, as she could only hear with her left ear, she looked that way and lost seconds in response time. The car driver had realised the danger and had hit the brakes, so the car was skidding on the wet road at this point, but it still hit her so sharply on the right knee that she was knocked clean off her feet. I looked round to see her in the air then hit the ground on her cheek. Fortunately her coat hood had been flipped over her face by the motion and covered the contact area, preventing any abrasions, but her cheekbone was fractured.

Immediately, people appeared and gathered round. The driver of the car proved to be a young lad who was supposed to be taking it to be cleaned for the owner, but got carried away when he got behind the wheel. I don't think he had a licence or insurance. Fortunately, one of our companions was a nurse, who was able to check that Val's face was the only part badly damaged, although her leg was extremely painful. One of the crowd was the security guard from a neighbouring building, where somebody important must have been living. His only contribution was to stand staring down at Val with his loosely slung Klashnikov pointing at her, until I told him to move away.

Meanwhile, Val was lying in the road where she had fallen with coats being pulled over her. The Embassy duty officer, Vincent Fean, had been contacted and he also came and then got in touch with the hospital which the Embassy used to warn of our arrival. Our nursing friend gave the all clear for Val to be moved, so, as our flat was fortunately nearby, I collected our car and we carefully loaded

Val into it and I drove her to the hospital.

There, she was a bit of a celebrity, with our Embassy doctor, the maxillofacial surgeon and a military doctor, whose position in the process I was unsure about, all consulting about treatment. As luck would have it, the cheekbone had broken cleanly and the surgeon was able to 'simply' hook the bone through the flesh and pull it back into position. And, although not broken, her leg was put in plaster to aid recovery. And that was pretty well that, so to speak. But not quite.

While Val was lying in hospital, the mother of the young man responsible for the trouble came to plead with us not to sue the family. It hadn't occurred to us to do so. The cost of the medical treatment was not going to fall to us, but was covered under the Diplomatic Service Medical Scheme, and we simply didn't think in terms of obtaining cash compensation. The poor woman's concern was that any award against the family would have been devastating for them. She was so grateful when she understood we were not going to pursue this, that she fell to her knees beside the bed, taking Val's hand, weeping over it and calling blessings on us. All very Middle Eastern and very embarrassing.

Something else which was very Middle Eastern was the standard of nursing, or, rather, the complete lack of it. After one night in the hospital, Val discharged herself and I took her home where I nursed her for the week or so it took before her leg was mended sufficiently to let her get about with something approaching ease. During this time, we had a steady stream of well-wishers from the Embassy and our friends in other diplomatic missions and the flat was full of flowers.

Of course, her face was very bruised, first by the impact, and then from the treatment. For a couple of months, she had a swollen face and steadily fading black eye, as well as an improving limp. But we tend to mend well on both sides of our family and now, in her mid seventies, she can walk as well as I can over the South Downs and there is little sign of facial damage and no limp. The fact that her leg shows no sign of damage I find quite remarkable, considering that she sustained an impact pretty well exactly on the knee joint sufficient to throw her through the air for several feet.

In November 1982, it was decided that, for the first time in many years, the Embassy should be represented at the Remembrance Day service at the Aleppo Commonwealth War Grave. As I was still the most frequent visitor to the area, I was chosen to officiate. I gathered together the small British community in Aleppo and performed the necessary formalities. I don't remember any clergy being present, though. This was the first of a number of occasions when I officiated at a Remembrance ceremony. As head of post, I laid the British wreath during each of my years in Antigua and then again in my first year in Khartoum.

I was due to be posted abroad again in 1983, but the announcement of where I was to go was delayed. I later found out that this was because I had been proposed for head of the two-person post of Antigua and there were doubts about the timing of the Independence of St Kitts and Nevis, which was also to be in my area of responsibility. Eventually, this was cleared up to the extent that I knew where I was going before I actually left Damascus, but only just.

When we came to leave Damascus, I was faced with a problem that cropped up often when I left a post – how to satisfactorily sell the car. As I have mentioned, there were very strict controls on importing cars to Syria, which in effect meant that departing diplomats had to sell to others with diplomatic status. In my case I accepted an offer from an officer in the French Embassy. He wasn't exactly in the French Diplomatic Service, but was, as I recall, a *'co-operant'*, which I understood to mean that he was, in effect, doing his national service in the civil, as opposed to the military, sphere. Anyway, whatever he was, he reneged on the deal after I left. This left me in the hands of the Admin Section to find a buyer and finalise the transaction.

If this situation had arisen before I had left, I could have driven the car home again. This would have involved the attaching of cardboard registration plates. Why was this? Well, before departure, diplomats leaving Syria had to hand back the special diplomatic plates they had been issued with. If you were driving the car out of the country, this meant you would have no plates on the car at all. To get round this, it was the general practice to commission a man to copy your plate exactly onto cardboard and depart with that on your car. In the event, in my case I didn't need do this, but I certainly saw the man in question about his business at his pitch near the Embassy on several occasions, so I believe it worked.

On the last couple of leaves from Damascus, we had been looking around Eastbourne for a larger house than our small semi-detached one in Polegate. After we left Damascus in December 1982, we made one more determined effort and during that time settled on a much larger four-bedroom detached house on the outskirts of Eastbourne. In the four and a half months we were in the UK between posts, we managed to sell the first and buy the second, moving in just under two weeks before we left for Antigua.

CHAPTER 8

ANTIGUA 1983 – 1986

We flew out to Antigua on 19th April, 1983. The full title of the country is Antigua and Barbuda, the latter being effectively little more than a small, nearly arid sand bar some miles from the main island. The total population of the two islands was only some 80,000, but for a time Barbuda harboured faint and ridiculously unrealistic dreams of a separate political existence. Antigua had only been completely independent for just over a year and the neighbouring islands of St Kitts and Nevis (forming one territory) were to become independent later that year and preparations for this took up a lot of my time during my first few months.

These two territories had been the last of the West Indian 'Associated States'; a status which was the halfway house between colony and full independence and which had been the designation since 1967 of the majority of the Windward Islands under British rule. The Associated States had been set up after the failure of the West Indian Federation, which had been an attempt to build a viable state from a widely dispersed scattering of British Caribbean islands. Rather than be re-adopted as colonies, they had been given this odd, self-governing status.

179

Montserrat and Anguilla were the only remaining islands in the group to be still 'overseas territories', although they did have self-government. Montserrat had been left out of the process at its own request. Anguilla, purely on grounds of geographic proximity, had previously always been lumped with St Kitts and Nevis, but in 1967, had objected strongly to being governed by the Kittitian politician, Bradshaw and had revolted against his government, forcing Britain to effectively re-colonise the island and appoint a British governor.

Even after their various independences, all the West Indian islands remained staunchly royalist, practically all retaining their links to the Crown and had local governors general as non-executive head of state representing the Queen and personally reporting to Buckingham Palace on matters of protocol in the continuation of centuries-old tradition.

As an example of this royalist pattern, the annual Antigua Independence Day celebrations were held on the Antigua Recreation Ground (commemorating the Jubilee of King George V), where the Queen's representative the Governor General, His Excellency Sir Wilfred Jacobs, Knight Grand Cross of the Order of Saint Michael and Saint George (GCMG), wearing British colonial white uniform, complete with ostrich feathers on an archaic hat, would take the salute with a march past by the Royal Police Force of Antigua and Barbuda, who, as likely as not, were playing the 'British Grenadiers'.

This sort of thing caused endless confusion to visiting American tourists, who could not get their heads round the idea of an independent country retaining the British monarch as head of state. And to point out that it was the same with Canada simply did not help – who the hell knew anything about Canada?

The island that was the exception to all this was Dominica, which, in a fit of absent-mindedness, to borrow a phrase, had opted for independence as a republic. The head of state was thus a non-executive president. As a figurehead, to all intents and purposes, he had the same position as his colleagues who were governors general, but he didn't represent the Queen and wasn't a knight, and therefore didn't have 'Sir' in front of this name. This rankled and some years after Independence, it was agreed that this republican figurehead would receive an honorary knighthood and then he was allowed to put 'Sir' before his name. So that was all right.

My post in Antigua was a Grade 6 position and I was still a 7E; a disparity about which I felt most strongly and about which I wrote to the Office on a number of occasions. This was all to no avail, although I see from the file that there were those who had some sympathy with me. Eventually my promotion came through with effect from the 1st of

September 1984, over a year after I started doing the job. There was one other UK-based member of staff; a secretary.

My new residence was on a hill a little way outside the capital, St John's and we flew the Union Flag from a flagpole in the front garden. There were only a couple of neighbouring properties. From the veranda, we had a very good view to the west over the sea to the neighbouring islands of Nevis (closest), St Kitts ('hull down' on the horizon) and St Marten (tip just visible beyond the other two on a clear day). Most evenings, sitting on our veranda, we could see the sun set and on a number of occasions we saw the 'green flash' as the sun finally sank below the horizon on a clear evening. Frustratingly, completely clear evenings were rather rare, as wisps of cloud seemed always to build up just as the sun reached the horizon.

The phenomenon was not really a flash; the red of the sun just before it sank below the horizon changed to bright green. The colour remained visible for a short while; easily long enough to look away and then back again to establish that what you saw was not the retinal after-image of the red sun.

Apart from the house, we inherited two pets; a cat and a dog called Trad and Turpin respectively. They were a real odd couple. The dog had been acquired by my predecessor as a small puppy when Trad was already established in the household and, although, or, on second, more recent, thoughts, maybe because, the cat was a neutered tom, he took it on himself to 'mother' the dog. This behaviour continued long after the dog was full-grown and three or four times the size of the cat. We often saw the cat grooming the dog, who was treated to the bat of a paw round the ear if he moved while a tricky bit was being cleaned.

My predecessor had had the habit of taking the dog for a short walk before breakfast and I continued this for a time. The cat always decided he would come, too, but would not deign to be seen with us; he would stalk through the bushes on the side of the path about fifteen feet behind, while making the most annoying wailing sound. There was no way I could see to stop this, so after a time I gave up these early morning expeditions.

The office in St John's was on a corner of St Mary's Street and consisted of the upper floor of a typical West Indian wooden building, the lower part of which was occupied by the office of a firm of surveyors owned by two partners from Britain, one Scots and one English. They were also our landlords.

Later in my posting, it was decided that we should move the office to a more modern building of brick and concrete not far away, but the scheme fell through for reasons of cost, the details of which I can no longer remember. But what I do remember, though, was the cynical attitude to security highlighted by the scheme. Even though the terrorist threat in Antigua was nil, one of the requirements for the new office was for a bullet-proof barrier in the reception area, window and counter. When the move was abandoned, I asked about bullet-proofing for our existing office, where all the walls were of one plank of wood and the receptionist simply sat at a desk in the room visitors reached on coming up the stairs. Oh, no, I was, told there was no money to spend on upgrading existing property, only on newly acquired buildings.

On my first day in post, as part of the handover process, my predecessor gave me the folder with recent incoming and outgoing telegrams to read. I glanced through them with little interest, until I came to one he had sent the day before in response to an enquiry from London about a request I had made for a freezer to be supplied from official funds. I was amazed to read that virtually the last thing about which he had sent a telegram was a recommendation that my request be turned down, as a freezer was not necessary. The man was leaving in three days' time and had had a freezer himself throughout his three-year posting; why had he done this? Probably because he had had to buy his freezer and it rankled that his successor should get one on the house, so to speak. A month or so later I reapplied, with my own endorsement and got one.

A short while after our arrival, I had not heard from Damascus about the fate of the car I had left for the Admin Section to sell for me. I had been in touch on the subject previously of course, and so I sent a reminder in the form of what I think must have been the shortest telegram text ever to be transmitted in the FCO system. Between the subject and signature, it consisted of no words, just a question mark. Thus:

Subject – Car
?
[signed]Crane

The High Commissioner in Bridgetown, Viscount Dunrossil, was about to leave on transfer almost as soon as we arrived and he and his wife paid a valedictory visit to both Antigua and St Kitts. Of course, Val and I had to accompany them. The visit to St Kitts went well enough, although his farewell calls tended to eclipse the fact that I was effectively paying my introductory calls at the same time. Two things stick in my mind from then. The first was an old white man who claimed his ancestors had arrived in St Kitts in 1666, thus pre-dating the arrival of the ancestors of the vast majority of the black population and who had taken strong exception to the Independence Constitution. He caught up with the High Commissioner and berated him at considerable length on the subject.

The second was that during our visit, the High Commissioner's wife made a tour of the island, on which Val was, by default, expected to accompany her. Val later told me that it was not a relaxing affair and at no time did Lady Dunrossil ask to be called by her Christian name. So for the two or three hours they were sitting in the car together, Val was required to address her formally by her title. This was a very old-fashioned attitude even in those days.

A month or two after we arrived in Antigua we had our first ship's visit. This went well enough, but it was early on in my learning curve as I was still feeling my way. However, after the frigate sailed, as they had the frequency of our emergency inter-island radio, we received a radio call saying that one of the sailors had developed extreme appendicitis and the ship was putting about in order to be in range for their helicopter to fly him for an operation in Antigua. The helicopter duly flew direct to the grounds of the one hospital on Antigua and delivered the 19-year-old sailor. It then took off immediately and returned to the ship, and the sailor was rushed into surgery.

The operation was successful and he was ready for discharge within a week or so. But he wasn't allowed to fly back home immediately, as medical opinion was that a possible embolism in the healing wound might react badly to the low pressure in an aircraft. However, there was nowhere for him to go and Val and I felt it would be a bit rough for him to be stuck in a hotel until he healed, so we took him in with us for about three weeks.

For Val this was nice. It was very much as if she had another son to look after, which suited her fine. It also meant that she had company while I was at the office. He was a polite young lad, who was returning home after having served in Falklands area and was thoroughly enjoying a relaxing time in Antigua. When he was well enough, a military medical team of a doctor and nursing specialist was sent out to accompany him home. They took him over and they all moved into hotel accommodation for a few days before returning to UK.

Although we enjoyed having him stay, there was never any comment of appreciation from the High Commission nor did the Ministry of Defence express either thanks or suggest that we should in some way be reimbursed for feeding an increasingly healthy young man for three weeks. The young sailor himself, though, had good manners and insisted on taking us out for a meal before he left.

Antigua hosted two US military bases; one Air Force and one Navy. They were left over from the lend-lease arrangements with the USA during the Second World War, when bases in British territories were provided in exchange for military hardware. By the time I was there they were pretty vestigial, particularly in the case of the Air Force base which was manned by one major and one sergeant. The air base appeared to have two functions, one was to monitor satellites and the other to act as a base for

Hercules C130s to track hurricanes in the Caribbean in the appropriate season.

The Navy base was larger and, among other things, acted as a communications link for the US Consulate on the island. The confusion in American minds about the status of Antigua in relation to Britain, the Commonwealth and so on was well illustrated when there was a change in the rear admiral in command in the area in which the navy facility fell (based on Miami, I think). Local notables, including Val and me, as well as the Governor General, Sir Wilfred Jacobs, and Lady Jacobs were invited. Having been ensconced in the hall where the ceremony was to take place, we were all instructed to stand for the admiral as he took the stage. Sir Wilfred was sitting in front of me and I watched closely to see what he would do. He, as effectively the head of state, was being asked to stand for a foreign naval officer. In the event he did stand. I spoke to the local Navy base commander about it afterwards, but he was unfocussed on the subject and, to be honest, wasn't very concerned.

An oddity resulting from the establishment of the US bases on the island at a comparatively early date was that the first electricity generators were installed to service the US bases so that the electricity supply was on the US system of 150 volts, 60 herz, rather than the 250 volts, 50 herz system used in the UK. This then became the standard over the island. All the other islands in the

British West Indies were standardised on the British system.

The most important thing on the horizon for my new job was the forthcoming Independence in September of St Kitts and Nevis. As I have already mentioned, my posting had been delayed while the Independence Constitution was being argued about. St Kitts and Nevis may have been one country, but they were two islands and Nevis, although the smaller had, like Barbuda, cherished a dream of attaining independence as a separate state. Eventually a type of federation was decided on, with a federal government in Basseterre, St Kitts and an island administration in Nevis. With the timing for all this settled, I had been able to go to post.

As the Independence arrangements took up a fair amount of time during my first months, I was often over in Basseterre, the capital of St Kitts in the months leading up to Independence, lodged at the Ocean Terrace Inn, a very comfortable billet overlooking Basseterre Bay. During this period a temporary assistant, a Grade 9 floater, was allocated to me to run the post in St John's.

The celebrations were to be attended by Her Royal Highness, The Princess Margaret Rose, Countess of Snowdon, representing Her Majesty the Queen. In advance of this, the Princess's Private Secretary, Lord Napier, and her personal bodyguard, Inspector Philpott, came out on a reconnaissance

189

visit. There was, I recall, some discussion about the required upgrading needed to the accommodation in Government House in St Kitts where the Princess would be staying, but, on the whole, there were no problems.

On the evening before the two returned to the UK from Antigua, we had them round for a meal. They asked for a snack, rather than a full meal, which we offered and which Val would have preferred to prepare. She cooked eggs and bacon, but embarrassingly had managed to burn some of it and the dish included some black bits. Nevertheless, the Private Secretary, a 14th Lord and 5th Baron, had been well brought up and insisted they were delicious, while the police inspector remained cheerfully non-committal.

Val accompanied me to St Kitts for the celebrations themselves. Although Independence Day was the 19th of September, the celebrations were to last for ten days from 10th to 20th September, with the Princess arriving on the afternoon of the 16th. Some of the various events did not concern us that much, but we were included in an invitation to a buffet on the Trinidad & Tobago Coast Guard Ship TTS Cascadura on 15th as well as a dinner on HMS Berwick 'in the presence of Her Royal Highness the Princess Margaret' on 17th.

The new state was not wealthy and so some of the arrangements round the Independence celebrations had a slightly homely feel. For instance, they had invited delegations from all the various countries with which they would have diplomatic relations and quite a lot had agreed to come. So many, in fact, that the country did not have nearly enough official cars to meet them all at the airport. So the call went out to all residents who owned presentable cars to muck in and help man a transport roster. This actually seems to have worked quite well and even netted another Rolls Royce in addition to the Governor General's venerable vehicle. As I was tied up with the British delegation the whole time, I didn't see how this went in practice, but I would very much have liked to have been there when the official French delegation arrived and discovered they were to be transported in a private car.

Princess Margaret's tastes needed some close attention. For instance, her tipple was Famous Grouse whiskey with Malvern Water. The spirit was no problem, but the Malvern Water was not to be found on St Kitts; in the event she took her whiskey with Kittitian tap water and nobody seemed to notice.

She also wanted to go for a swim and this presented a challenge. Clearly, she needed some privacy, but there were no sufficiently secluded beaches on the island and the pools in the various hotels on the island were too public. Eventually, I was pointed in the direction of an old sugar plantation house at the far end of the island owned by a retired American, which had a private pool built into the shell of an old outhouse; just the thing. He was very flattered to be asked to loan his pool to Her Royal Highness for a couple of hours and was delighted to agree.

Margaret was well acquainted with the West Indies, of course, frequently holidaying on Mustique in the territory of St Vincent, further to the south and she had also represented the Queen at Antigua's Independence in 1981, but, as far as I know, she hadn't been to St Kitts before.

A VC10 of the Royal Flight couldn't quite make the trip without having to refuel in case of a head wind, so the Princess's party, which included her equerry, lady-in-waiting and hairdresser, travelled out in the upper deck of a British Airways Jumbo. There was no scheduled flight from UK to St Kitts and this one was the regular service to Barbados via Antigua which was diverted to land additionally at Golden Rock Airport, St Kitts. On arrival, the idea had been that passengers from all other flights would be delayed, either in the terminal or on their planes, until the welcoming ceremony was over. Well, that went wrong: no such limitation was apparent and the royal party was the object of much interest among the other passengers strolling across the tarmac.

Before this, something else that nearly went wrong was the misplacing of the Princess's standard to be flown from the official car, the Governor's rather elderly Rolls Royce. As we were waiting in the VIP lounge for the plane to arrive, I reminded the Governor that he would have take down his pennant and replace it with hers when they left the airport together in his car. Where was Her Royal Highness's pennant, he asked me. I hadn't seen it, so asked the diminutive and slightly eccentric Deputy High Commissioner, David Montgomery, who was among the party from Bridgetown.

The result of my inquiry was impressive. A terrible Glaswegian oath (for he hailed from that fair city) rent the air. It appeared he had indeed brought the pennant from Bridgetown, but had secreted it in a safe place under his bed in the hotel, where it remained. In other words, he didn't have it with him. However, he knew a man who could help. He shot over to the startled Police Commissioner, who was amongst the gathered reception group, commandeered his new Ford car (recently supplied under a British aid package), together with driver and careered off from the airport to the hotel, scattering Kittitians widespread.

In the event, he actually did get back before the plane finished taxiing and was able to take his place in the receiving line and the Princess left with the correct pennant flying.

At the receiving line on the tarmac, being the most junior official present, I was at the end and so, when matters were delayed slightly, I was the one the Princess was left talking to. It must be one of those things that one learns to cope with when one is working one's way down a receiving line. If one has time left over, don't stand there looking around, wondering what's gone wrong (somebody will be dealing with that), but do something. In this case, talk to the nearest person available. We had a short chat, as I recall it, about the journey: I asked an inane question and she gave a non-committal reply, but a photograph of the occasion has survived. Then the cars arrived on the tarmac and we all moved off to Government House for tea or, in her case, whiskey and water.

The following day, we, the FCO party, all congregated at the Ocean Terrace Inn before moving on to Government House for a meeting. As we arrived at the gate, the Princess's motorcade was sweeping out. Consternation! - she wasn't supposed to be going anywhere at that time. We went in and spoke to the Governor who told us that she had decided to go swimming that morning instead of the following day as in the programme and the motorcade was off to the private swimming pool that I had identified at the other end of the island.

It was fortunate that it was at the other end of the island, as this gave me time before they got there to get back to the hotel and phone the American owner and warn him. The poor man was rather concerned. He hoped Her Royal Highness wasn't going to stay very long as he had guests coming for lunch. In the event, the swim was fairly brief and I assume his lunch party later went off well, although I have no doubt what the main topic of conversation was.

I was, and continue to be, rather mystified as to why she did this. She knew the place was a private estate and that arriving without notice, as she clearly intended, would cause problems. I have only one theory to put forward. She regarded the West Indies as a fun place where things do tend to go wrong and she found this amusing. So to help things along this path, so to speak, to turn up out of programme would be entertaining: it would add to the stock of jolly anecdotes about the area. Whatever her reasons, though, I'm afraid it has always struck me as being very impolite.

The Princess was to formally open Sandy Point Primary School in the morning of the 18th. This was some way from Basseterre along the coast road and to get there, it was necessary to pass the historic site of Brimstone Hill, a British fort of the Napoleonic era. It got its name from a volcanic vent which continuously leaked sulphurous gas into the air. It was on top of the hill and was reached by a narrow, winding road

I was travelling in the elderly Jaguar provided by the Kittitians with three fairly senior British officials: the Deputy High Commissioner, the Head of the Development Division (DevDiv) both from Bridgetown and the Head of West Indies and Atlantic Department (WIAD) from the FCO, who were all travelling in the back. Naturally, this was rather crowded for them and, early into the journey, the Head of DevDiv asked me rather pointedly why there were three councillors sitting squashed in the back of the car and one second secretary sitting comfortably in the front. I said that I had not arranged the seating in the vehicles. Oh, he asked, who had then? David Montgomery, I said. There was a short pause while the other two digested this as he was in fact sitting between them. He was challenged, but I can't remember his explanation, although he clearly enjoyed the situation.

The Head of WIAD then insisted that there was enough time for us to visit Brimstone Hill before we reached Sandy Point. This was true, but I pointed out that the Jaguar was well past its prime and carrying five people up the long steep hill might be too much for it. This objection was brushed aside and we duly drove to the top of the hill. However, as I had feared, the engine overheated and a rubber radiator hose split. The driver managed to nurse the car as far as Sandy Point, but on the journey back to Basseterre we were transported in the personal vehicle of a police officer. I cannot recall the Head of WIAD apologising to anyone or acknowledging I had been reasonable in my doubts.

At Sandy Point School itself, we were milling around awaiting the arrival of the royal party when the BBC Americas Correspondent, one Martin Bell, asked me how he could recognise the car with the

Princess in it. I said that was easy it; was the Rolls Royce. Oh, he said, suddenly very interested, you've flown one out for her? (Pretty unlikely, I'd have thought.) No, I replied, they already have one here and he immediately lost interest.

The actual Independence ceremony itself was held at midnight at Warner Park, Basseterre, the regular setting for formal functions in St Kitts. Rain threatened, but held off, the Royal Marine band, brought in for the occasion, played, the Union Flag and the old St Kitts and Nevis state flag were both lowered and the new flag of the Federation of St Kitts and Nevis was raised. Governor General (promoted from Governor) and Prime Minister (promoted from Premier) were sworn in and the Independence Documents were handed over. I had been curious about what these last actually were. It was a bit of a let down to find that they consisted simply of a copy of the Independence Act passed by Parliament in London, bound in rather nice red leather.

Due to the slightly odd relationship between the islands, the following day a portion of the celebrations had to be held on Nevis and the best way to travel between the islands was, of course, by air. The arrangement to get the official party across was that a Leeward Islands Air Transport (LIAT) Twin Otter would be used. This took 19 passengers and there were only just enough seats as sundry hangers-on, including Her Royal Highness's hairdresser were to accompany us. There was some slight confusion about protocol for boarding and seating on the plane; initially, I was told that the Princess liked to avoid waiting around on the plane and would be boarding last. However, this didn't happen in the event, so Val and I ended up boarding before everybody else and then had the difficulty in being unable to stand up in the small plane as the Princess got on.

The cars on Nevis were to be provided by the Nevisians, but they didn't have enough police drivers of the necessary calibre, so the drivers from St Kitts would go over by air, too. They were to drive the royal motorcade to the St Kitts airport and smartly depart in a couple of small aircraft, while the main party prepared to board the Twin Otter. The drivers would thus arrive first and then be ready to resume their duties in the Nevisian cars.

This went well. In fact, it went slightly too well. Nobody seemed to have understood the importance of sticking to the timetable as opposed to performing their duties as quickly as possible. As a result, the party gained slightly on the timetable at each stage, until we arrived at Newcastle Airport in Nevis at 11.00, instead of the scheduled 11.15.

The first item on the programme in Nevis was the swearing in ceremony of the Nevis Deputy Governor General and of the Nevis administration. A short distance into our journey from the airport to Charlestown, the capital of Nevis, we passed the new Nevisian First Minister, Sim Daniel, heading to the airport to meet his royal guest. Having passed him, of course, we couldn't see what happened next, but I imagine there was a lot of screeching and dust involved as he had almost caught up with us when we arrived. Well, he had to as he was also being sworn in.

We followed the Royal party for most of the day. After the swearing-in there was a visit to Government House for refreshments and a photo opportunity for Stanley Gibbons to display their new stamps. This last seemed to me to be a pretty crass commercialisation of a state occasion.

Next, there was lunch under a canvas awning at a beach-side hotel in Charlestown. This last strained the organisational resources of the Nevis administration considerably. For instance, having arrived ahead of the main party, I had a quick glance at the nameplates and saw that Timothy Raison, the FCO minister representing the British Government, had been placed well below the top table. I immediately swapped his nameplate for another on the top table and nobody seemed to notice. The serving of the food to so many people meant that those on the lower tables, including Val and me, hadn't started their dessert before the Princess rose to depart, so we still had, shall we say, some appetite left at the end of our meal.

We were grateful not to have to be with the Princess for any of the other events of the day, which included a visit to a hospital and the opening of another school. However, we did accompany her back to St Kitts by air in the afternoon, with the police drivers doing their quick-change act in reverse, so to speak. It didn't matter if we got back early this time.

On the 20th, the Royal party returned to Britain from Golden Rock airport, with the BA Jumbo again being deflected from its regular route between Bridgetown and London. But, before this, there was a final ceremony at Government House, where all those involved in the visit were received by the Princess and given small mementoes, which were graded according to seniority. The Governor General, Sir Clement Arindell and the High Commissioner, Giles Bullard, were given large, full-colour portrait photographs of Her Royal Highness, whereas I was given a fairly small black and white picture of her, taken a little while before, I think, and a small leather-covered notebook.

There were some aftershocks following the end of the Independence celebrations. First of all, nobody had remembered to formally thank the pilots of the LIAT Twin Otter who I knew had been specially chosen for the task, so I did so in suitably glowing terms on behalf of Princess Margaret. I copied my letter to Bridgetown, but no one commented.

However, the High Commissioner did write to the new Kittitian Prime Minister in appreciation of the efforts made and I recall he quoted Kipling's 'Recessional'; "The captains and the kings depart…." I have no idea what the Prime Minister, Dr Kennedy Simmonds, made of it and it struck me as ambiguous. It could be referring to the withdrawal of Britain from one of its last remnants of Empire – or simply to the fact that there would be some peace for the new state now all the formal activities were over.

Then there was the letter from an enterprising fisherman from Saint Kitts who claimed that the visiting British warship had fouled his nets and submitted a detailed account for the damage allegedly caused. I passed this on to the Naval Attaché in Bridgetown, who told me that this sort of thing was quite common in the West Indies and that there was no way of establishing that the claim was valid. It was also strongly suspected that the man and/or his colleagues would have submitted a similar claim to the French, American and Trinidad and Tobago governments for similar damage caused by their ships in the area during the period. The Royal Navy simply paid up and I assume that this applied to the other naval authorities as well. Interestingly, I never received any similar claim from fishermen following visits from the various British naval vessels to Antigua during my three years there.

This was not the last time I was to meet Princess Margaret. Some months later, I received a phone call out of the blue to tell me that she would be landing at Antigua airport within the hour. The plane she was travelling on, a regular BWIA flight from St Vincent to the USA had developed a problem and was going to have to land unexpectedly and Antigua was the closest suitable airport. Another plane would be diverted to pick her up later in the day. The Governor General had also been informed, so we both went to the airport. The Princess was travelling privately and so had only Inspector Philpott with her. The visit was fairly brief, but not without event. As in the case of the swimming pool, the Princess again displayed a certain wilfulness.

There was a small VIP lounge in the airport where we all assumed she would wait. However, after getting off the plane she showed great reluctance to go into the terminal building and chose to stand outside on the tarmac. This would have been fine except that another large plane had landed and the passengers were streaming across the tarmac, heading towards the terminal building in front of which she was standing.

She had already attracted the attention of the passengers in the transit/departure area. This was open to the air, bounded only by mesh fencing and those inside could easily see what was going on a few yards away on the tarmac. They were mainly American tourists who clearly regarded the sighting of the Queen of England's sister as one of the highlights of their holiday. They would like to have a picture for the folks back home. Trouble was, she was facing away from them. So they set up a cacophony of calls and whistles in an effort to get her to turn round. She remained standing looking out across the airport, ignoring both them and us, who were trying tactfully to get her to go inside.

In the middle of all this arrived the Canadian High Commissioner accredited to Antigua, but resident in Kingston, Jamaica, who I knew slightly and who was passing by from his post. He recognised Princess Margaret and asked me if he could be introduced. I obliged, but she pretty well ignored him, too, barely acknowledging his presence. I believe I committed a *faux pas,* and breached protocol, by taking the initiative in addressing her. But, as she was the sister of the head of the state he personally represented, it seemed to me perfectly reasonable that I should introduce him to her.

Eventually, just before being engulfed by a stream of North Americans bearing down on her, Her Royal Highness deigned to accept the suggestion that it might be better to go indoors. There were no further alarums and she duly left on the diverted plane shortly after.

In October 1983, the US invasion of Grenada had repercussions around the West Indies, including Antigua. A coup on Grenada, a Commonwealth Caribbean island south of my patch, had caused considerable dismay in the region as the new regime was hard-line Marxist and allied itself with Cuba. There were a number of US and Canadian students on the island and this was seen as a cause for concern. Steps had been taken to arrange a charter flight by LIAT to evacuate them, but, for some reason, this needed the agreement of all the countries that were joint owners of the airline, which included Antigua. I was instructed to approach Prime Minister Bird to ask for this agreement. I had the chance at a reception that evening at the residence of the local Anglican Bishop. Bird was quite short in his rejection of the idea, claiming it was unnecessary.

The following day I received a phone call from the Commissioner of Police in St Kitts asking if I could intervene with British Airways. The airline was insisting that the rifles the police contingent from St Kitts & Nevis were taking to Barbados be carried in the hold and not in the cabin. Could I persuade them to change their minds? What on earth was this all about? It seemed to me perfectly reasonable that firearms not be carried in the passenger cabin of a regular civilian flight, but why was the request being made at all? It took very little questioning to extract from the Commissioner, a very straightforward man, not at all at home with dissembling, to find out that there was a plan to gather East Caribbean forces in Barbados in order to provide a regional element to the US invasion of

Grenada. St Kitts & Nevis had no army or defence force, so police were being sent. I regretted that I couldn't help him.

It seemed clear to me that, if St Kitts & Nevis was sending some policemen, then Antigua & Barbuda was surely sending some of their (very) small army. So I phoned the commander of the Antigua & Barbuda Defence Force and asked him, not if he knew about the intervention, but how many men he was sending to Barbados. As I hoped, he assumed that I knew all about the plan and told me; a couple of dozen, I think.

Next (and in retrospect, somewhat naively), I phoned my US counterpart to ask if he had heard anything about this. He mumbled something about not having seen his messages from the Navy base that morning. That was not at all what I had asked him and I clearly wasn't going to get any more. This needed a classified message to Bridgetown.

So I got out our primitive coding machine and laboriously encoded, and then transmitted, the information. Shortly afterwards I received a phone call saying they knew the information in my telegram already, thank you, but hadn't thought it necessary to tell the island posts. They didn't congratulate me on finding out for myself and I was not terribly impressed with their attitude.

During the fighting, my colleague on the island of Grenada, John Kelly, remained at his post and was joined at one point by David Montgomery, who had managed to wrangle a lift on a plane from Bridgetown in order to join in the excitement. At one point David could be heard over the High Commission emergency inter-island radio animatedly describing the action, or what he could see of it from the roof of John's office.

The briefing we received after the dust had settled included a copy of the letter supposedly written by the unfortunate Governor General of Grenada, inviting the US-lead intervention.

During all the various upheavals and coups, no Grenadian politician had got around to changing the country's constitution, so that nominally the Queen remained head of the Marxist state, with the Governor General as her representative. He was, of course, non-executive and supposed to act only on the advice of his government. This point was either not understood by the Americans or was completely ignored by them and they lifted him from his own front lawn by helicopter and persuaded him to write the required letter from a US warship, but back-dating it to before the arrival of the forces. The telling point was that, if he had written the letter in Government House, as was alleged, it would have been on his own headed paper, and it wasn't.

In any case, even if he had written the letter as alleged, constitutionally, the situation would have been unclear. Normally, it would have been illegal for him to invite foreign forces into the country off his own bat without the advice of his government. It was argued, though, that there was no longer a properly constituted government to advise him and that he could act on his own initiative. Anyway, it was all water under the bridge.

Following the invasion, Margaret Thatcher let her views on the American action be known in no uncertain terms. She was particularly incensed that a country of which the Queen was head of state should have been invaded. However, as the country in question had been independent for a number of years, it was strictly nothing to do with the British Prime Minister.

Whatever the rights or wrongs of this point, her outburst caused me to be summoned to a cabinet meeting of the Antiguan Government to be requested to let the British Government know of their dissatisfaction at Mrs Thatcher's statement, as it was interference in the internal affairs of an independent state. This I passed on by telegram to the FCO with a side copy to Bridgetown. I then received another phone call from Bridgetown, this time from the High Commissioner himself, pointing out that I should have addressed the message to him, with a side copy to the FCO. He was technically correct, of course, but his taking the time to tell me so personally didn't seem to be necessary.

The scope for visiting neighbouring areas from Antigua was strangely limited. There were no regular ferry sailings between the islands with the exception of one between Saint Kitts and Nevis and the normal method of transport was by air. This made it quite expensive and so, apart from one or two official visits to neighbouring islands, Val and I only made one private trip in the area and that was to Nevis. This was towards the end of our time and our newly arrived small son, Bobby, was with us.

During this trip I decide to go and watch a cricket match at Charlestown recreation ground and I took a bus from the hotel where we were staying down to the town. My arrival at the cricket ground unfortunately caused a small stir, as I was recognised, and the police insisted that I should have had an escort. Moreover, the Premier, Sim Daniel, was watching the game and I was ushered into his presence, much to both our surprises and ended up benefiting from a free lunch. I don't remember catching the bus back up the hill, so I think I must have had a lift in a police car pressed on me.

The inability to travel incognito was reinforced when we tried to leave as private individuals from St Kitts airport. Again, I was recognised by the policeman on duty who insisted we should be ushered into the VIP lounge. All very flattering, but also a good illustration of the goldfish bowl affect of living in such a small society.

The small, almost village type of society in these islands was also brought home to me on another occasion. At a party I became aware that I was being complemented on my telephone manner.

As far as I knew I had never spoken on the phone to the woman concerned. Then I remembered she worked for the telephone company, Cable & Wireless, as an international operator. It was, it seemed, quite acceptable locally to listen in to private conversations and openly discuss them afterwards.

One of the recurring chores during my time in Antigua was dealing with Royal Navy ships' visits. The vast majority of the visits were by frigates, which were either returning from station near the Falklands or part of the regular naval presence in the West Indies. During my time, though, we also had visits from one aircraft carrier, one small submarine and two survey vessels. The pattern for the visit was always the same. I received notification of the time of the visit and made sure that there was a berth available and then I had a message from the ship itself with a regular list of requests. These involved identifying chandlers to supply the ship, hiring a car for the use of the captain, arranging a formal cocktail party on board for members of the British community, local leaders, senior military officials and so on; a smaller party for the officers and another for the senior petty officers. Both these last two required us to identify and invite a suitable selection of (relatively) unattached ladies.

Of course, the details of these arrangements varied with the vessel. For the submarine, which was not a nuclear one, but of the conventional diesel-electric type and a very small, cramped vessel, practically the whole crew disembarked and were put up in a hotel on the island, with only two or three left to monitor equipment and to maintain a presence on board.

The cocktail parties on board the ships were usually on the deck in the case of the frigates, but in the case of the aircraft carrier there was plenty of room below decks for a real celebration and, in addition, for a marching display by the Royal Marine contingent on board.

Again, in the case of the submarine, this was different and quite an experience. The only place on the vessel where you could expect to stand upright without danger of banging your head was in the central control area (was it called the bridge?) just under the conning tower.

Access to the submarine was through a hatch in the deck and down a ladder. Advance information about this was particularly important for female guests, regarding the question of skirts or slacks and I had a bit of discussion about whether this had been made sufficiently clear with the comfortably sized wife of one of the local merchants. Clearly the number of guests in the circumstances was severely limited as we were in what was effectively the control room of a warship and the occasion was punctuated by the occasional firm request: "Please don't touch that!"

On one occasion, during a regular frigate's visit, the night before sailing, one member of the small squad of Royal Marines on board had enjoyed himself and rather taken a shine to life in the West Indies. On the morning of the sailing, when I went down as usual to the port to bid farewell, I was asked by the Royal Marine captain in charge of the contingent if I could kindly give a lift to him and two burly marines to winkle out this colleague of theirs from a brothel. This was the first occasion I had had to identify, let alone appear anywhere near, the Antigua brothel. However, I was quite strongly motivated to help, as the captain of the ship was determined to sail on time and, if the marine were to remain behind, I would have to make arrangements to get him home. In the event he was persuaded to come quietly, without much physical effort and I delivered the lot of them back to the ship in time for the scheduled departure.

The two survey vessels, HMS Fox and HMS Fawn, were a novelty. They were actually working in the area and therefore were around for, I think, about a month. They were very small vessels and when crossing the Atlantic, the medical officer, who was shared between them, had been helicoptered off the deck as he had developed extreme seasickness. This was an irony not lost on the sailors. Apparently in such extreme cases the patient develops an antipathy towards sea travel to the extent that they can effectively never go to sea again. What that does to the career of the naval officer I can only speculate.

The vessels had, unusually, a Land Rover which the sailors would drive around the island while making their surveying measurements. One evening, having sampled the local rum punches, they managed to drive the vehicle through the wall of a local lady's garden. The vehicle was so severely damaged as to be beyond local repair, although they managed to get it back to their ship. The sailors involved were then told to volunteer to rebuild the wall. The final ignominy for the Royal Navy was that, when the vessel finally sailed, the Land Rover, which had to be returned to the UK, was to be seen, battered and bent, lashed to the deck of the departing vessel.

After the one Post Inspection I had during my time in Antigua, I learned that my entertainment allowance specifically covered visits by two Royal Navy ships a year. However, I was at that time regularly having visits by four ships a year, each of which involved my providing entertainment. I was considered in Bridgetown to be extremely surly and unco-operative when I pointed out that I would be unable to accept more than two visits a year from then on, otherwise it would mean either being unable to entertain the captain and his officers sufficiently on every visit, or that I would have to cut my regular entertaining.

The US, Dutch and Canadian navies all also paid courtesy visits during my time. The pattern was always much as the Royal Navy visits (maybe there's a NATO standard for this?) However, because of a ban on alcohol on board US ships, their visits were never as popular as the others,

Before he left, my predecessor had recommended an OBE for a diminutive and fierce lady who had run a kindergarten on the island for many years after arriving from England. In her younger days, in the 1930s, she had been a rally driver and tended to drive her elderly Mini as if she was still competing. Eventually, she was persuaded to hang up her driving gloves in the interests of public safety. She was awarded the OBE in the Queen's Birthday Honours for services to the British community in Antigua and the award was on the UK honours list. However, Antigua was a realm and was still participating in the honours system in its own right. This meant it had its own list put forward by and on behalf of Antiguans.

Unfortunately this distinction had been overlooked by the lady, who, having told her close friends of the honour, was mortified when her name wasn't read out with the Antiguan recipients on the local radio on the morning of the Queen's Birthday. She phoned me in some dismay to ask why her name seemed to have been missed out. I explained the difference between the two lists and assured her that

213

the High Commissioner would be presenting her with the award personally on a forthcoming visit. This really didn't help matters as she had been expecting the presentation to be at Government House at the hands of the Governor General.

Oh, dear! I tried to play up the relative greater importance of the award on the UK list, but she was clearly disappointed, even when we had a *vin d'honneur* for her at my residence at which the High Commissioner duly made the presentation.

At about this time the High Commissioner became aware that on the various subordinate islands his representatives were habitually flying the Union Flag on their official cars. Up to this point he had apparently assumed that the flag was flown for him when he visited and had not realised when he departed the officer on the island continued to do so. He clearly considered that this was not necessarily correct and we were instructed to ask permission from our various host governments for the practice to continue.

This was a slightly odd request, as it was clearly something that had been going on for some time and the host governments were presumably not at all bothered by it. Moreover, as I pointed out in a letter to Bridgetown, the request in the case of Saint Kitts was going to sound very peculiar as they actually provided the flag (and, indeed, the car) every time I visited. Nevertheless, we all complied with the request, permission was duly formally given by the various governments and the practice continued exactly as before.

In the case of Saint Kitts, the flagstaff from which the Union Flag flew on the car was a small pole on a fairly strong magnet which was simply placed on to the bonnet of the ancient Jaguar which still served as the official car. This was fine while the car was travelling at no more than 20 to 25 miles an hour, but on one occasion when I was rather late for an appointment and the driver speeded up, each time we passed the speed of about 35 miles an hour the magnetic adhesion failed and the flag fell off. This of course necessitated the driver stopping, getting out, going back down the road, picking it up and putting it back again. Thus, I was even later, so I suggested that he keep it in the car until just before we arrived at the destination and then replace it.

While I was in Antigua the then Archbishop of Canterbury, Dr Runcie, paid a pastoral visit. Before he came his chaplain, Terry Waite, who later became world famous for his experiences in Beirut, paid an advance visit to make arrangements with the local Anglican community. I was not formally involved, but as Dr Runcie was head of the Anglican Church, it was useful that I was kept informed. Terry came to the house for a light meal during his visit to discuss the arrangements in general terms. I remember him as a tall, burly, bushy man with a strong charisma who tended to stand slightly too close for comfort in terms of personal space.

When the Archbishop did arrive, travelling in a private aircraft provided by a friend, the original plan was that he would have a fairly relaxed visit to the island and preach one sermon at St John's Cathedral. However, by the time he had arrived this had been changed, much to Terry Waite's annoyance, to require Dr Runcie to preach a sermon in each of the six Anglican churches as well as the cathedral. I remember Terry commenting to me that the schedule was almost killing his boss.

I attended the special service in the cathedral. His sermon was, from the British viewpoint, pretty conventional. However, for West Indians, it was somewhat bland and not up to the expectations of some of the listeners. There was no fire and brimstone, but more of brotherly love and turning the other cheek. This was not at all what West Indians want from their Archbishop and I felt there was some disappointment.

One of the main recreations available in Antigua was scuba diving. As I said previously, it was something I had dabbled with when we were in Abu Dhabi, but had not completed the tests to obtain the necessary certification. In Antigua, we made the acquaintance of a young American who was a qualified instructor and our children and I very soon managed to obtain the necessary qualification.

216

Following this I joined the Barbuda and Antigua Diving Club (named in that order so that it could be called the BAD Club) and went on a number of very interesting dives around the island. I also bought a face-mask with lenses ground to my prescription so that I was able to see pretty much as well as anyone else under the water.

Unfortunately, because of her old ear trouble, Val was unable to join in, although she came for the picnic and sunbathed while the rest of us swam. The children, when they came out for the school holidays, were very keen divers, although Stephanie sometimes had difficulty with the pressure on her ears and on occasion was not able to dive with the rest of us.

In my case, although I was an adequate diver, I have always been a very poor sailor. As a result on the dive boat, the call was "Let John go down first" and I was kitted out with my tank, weights, belt etc. and allowed to dive before the rest. The water movement was minimal below about 6 feet and there was no question of motion sickness there.

Some of the dives around Antigua were extremely good; the water was clear and the natural flora and fauna enchanting. On one occasion I tried a night dive. I did not own a wet suit, as it was invariably warm enough during the normal daytime dives. But, during a night dive, the body heat you always lose once you are in the water could not be replaced quickly when you came to the surface, because there was no tropical sunshine. As a result, on this night dive, I found that I was as cold as I have ever been: my internal temperature was clearly extremely low.

On the other hand, there were pluses with a night dive. Not only do you see nocturnal life for the first time, but, oddly enough, colour visibility is better. This is because you will be diving with a torch and the light produced is white in contrast with the sunlight during the day which is filtered through several dozen feet of water and gives everything a bluish tinge.

Although Antigua was not a consular post and I couldn't issue passports or visas, the most interesting consular cases in my career cropped up here. They all had a slightly, but distinctive, West Indian flavour about them.

There was a suicide where the deceased was buried in the wrong plot; the dipsomaniac air hostess who kept returning on the flight deck of BA planes every time she was sent home, the London policeman who had retired to Antigua, but ran out of money, the man who thought he was a secret agent and that I was his control, the elderly couple convinced they were being pursued by gangsters and the young man who wanted to be repatriated to South Africa and kept spending the money his mother sent before managing to buy a ticket. On this last one I did what you should NEVER do and loaned him the money from my own pocket. Naturally, in spite of his protestations, I never heard from him again. Then there was a rape case which made the British papers and a man travelling with somebody else's wife and child who was robbed of his yacht.

One day in spring 1985, I was in my office, talking to a colleague visiting from DevDiv in Bridgetown, when Val came in. This was completely unexpected, and she did not normally intrude when I had people with me; in fact I don't recall her ever doing it at any other time. There was a serious reason on this occasion, though. As she apologised for interrupting, she handed me a scrap of paper on which was written "Mrs Crane – pregnancy positive." I didn't show it to my visitor or mention it and he made no comment and I like to think I didn't skip a beat in my conversation, but of course my mind was no longer on the British aid programme.

And so I learned that we were once more to become parents. Our other children at this time were aged 19, 16 and 13 and we were both 42. I was surprised, but Val was delighted. It certainly changed the subsequent pattern of our lives until 2009, when the new arrival finally left home after university and started work in London and we could get on with being empty-nesters.

The reaction of people at the time was quite interesting. It was clear that the baby hadn't been planned and there was much 'nudge-nudge wink-winking' to be put up with. And the gynaecologist, a leading doctor on the island, assumed we would be requiring an abortion, which was interesting, as at that time and place, abortions were illegal and he was also a prominent opposition politician. Val was also offered the possibility of an abortion by our local hospital when we came back to Eastbourne in the summer and she went for her check ups. However, we are both against the idea of abortion in principle and were very happy to have another child, a decision which, I can emphatically say, neither of us has ever regretted.

The baby was due around Christmas and, in view of the perceived higher possibility of complications due to Val's age, the medical advice from the Office was that she should come back to England for the delivery. We were due to go on leave that summer, but the Office would not pay for another journey for Val at Christmas so soon after a leave journey, so she would have to remain in the UK when I returned to post. There was a way for me to be present at the birth, though. The regulations allowed for one parent to return to the UK in lieu of the holiday journeys of their children.

A Christmas at home with all the family was just fine, so I returned alone to Antigua on the 10th of September and then came back to England on 20th December for Christmas and for the birth of Robert Peter, who arrived nine days later.

While Val was in the UK awaiting her confinement, the Queen visited the West Indies, including both my patches. She was travelling on the Royal Yacht Britannia and the trip was to include all the islands from St Kitts down to Barbados. As I have already said, West Indians are typically very royalist and the Antiguans were politely critical that Her Majesty had not visited them since, I think, 1966. To those who complained to me, I pointed out that the town where I live had roughly the same population as Antigua and Her Majesty had hardly visited there at all. This was not regarded as at all relevant.

It was an important constitutional point that, since her last visit, the island had attained Independence as a realm within the Commonwealth and so Her Majesty was now coming as Queen of Antigua and not as that of the 'imperial' power as previously. And as this was the case, I was not involved in the arrangements, such as the guest lists for the various functions; that was the job of the Governor General.

The change was hard for a number of people, both Antiguans and British, to hoist on board. On the one hand I had to explain to local school children that I had no Union Flags to hand out for them to wave as the Queen passed. While, on the other, I had to explain to expatriates that I could not intervene in the question of people who had been introduced to

221

Her Majesty last time being missed off lists this time. In fact, I explained, I was not going to be at every function myself.

My mother had been very concerned that Val was going to miss out on a chance to meet the Queen and offered to pay her return fare to be with me during the royal visit. But, although far from being a republican, Val wasn't that bothered and chose to stay in England.

I met Her Majesty formally on HMY Britannia at the start of the visit. I had been briefed that I should not be too firm in my handshake, as the poor lady would have to shake many hundred hands each day. This suggested to me that her hand would be fairly relaxed. Not a bit of it; one of the two things that impressed me about the Queen was her firm handshake, the other being her lack of height. She is quite petite.

It had been decided that there should be something for Her Majesty to open while she was on Nevis. There was an electricity generator, which had been part of the British aid programme, but this had been opened twice already; once by the Nevisian First Minister and then by the British High Commissioner. There was serious consideration given to a plan to turn the motor off again to allow the Queen to formally switch it on once more. But reason prevailed, when it was pointed out, that switching off the power supply to the island to mark the Royal Visit, would please neither the citizens of

Nevis, nor Her Majesty.

The only other recently completed project available was an abattoir and so it was decided that she would declare this open. Reason, having got a foot in the door, now dictated that the Queen wouldn't actually have to be directly involved in bovine slaughter, but would simply unveil a memorial plaque.

The plaque, having been prepared and placed on a suitable wall, was covered by two small curtains that were to be parted by pulling on a cord at the side. Fine, except the operation was not tested in advance, so that when the Queen, after a few apposite words, pulled the cord, the whole thing, curtains, pulley and rail fell without the curtain parting and hung there swaying drunkenly from a hook on one side. The plaque was revealed though and when the First Minister, Sim Daniel and companion minister, Ivor Stevens, rushed forward to put the whole thing back up for a repeat performance, Her Majesty expressed her strong view that the abattoir was well and truly open and moved on.

Giles Bullard had decided that he should be present on each of the territories he was accredited to when the Queen arrived. Thus, he would he meet her at St Kitts, then Antigua and so on down the chain to Bridgetown. This meant that I, too, had to meet her twice, accompanying him on my two islands. Thus, the morning after the first reception in

Basseterre, St Kitts, we took the earliest flight to Antigua for breakfast, before lining up to meet the royal party on their arrival at St John's harbour, Britannia having sailed over during the night.

The reception line-up on the jetty was in strict order of precedence, so, as my head of mission was present, I was well down the line, not far ahead of the US navy base commander. He and his wife were determined that their teenage daughter, who was not on the reception list, would meet the Queen and they had clearly dressed the girl for the occasion. This was embarrassing for Ena Pereira, the Antiguan Head of Protocol, who was hard put to stop the Americans pushing their daughter back into the line after she had been politely removed. They tried three or four times before giving up.

We had, of course, met all the royal party the day before in St Kitts, but they had for the most part been meeting people in receptions for a long time, so I was faintly flattered when two of them actually remembered me from the previous day. The Queen's equerry, Major Hugh Lindsay, greeted me by name as he went past. "Morning, John." "Morning, Hugh." (He was to die three years later in an avalanche at Klosters in Switzerland while skiing with Prince Charles.) And the Duke of Edinburgh, as he shook my hand, said: "Aren't you the British Representative?" When I confirmed this, he called the information to the Queen, but she was by now two people further down the line and replied to him rather tetchily "Oh, do come on!" So much for 'trusty and well-beloved' on my commission!

By the end of the day word must have percolated to the royal party that the High Commissioner intended officially meeting Her Majesty on arrival on each of the next five days as she processed down the chain of islands. This seems to have struck them as bizarre as it did me and so he and his wife were invited to travel to Bridgetown on Britannia. On the voyage he was knighted, probably during the evening that he left Antigua.

The knighthood was conferred because one of the territories he was accredited to, Dominica, was, as I have mentioned, a republic. It is the convention that, during a royal visit to a country of which Her Majesty is not head of state, the head of mission is appointed a Knight Commander of the Royal Victorian Order (KCVO). In the other six countries where he was accredited, the Queen was head of state, but one republic out of seven states was enough for a knighthood.

When Prince Andrew became engaged to Miss Sarah Ferguson, this lady decided to take one last private holiday before becoming part of the Royal Family. Antigua was the chosen destination as she had been at school with Florence, the daughter of the French film actor, Jean-Paul Belmondo, who had a holiday home on the island. Sarah may not have yet been part of royalty, but she was already well in the public eye and had also been allocated a Royal Protection detective who, whether by chance or intention, had quite a resemblance to her fiancé. Both the Governor General and I were, of course, informed and told that the visit was not to be publicised. Fat chance!

The Governor General and the Police Commissioner as well as myself turned up at the airport. On arrival, I suggested that I should go to the plane to meet Miss Ferguson as I was often at the airport meeting people while His Excellency and the Police Chief weren't, so it would attract less attention for me to walk across the tarmac. In the event, although I did walk out, BA of course knew of their passenger and sent a motorised buggy out to the plane to pick up her and her detective.

After I greeted her, the detective told me that they had the press on board, too. I asked how on earth had that happened. Apparently, a reporter and a photographer from the Daily Mail had followed her everywhere she went in Britain and, when she got to the airport, they simply bought two tickets on the same plane. They had had the chance to report where they were going with the result that a local photographer was also on hand and took a picture, which the following day appeared in the Daily Mail, of Sarah Ferguson seated beside me in the BA buggy.

They had done their homework well and knew about the Belmondo connection, so it took them very little time to find out where the Belmondo residence was and the house was besieged by an ever-increasing crowd of reporters and photographers for the remainder of her stay on the island. I believe there was an agreement that the press would be given a few opportunities for beach shots on the understanding that Sarah was left pretty much alone for the rest of her time in Antigua.

This lasted until her departure. No subterfuge this time. The Governor General and I went to see her off and walked with her to the plane from the departure lounge. It was night time and in front of us a veritable army of press photographers was walking backwards taking flash pictures. It was almost physically uncomfortable and I kept well to the side.

During our last year in Antigua the entrepreneur, Peter de Savary, bought up and relaunched a hotel on the island and Prince and Princess Michael of Kent came for the formal opening. De Savary also brought his parents out and the Governor General felt that, as royalty were about, he should provide some entertainment for the party. We were included and attended the small drinks party at Government House. It was a rather strained affair.

Later Sir Wilfred and I were invited to the opening of the refurbished hotel. We were both rather sidelined, as our host was clear in his mind that the most important guests were the Prime

Minster, V.C. Bird and Their Royal Highnesses. So, when Prime Minister Bird arrived, the Antiguan National Anthem was played and when the Prince and Princess arrived, the British one. I was sitting next to Sir Wilfred and neither of us felt this was the way things should be happening. As effective head of state, he should have had his national anthem, and I was just a bit doubtful about minor royals getting the national treatment.

Still there was a consolation. One of my pet pedantries is, as I believe I've mentioned, the correct flying of the Union Flag and they had got one upside down. I was probably the only person there who noticed and certainly the only one to be bothered, but I pointed this out to one of the young ladies bustling around. She, bless her, instead of simply leaving it and getting on with her job, took it on herself to pick up the microphone and drew attention to the error by apologising for it to all and sundry. I don't suppose her boss was very pleased.

At the end of my time in Antigua I was once more due London posting. Val, Bobby and I left on 21st of September 1986 and were upgraded to first class on the BA flight back, thanks to our acquaintance with the local BA station manager. This was the only time I have ever flown first class, but it didn't strike me as being worth the extra money others would have paid. And I got the impression that our fellow passengers in the cabin were not impressed with sharing their journey with a seven-month-old baby, even though he was quiet for the whole journey.

CHAPTER 9

LONDON 1986-1989

Back in the FCO my new job was in Nuclear
Energy Department, where I was desk officer in
charge of relations with the rest of the world in the
areas of civil nuclear power and radioactive waste.
So I instantly became the FCO 'expert' on the
subject, even though, of course, I had no background
in nuclear physics (or any other physics, come to
that, apart from my 1958 'O' level), but the FCO
never bothered about little things like that. I actually
found it rather a fascinating subject that has tended
to generate considerable, and largely misinformed,
interest in the public mind.

While I had been in the West Indies the
Chernobyl nuclear accident happened. Following
this the world was full of the sound of stable doors
being nailed shut as governments rushed to reassure
their anxious, but generally ignorant, electorates that
they, the authorities, were taking steps to ensure that
such an event could not happen again. Or, if it did, it
would not affect their own country. Or, again, if it
did, then they would be able to point the finger at the
perpetrator.

The UK, as a leading civil nuclear power, was
in the forefront and moved to reassure its European
neighbours about its response to any future nuclear

accident on its soil. Ignoring the fact that most nuclear scientists in the various Western countries were in close contact with their opposite numbers on a regular basis anyway, the politicians were keen to reassure everyone that they had DONE SOMETHING. So the International Atomic Energy Authority encouraged a series of agreements between countries. These agreements were to enshrine the commitment of each state to tell its neighbours if there were to be a nuclear accident in its territory, difficult though it was to imagine that they would do otherwise.

It was all mainly cosmetic, of course. The circumstances of the Chernobyl accident were eventually well documented and the peculiarly Soviet-era faults in safety checks and operating procedures were understood. These, it was generally agreed, were practically impossible to replicate in the West as the successful containment of the Three Mile Island accident subsequently proved.

At the time I took over the desk, the process of establishing these agreements was just beginning. One of my first jobs was to start the drafting process. The details were much the same in each case, although some countries had particular concerns and separate negotiations were held with each. The first of these agreements to come to completion was with Norway. I was part of a team that negotiated this during a very pleasant visit to Oslo in the summer of 1987, followed by an equally pleasant visit by overnight ferry to Copenhagen. There we 'negotiated' an almost identical agreement with the Danes.

The reason for the similarity, we were cheerfully told by the Danes, was that their Norwegian cousins had faxed a copy of their agreement while we were on the ferry and the Danes thought this wording would do them very nicely, too. So we had nothing to do and spent a couple of days sightseeing around Copenhagen. I hadn't realised until we got there that, from Copenhagen, when looking out to sea, the view was dominated by the Barseback nuclear power station on the coast of Sweden, which has since been decommissioned.

The most important of these agreements was with the Soviet Union, as it still was – just. I was part of a delegation of four; two from the FCO and two from the Department of Energy that went out for the negotiations. We flew to Moscow where we were accommodated in a city centre hotel, full of foreigners. The actual negotiations were over fairly easily, after all there was not much disagreement about what we both wanted. And notifying an accident did not imply access to any sites or the provision of much secret technical information.

So we had a chance to look around. We visited the bits of the Kremlin open to tourists (quite a lot of tourists) and were taken by our Soviet hosts to see a show and to a meal in a restaurant. These were both interesting experiences in their way.

The play, of course, was in Russian and our host had to lean over and translate as the plot unfolded. I can't remember the details of this now, but at one point there was considerable laughter. We were told that the joke was that when the girl asked the boy why he hadn't declared his love earlier, he replied that that had been 'before glasnost'. This was in April 1988 and the cracks were starting to show in the Soviet system.

The evening was not exactly enhanced by the argument we had when trying to return to our seats after the interval. As we sat down, the harridan, who was performing the function of usherette, came over to argue that we had no right to sit there. I can only think she was after money, because the objection was clearly ridiculous as we had been sitting there during the first half of the show. Our embarrassed host remonstrated with her and she eventually gave up, but it was a bit of a flaw in the evening.

The restaurant we were taken to seemed to be regarded as a very select establishment and there was a queue outside, but we were honoured guests and our hosts were senior officials, so we walked past the waiting line. When inside, the only part of the meal I can remember was the meat. This was presumably the top quality available, but none of the British side was able to get their knife through it, let alone chew it. Amazingly, our Soviet hosts chomped their way through the whole thing with relish.

Heaven knows what they normally ate.

I later discovered that the inevitable Soviet obsession with security was undiminished and had affected me. Not only did my beard trimmer never work again, but I later found that the hand Dictaphone I had with me had recorded on it the sound of a train – on the whole tape, as far as I could tell. I assume that I was used as a training exercise for KGB recruit spooks; certainly they gained nothing, but did show what they could do.

The next stage in the general process was the formal signing of the agreements. In the case of Norway this was arranged at ministerial level, when a Norwegian minister was due to pay an official visit to London later that year. She could only fit the signing in at eight in the morning, so it had been decided there would be a champagne breakfast or, more exactly, champagne at breakfast time and there should be a picture of the event.

I had to leave Eastbourne hideously early in order to arrive at the Office before seven in time for a meeting at eight, but I did it, to find the minister's Assistant Private Secretary (APS) busy organising the event in one of the ornate Old India Office rooms on the first floor. The ceiling of the room was high and as I came in there was a workman some twelve feet up a ladder in the middle of the room, with another holding it. The one aloft was checking light bulbs in the chandelier and replacing the faulty ones, as well as cleaning the fitting. When they had finished they folded the ladder and left.

Some minutes later, the APS went over to the light switch and flipped it to check that all was well. There was a click and twenty-three of the twenty-four bulbs lit. The twenty-fourth fell from its socket and bounced on the carpeted floor. There was now no way anybody could reach the chandelier to replace the bulb. I picked it up and looked at it then considered the light fitting for a moment. It didn't seem likely that anybody was going to stand and count the bulbs. We would have to get rid of this one, though. Inspiration struck me. I took down one of the grand vases from the mantelpiece, put the errant light bulb in it and replaced the vase. The bulb may still be there.

Rather than use the main FCO entrance, which would mean the visitors walking from one corner of the main building to the other, it had been decided that they should come in by a side entrance in King Charles Street, which was much handier for the room. This door wasn't being regularly used at the time, but I had been promised that it would be opened specially for us that day. I went to check that all was well. At first, I was reassured to see a uniformed security officer apparently in the process of unlocking the door. As I came closer, though, it was clear that he was actually struggling with it and the door was not budging in spite of his efforts.

I asked if he knew the door should be open for

the Norwegian delegation at eight. He assured me it was going to be all right. He was just waiting for his colleague to come and help. I did not feel completely happy with this comment. It seemed clear now that he had been wrestling with the door for some time without success. I joined him in his vain attempts to shift the restraining bar. With a sensation of panic looming, I struck the recalcitrant bar hard. My hand slid along the metal and a sharp edge gouged a small furrow in my wrist. As I watched in dismay, blood slowly welled up from the cut onto my shirt cuff.

Having patched myself up, I went back upstairs and called the Housekeeper's Office to be assured that there would be no trouble with the door by the time the Norwegians arrived. Unfortunately, this deadline was now only ten minutes away.

Time for Plan B: the visitors would simply have to come through the main entrance, after all. I went down a corridor, out through the main entrance, back up the road and stood at the foot of the steps leading up to the designated, but stuck, door. I could hear the faint noises of the security officers' efforts on the other side the door, but there was no sign of it opening. I looked up the road as a black Mercedes from the Norwegian Embassy drove down the length of King Charles Street and drew up opposite the door. I stepped out into the road to greet the occupants, who were all female.

"Welcome, minister," I said. "I'm afraid there's

been a bit of a problem and if you could just go back down there to the main entrance…"

"No, I'm not the Minister" said the lady I had addressed. "I'm the secretary. That's the Minister", gesturing to her companion exiting the car on the other side. As it happened, the Minister hadn't caught what I said.

Just then, I heard a muffled click followed by a thud from the top of the entrance steps behind me. I turned to see both halves of the door suddenly swing open to show a grinning security officer. It was one minute past eight.

Back to Plan A. We all ignored my earlier greeting. "If you'd come with me, Minister," I said to the correct person, gesturing up the steps.

I led my Norse trio up into the building and then round to the rather grand staircase up to the room where the assembled British team was waiting. Just outside the room, there was a coat rack and I helped the women off with their coats and hung them up. They seemed to regard this as being the height of gallantry. Apart from the Victorian opulence of the décor, this was probably the only positive impression they had of the whole proceedings.

They moved into the room, introductions were made and I was able to relax a little. I glanced up at the chandelier. No more light bulbs, I noticed with relief, had fled their perches. I looked around. The photographer should have been there by now, but I couldn't see him. I went to the phone and called News Department. They were afraid there'd been a bit of a delay, but they'd get somebody along in a minute. This was delivered in what was apparently intended to be a reassuring tone, but was worryingly somewhat lacking in conviction.

The British minister said he thought they were ready to move on to the signing. Was everything ready? Not quite replied his APS; the photographer is not yet there, but we have been told he is on his way. Her boss was clearly not entirely happy with the delay and a couple of minutes later, having grown increasingly less happy, he consulted his Norwegian counterpart. She told him she had another meeting soon. So the Ministers decided that they would go ahead without a picture.

The pens were checked, the document folder opened and the two ministers were invited to sign. The champagne was produced with a flourish, but only token sips were taken.

The speeches were just beginning to get under way when, just too late, a young man appeared at the door with a camera, but didn't seem so sure of himself. The APS approached her boss to inform him that the photographer was here now. Maybe he and the Norwegian minister could pose over the document again for a picture? He agreed quite tersely. The Norwegians were looking slightly surprised: this inefficiency was all so much at odds with the quality of the surroundings.

The two ministers again formed up at the green baize table and held pens over the document in pretence of signing. Now I looked more closely at the camera the photographer was holding, it had the appearance of a type at home taking snaps of the family in the garden and had clearly had greatness unexpectedly thrust upon it in now being pressed into service for the recording of events of state. Nothing was intrinsically wrong with that, except that, in spite of its simple appearance, the bearer of this instrument seemed not to be fully conversant with its operation; or, at least, with the flash attached to it.

The unfortunate amateur photographer blushed, muttered, apologised and wrestled with his inadequate apparatus as both ministerial tempers started to look decidedly dog-eared. It also looked quite likely that in a very short time, helpful amateur photographers in the group would be advising him what the problem was and what could best be done to right it.

The British minister, who was losing face and temper in equal measure, demanded to know what the matter was now and the Norwegian minister was muttering that perhaps they could, after all, do without the picture as she really should be leaving. At that moment, suddenly and smoothly, there entered the real photographer, newly released from the clutches of British Rail or London Transport, with a proper, professional camera, complete, as he duly demonstrated, with a working flash.

So, the performance was gone through again. In what appeared to be faint disbelief, the two ministers stood at the green baize table for a third time. The real photographer duly took proper and flash-lit pictures, but I never did see them.

There were other agreements in the series, but these were either signed overseas by ambassadors or by our ministers visiting the corresponding country. There were no other signings in the FCO.

One of the aspects of my job was to pay familiarisation visits to various nuclear establishments around Britain. As part of this process I visited the nuclear power stations at Dounreay and Dungeness as well as the reprocessing plant at Sellafield. Strangely, although I was the only person in the department with the responsibility for nuclear matters, every time I paid a visit, I was accompanied by at least one other departmental colleague.

The visits to Dounreay and Dungeness were relatively unmemorable, in particular as Dounreay was in the process of being decommissioned, but the visit to Sellafield was extremely interesting. The tour included a visit to the storage ponds where spent fuel rods from nuclear power stations were kept while they cooled. The amount of water providing shielding between us and these highly radioactive rods was approximately 8 feet; little more than the deep end of a decent swimming pool.

We were given a complete tour of the establishment. While we were inside, there was a continual beeping noise, which we were told was a warning device. It seems people react more strongly to the interruption of a continuous sound, than to the introduction of new one and if this beeping were to stop, this would be a warning.

On entering the reprocessing plant, we had to put on white coveralls and a white hat and on the way out we had to remove these and put them in a special receptacle together with a piece of tissue into which we had blown our noses. These were all then classified as a low-level radioactive waste and disposed of accordingly.

There was a TV crew making a programme about some aspect of the nuclear industry on site while we were there and they accompanied us for part of our visit. We were told that we would probably feature in the finished product. However, as luck would have it, a week or two later, there was a visit by a junior minister. His presence trumped ours and we didn't appear in the programme after all.

NED was the contact point for complaints from other countries about the perceived radioactive pollution of the seas by British nuclear facilities, particularly Sellafield and Dounreay. This was mainly from the Irish, Norwegian and Icelandic governments and from environmental groups.

With a degree of irony, we were also involved with complaints by the Channel Islanders about just such pollution from the French reprocessing plan at Cap de la Hague on the coast of the Cherbourg Peninsula.

While I was in the department, it was decided by an environmental group in Norway that they would launch a mass complaint to Mrs Thatcher, the prime minister at the time, about plutonium contamination of the North Sea stemming from Dounreay. This took the form of a postcard with a printed message and space for the signature. Several hundred of these were sent, addressed to 10 Downing Street. Nobody there was particularly interested, so they were all sent to the FCO, where they eventually landed on my desk. I looked through them; some had personal additions, but mostly they were just printed cards. In the end I kept them for a time after counting and recording the total and then, after a couple of months, during which time nobody took the slightest interest in them, threw them away.

The continual inspection system in the FCO produced a revamp of the nuclear energy portfolio later in 1988. Thus, the military aspect of NED's work was taken away and put with other aspects of non-proliferation (i.e. rocket technology) and the civil nuclear bit was added to the science side of things to form Science, Energy and Nuclear

Department (SEND), so I became a member of that. This involved a move from the top floor of the India Office Building to the ground floor of the main old Foreign Office building overlooking the Cenotaph in Whitehall. This was a few yards from the entrance through which the Royal Family pass when attending the Armistice Day ceremony. This door is not normally used at any other time.

Having gone from sharing a room with a colleague dealing with handling Britain's efforts to restrict the spread of military nuclear technology, I now shared with one who was concerned with the price and availability of oil supplies. We had no responsibilities in common. However, this did not deter an inspection review recommending a few months later that there must be 'synergy' between myself and the oil expert, even if only because we sat in the same room and both looked after different aspects of power (nuclear and oil). This was, of course, nonsense and we both ended up having to try to get a working knowledge of a completely different subject from the one we normally dealt with.

In the wake of the Chernobyl disaster, it was decided that all British diplomatic missions overseas deemed at risk should be protected in the event of another civil nuclear accident. So a list was drawn up of all posts in countries in the world having nuclear facilities, and another of posts in countries

243

bordering these. Those in the first category were all issued with a supply of potassium iodide pills and a radiation detector and instructions on how to use them both. They all also had a covering letter signed by me. Nine years later, as I was doing some tidying up before leaving Khartoum, I came across the post's copy of my letter. It had been completely ignored and, indeed, I had forgotten that I had sent a copy to Khartoum. I suspect that there are unread copies of this letter still filed away in various posts in the backs of cupboards world-wide together with languishing supplies of potassium iodide pills and mouldering radiation detectors.

Towards the end of 1989, my turn for an overseas posting came up again and I was told I had been selected for the number two post in the British Consulate General in Jerusalem. This was an Arabic speaking post, but as I had not been in such a post since I left Damascus in 1983, my entitlement to a language allowance had lapsed after the designated five years and I would have to retake the exam. I hadn't found passing the first time easy and I wasn't at all confident that I would find it any easier this time. Anyway, off I was sent to brush up my language skills again. MECAS had long since been closed, so this time I went to the FCO Language School which was in a building just off Millbank. This, plus my political briefing took up a large part of my time in the months immediately before I was due to go to post.

One day while I was travelling to the Language School, a journey which took me past the Houses of Parliament, I witnessed a rather strange event. As I was walking along the other side of the road from the House of Lords entrance, I heard a vehicle skid on the wet road and looking round was just in time to see a man being hit by a Ford Transit van and knocked along the road. It appeared that the unfortunate man was a tourist who was crossing the road and, as was often the case with foreign visitors, looked the wrong way. People passing by rushed over and the van driver, who was clearly shaken, was standing at the back of his van puffing on a cigarette. The policeman on duty outside the House of Lords had apparently quickly phoned for an ambulance from his kiosk. People were gathering round the victim who was lying on the road in some pain and a coat was put over him. His shoes, which had fallen off, had been placed by his side.

In the midst of all this, an elderly man came up and, after hearing the victim's companion speak, asked if the injured man was an American and his friend said he was. To everybody's amazement, well, to mine, at least, the old man then took a handful of loose change out of his pocket and put it into one of the shoes of the injured man. The donor of this rather small largesse said nothing more and, with no explanation of his action, simply walked off.

I can only assume that this was intended as a gesture of thanks for American support during the War; the man was certainly of the right sort of age. However, he had said nothing apart from establishing the victim's nationality. What the two Americans made of it I would be fascinated to know.

All the while, we were still waiting for the ambulance, so I went back over to the police box at the House of Lords entrance and asked the policeman to repeat the call for an ambulance as the injured man was still lying on the cold wet road and eventually the emergency medical services appeared.

On the 23rd of November 1989, accompanied by young Robert, we flew out to Jerusalem– where I later actually did again pass the Arabic exam, to my relief and slightly to my surprise. So ended my last home posting.

CHAPTER 10

JERUSALEM 1989 – 1993

We were happy to be posted to Jerusalem, partly because it was as close as could be to the centre of the Middle East problem, always a focal point in the Arab world, and partly because I would be working under Ivan Callan whom we had met many years before while studying at MECAS and with whom I got on well.

First, a bit of background to the political situation in Jerusalem. At the time of the establishment of the State of Israel in 1948, there were a number of UN resolutions which were supposed to apply. Most have been overtaken by events, but the one dealing with the status of Jerusalem is still regarded as valid. This said that the eventual status of the city would be finalised by an international agreement, but meanwhile the city would be legally a *corpus seperatum*; that is part of neither the Arab nor Jewish states. This has been held to mean that the city boundaries as at 1948 remain and that nowhere within this area can be annexed by anybody, prior to a permanent settlement. Of course, from this it follows that, as Jerusalem is not part of Israel, it cannot be the capital of the country.

To deal with the fact that the city was actually

split between the two sides in 1948, it was agreed that the practical (*de facto*) administrations were Israeli and Jordanian (as it was at the time), but these were not regarded as legal (*de jure*). After the 1967 war, when the Israelis occupied the whole of the city (as well as the whole of the former British Mandate of Palestine), a new stance had to be adopted. This was that, while the Israeli administration would be recognised as *de facto* in the western (Jewish) part of the city, it would not be so recognised in the eastern (Arab) part and would not be *de jure* anywhere in the city. (I hope you've got all that.)

That was the theory. In practice since 1967 the Israeli government has always claimed that Jerusalem is the 'eternal and undivided capital of Israel'; and to bolster this claim, the Knesset (parliament), president's official residence and most government ministries are all in Jerusalem. Moreover, it has continuously worked to eradicate the old boundary of the city by building new Jewish neighbourhoods around the eastern (Arab) perimeter.

However, up until 2018, only two countries, apart from Israel itself, accepted Jerusalem as the capital; El Salvador and the Dominican Republic. This is why, until the US change in policy, they were the only two states to have embassies in Jerusalem; all the others were in Tel Aviv. The Netherlands, for a time, also had its embassy in Jerusalem, until the error of its ways was made clear by its European partners and it, too, moved to Tel Aviv.

While their embassies were in Tel Aviv, those countries that had had consular representation in Jerusalem, hung on to it. So, apart from ourselves, there were Consulate Generals of the USA, France, Spain, Greece, Turkey, Italy, Sweden and Belgium. Again, as Jerusalem was held to be not legally part of Israel, all these could not come under their respective embassies in Tel Aviv, and so all reported direct to their capitals. This frequently had the effect, at least as far as we were concerned, of the two missions producing contrasting reporting on events that were of common interest.

Other oddities resulting from the situation were that the ambassadors had no representational position in Jerusalem, as it was not part of the country to which they were accredited, and they could only pay official visits there if accompanied by, and technically introduced by, their local colleagues, the consuls general. Also, although the Consulate General covered the whole of the pre-1948 city of Jerusalem, as we did not recognise *de facto* Israeli administration of the eastern part, captured in 1967, we could not take part in any official Israeli activities in that part.

This was famously played up by Teddy Kollek, long time mayor, when hosting the Jerusalem Day celebrations one year. These take place in the summer, when this part of the world is hot. The boundary between East and West Jerusalem runs round the wall of the Old City. Mr Kolleck arranged for the official liquid refreshments to be placed just inside the wall and thus in the Eastern part, in other words in an area the thirsting consular officials sweating in their collars and ties were forbidden to go, as it was an official Israeli function. It happened before my time, but was remembered vividly by those who had been present.

As I have previously mentioned, I had been to Jerusalem and Israel once before, when I was on a familiarisation visit, just before being posted to Damascus. When we arrived this time, the 'Intifada' was in full force. The Arabic word describes the movement such as a dog makes shaking off water after a swim and was intended to represent the shaking off of Israeli occupation. This was completely misleading and wildly optimistic; rather like the idea that a zebra could shake off an attacking lion which was on its back with its jaws sunk in its neck.

The possibilities for meaningful acts of Palestinian defiance were severely limited; direct military confrontation was only possible at a very low level and the token activity of stone throwing was hardly going to cause the Israeli Border Police much pain. The most prevalent activities were commercial boycotts, known as 'strikes', and the ban on manifestations of pleasure by Palestinians.

These actions completely crippled the Palestinian economy and hardly bothered the Israelis. This has been described as the Palestinians saying to the Israelis 'I'm going to hold my breath until you turn blue in the face.'

For the Arabs, as so often in politics, principle always took precedence over practicalities. So, for instance, when the Palestinians had the chance to put up candidates for the Jerusalem city council, the political decision was taken to boycott the elections on the grounds that the so-called unified city was a Jewish imposition and they would have nothing to do with it. One prominent businessman, Hanna Siniora, had considered standing, but, after several attacks on his interests and family, he changed his mind. So there was no Palestinian representation on the council, which administered the whole city, Arab and Jewish.

The Consulate General was very small when I arrived; a Consul General, Consul, Vice Consul/ Management Officer and secretary were the only UK-based staff, although a second Vice Consul was added during my time to support political reporting. On arrival, I discovered that my predecessor as Consul was at daggers drawn with the Consul General and they hardly spoke to one another. I can't recall what the problem was originally, but it seemed to stem from, shall we say, character incompatibility.

Jerusalem was the first post I had been in which was equipped with computers and personal radios. The former were designed to be completely secure as the cabling between them was not copper wire, which would radiate a signal that could be read with suitable equipment, but by fibre optical cables which did not radiate at all. The radios, on the other hand, were completely insecure; anybody with a receiver tuned to the correct frequency could hear everything that was said. The telephone and telex links were similarly insecure. Israel shares the dubious distinction of being one of the three states which were certainly listening in to our conversations during our postings. The others were Syria and Sudan.

Another point of similarity with these other two countries was the prevalence of archaeological remains. It was practically impossible to go anywhere in Israel or the Palestinian Territories without passing by, over or round ancient remains, many of them identifiable from biblical or other historical references. As travel in Israel was safe and easy, we often made trips around the area. In contrast, in the Palestinian areas, it was not so easy for personal security reasons, although I did manage to see a few famous sites in the West Bank with the UNRWA Representative's office. The Representative himself was a former fellow student from MECAS, Yves Besson, who, at that earlier time, had been in the Swiss diplomatic service.

In Jerusalem we had an armoured Range Rover for visiting areas prone to violence. This appeared a standard machine from the outside, but had armour plating installed inside the outer skin, around the cabin and extremely thick, bullet-proof windows. As a result, it weighed in the region of four tonnes. On the other hand, it only had a standard Range Rover engine with an automatic gearbox. So on a hill you would put your foot down, the engine would whine, and the car would move off quite slowly. Although the suspension was suitably reinforced, it rolled very heavily on corners and had special, high-pressure, reinforced steel-belted tyres.

There was also a communications system, with a microphone and speakers on the outside and the equivalent equipment on the inside so that, in theory, you could talk to people outside without opening the doors or windows. In fact, both front windows would come down about half inch and invariably this meant that, as no one outside could work out what you are trying to do with the speaker system, a window was always opened for communication.

This was the Consul General's official vehicle, but we also used it for trips outside Jerusalem to various parts of the Palestinian Territories, mainly to Gaza, although during my time I don't remember anyone actually being protected by it. All other vehicles, including our personal ones were fitted with shatter-proof polycarbonate in place of glass.

This was to protect us from occasional stone throwing by Palestinian youths.

Living in Jerusalem, we were supposed to keep up contacts with both Arabs and Jews, although, as the Consulate General was widely regarded as the *de facto* British Embassy to Palestine, by far the majority of our contacts were with the Arabs. We did, however, continually pass between the two parts of the city and this was an unusual experience. This is, I think, the only place where it is possible to pass from one society to another without going through any formal barrier. Nicosia must be the closest in terms of proximity between communities, but there is there no such ease of passage between the two halves.

We kept in touch with the Palestinian politicians in the area. They were known as the 'Internal Leadership'. The 'External Leadership', was, of course, Yasser Arafat and the PLO, at that time in Tunis. The identity of these internal leaders was supposed to be secret, but it was widely known that they were headed by Faisal Husseini, supported by a number of other local activists, including Hannan Ashrawi, Sari Nuseibi, Riad Maliki, Sa'eb Erekat and others. If we knew this, it is quite certain that the Israeli internal security service, Shin Beth (also known as Shabak), did too, so it was all a bit of a sham.

Faisal was a member of one of the leading Jerusalem families, whose father, Abdul Qader

Husseini had been killed while leading the Arab forces trying to stop the Jewish attack on Jerusalem in 1948. Faisal himself later died of a heart attack while visiting Kuwait in 2001. Hannan was professor of English Literature at Bier Zeit University and was later, for a time Minister of Higher Education in the Palestinian Administration. Sari, another professor and married to an English wife, Lucy, had a brother, Zaki, whom I had met in Shaikh Zaid's entourage in Abu Dhabi. Sa'eb and Riad are the only ones, I think, to be still (2018) active in the Palestinian Authority.

We also kept in touch with the Gaza political world, including the fundamentalist Muslim movement, Hamas. This was widely believed to have been set up by Shin Beth to counter the PLO's influence. If so, it was a prime example of the law of unintended consequences. The leader of Hamas at that time was the blind paraplegic Sheikh Ahmad Yassin, but he was in an Israeli jail, so the temporary leader was Dr Abdul Aziz Rantissi, who had been the sheikh's medical attendant while he, too, was in jail. The third in line was Dr Mahmoud Zahhar on whom I often used to call during my Gaza visits.

Shaikh Yassin was subsequently released from jail as part of one of the occasional exchange agreements between the Israelis and Palestinians. Both he and Rantissi have since been assassinated by Israeli military action. I hear from the news that Zahhar is still prominent in the Hamas leadership:

He visited Khartoum in the early 1990s when I was there, but I didn't meet him then.

We took up playing badminton again in Jerusalem. To do this we had to visit the west of the city as few Arabs play this game. We found a social group among the Jews to join and played pretty well during the whole of our time there. It was a popular game among the Russian immigrants and often about a third of the turnout would be shouting at each other in Russian.

This was towards the end of the Soviet Union and many Russians were being allowed to leave for Israel provided they were Jewish. However, the Israeli 'Law of Return', which lays down that all Jews have the right to settle in Israel, had an unforeseen side effect in the case of many of these Russian immigrants.

The Israeli government had decided that the definition of 'Jewishness' would be the same as that applied by the Nazis in Germany. That is, it only needed one grandparent to have been Jewish or to be married to such a person, in order to qualify. Many of the Russians eager to leave their homeland were able to satisfy this minimal requirement, even though they themselves might actually be Russian Orthodox Christians. The odd result was that there was an upsurge in Russian Orthodox churches being established in Israel to cater for these people. I see that the interpretation of the Law of Return was changed in 1999 so that adherents of other faiths would not be eligible, but they were when we were there.

Religion sometimes directly affected the Consulate General, such as British Christians coming to Jerusalem in the belief, either that the Second Coming at The End of Days was at hand, or that they actually were the Messiah. The ones with the strongest delusion would normally either be dressed in white or often not dressed at all. The Israeli police, who were responsible for dealing with these people, had a special department set up solely for this purpose.

Once, during my time in Jerusalem, we had a case of a British woman with religious delusions about The Second Coming, who had brought with her a nine-year-old daughter. As she was convinced that time was about to end, she had made no provision for food or accommodation and they had been living rough in a stairwell somewhere in the city. She was persuaded to come to the Consulate General, where I singularly failed to establish a rapport with her. She was convinced that I was 'evil' and refused to speak to me. Fortunately, she saw the Vice Consul in a better light and was prepared to talk to her.

In these cases, our main aim was to get the person back to the UK, where they could receive treatment. By far the easiest way of doing this was to draw the attention of the Israeli Police to the fact they had overstayed their visa, as was usually the case, so that they were then deported. This achieved the aim of getting them home, while saving us the bother of making the arrangements and saving the British taxpayer the cost of the ticket home. This is what we did in this instance.

The woman herself was technically arrested and taken in a police van from the Consulate General to the airport, but under Israeli police rules, as the daughter had not been arrested, she could not travel in the police vehicle. This separation from her mother left the girl distraught to the point of hysteria. To get round this, it was arranged that she would travel with the Vice Consul in a Consulate General car immediately behind the police van, so that the daughter could keep in sight the vehicle that she had seen her mother enter. In this way they were both delivered to the airport.

Although it could be ensured that they both got on the plane to London, there was no mechanism for ensuring that there they would be met by social services at Heathrow, nor that they would not simply come straight back. This was a shortcoming of the system in general when people were deported back to the UK with social or medical problems.

It was impossible in Jerusalem to avoid the presence of religion. It was the first time I had been in a place where everyone needed to know the exact

258

religious stance of others. This was not only because of the difference between the Jews, Christians and Muslims, but also between the various sects and subdivisions of these religions. The range of Christian sects, all of which were represented in Jerusalem, was striking. In Britain we tend only to be aware of Protestant and Catholic churches and, to a certain extent, the Greek Orthodox. 'Protestant' generally is taken as including Methodists, Seventh Day Adventists, Wesleyans, Lutherans and so on. However, in Jerusalem, the full range of eastern churches was also represented; Greek Orthodox, Armenian Orthodox, Syrian Orthodox, Syrian Catholic, Armenian Catholic, Maronite, Abyssinian Orthodox and many more.

Amongst the Jews there are the Orthodox, the Ultra-Orthodox, the Reformed Jews, as well as those who were Jewish in name only and not very observant. On top of all this, there were odd mixtures such as the Messianic Jews, who believed that Jesus of Nazareth had been the Messiah, but persisted in following Jewish orthodox practice.

And then there was the Naturei Carta. These are a sect of Ultra-Orthodox Jews who hold the belief that the state of Israel may not be established until the coming of the Messiah. As they believe the Messiah has yet to come, then the state of Israel is clearly an abomination and they do not recognise it. However, they do realise that there is the need for some administration of the area known as the Holy

Land and this position they are prepared to cede to the Palestinians. At one time this group was described as Yasser Arafat's Jewish advisers.

Jerusalem turned out to be the place to meet people. Visitors while I was there included the then Archbishop of Canterbury, Dr Carey, Archbishop Desmond Tutu, Patriarch Alexei of Moscow, Douglas Hurd and Michael Helestine.

Archbishop Tutu visited Jerusalem over Christmas 1989 and paid an official call on us. Desmond Tutu was a striking man. In the flesh he looked exactly like his image on the TV. He was physically small, but with strong charismatic energy. The impression I had was of a small, tightly wound spring.

Soon after we arrived in Jerusalem, Dr. Carey, the recently announced nominee for Archdiocese of Canterbury, paid a semi-official visit. Although he was not yet formally enthroned, he was, in effect, treated it as if he were already holding that position. His host was the Anglican Bishop of Jerusalem, Samir Kafity, who held a sort of formal reception at which both Val and I as well as the Consul General and his wife were present. We sat around the room in the traditional Arab style and Bishop Kafity decided to make introductions. Unfortunately, as Val and I had only just arrived, he didn't really know us and confused Val with Mrs. Carey who was introduced as my wife. This caused some embarrassed amusement.

Having met his predecessor, Dr. Runcie, in Antigua, I was to meet Dr. Carey twice more during my career; once when he came to Jerusalem after having been formally enthroned and the second time, when he paid an official visit to Khartoum shortly before my retirement.

In February 1990 Val had to return home on the death of her mother. This was not really unexpected, as she had been going downhill for some time, but Val was unhappy at not having been with her at the end. As Bobby did not accompany her, I had to run our Jerusalem household for a week or so. In this I was grateful to have much help from friends and colleagues.

Later in 1990, a fact-finding mission of three Labour MP's, Anne Clwyd, Alice Mahon and Dawn Primerolo, visited Jerusalem. They called at the Consulate General for general briefing, on which I was asked to sit in. They asked if we could provide secretarial assistance for them there and then and were rather put out to be told that, if they could record their words on a cassette, we would see if time could be found for transcription a bit later. They appeared to think that British diplomatic missions should provide this sort of instant support for visiting members of parliament, as a matter of course. I don't know if they complained on return to

London, but we received nothing in Jerusalem.

An official visit by Douglas Hurd as Foreign Secretary also in 1990 did not go well. As is usual with these visits, he called on the Israelis a day or so before the Palestinians. One of his last appointments before coming to us was to hold a meeting with some Israeli politicians without any officials present. This was taken advantage of by the Israeli side to claim an acceptance by Hurd of a position that was anathema to the Palestinians. I can no longer remember exactly what this was, but the immediate reaction from the Palestinian leadership was to refuse to meet Hurd the following day, as arranged, unless he first publicly resiled from this alleged position.

The problem took us rather by surprise, although the offending statement was carried by Israeli radio in Hebrew the night before. We didn't monitor the Hebrew news; in fact there were no Hebrew speakers in the Consulate General. Hebrew language monitoring was done by the Embassy in Tel Aviv and they weren't aware of the idiosyncrasies of Palestinian concerns. The story was carried in the English language Jerusalem Post the following day, but, with our early start because of the visit, we hadn't had time to read it before we started out.

The programme started with a motorcade leaving from the King David Hotel, where Hurd was staying. The Israeli driver in the lead car had misunderstood our first destination, which was to be the UNRWA compound in East Jerusalem and instead headed off for the UN HQ building in West Jerusalem. We eventually got things heading in the right direction but, when we got to the UNRWA compound, few of the Palestinian staff would meet their guest. This was the first time we realised there was going to be a problem.

The Consul General had to accompany the Secretary of State, so it fell to me to try to persuade the Palestinian leadership to keep their appointment with him. This they stubbornly refused to do. At one point I was to be found arguing with them in the road outside the St John's Eye Hospital in East Jerusalem, while the official programme with the Secretary of State and Consul General continued inside. Mr Hurd was due to give a press conference at midday, I pointed out, and he would put the record straight then. No, they said, they must have the retraction first.

I think they accepted the point that, in taking this stance in response to something the Israelis had put out, was to allow their enemy effectively to control the argument, but they were frightened of the Palestinian 'street', the word used as shorthand for the politically active populace. In other words, they could not, and made no attempt to, influence the views of the mob. In the end, they failed to meet Hurd and thus substantially damaged their case, but then that was typical.

Ivan Callan was transferred at the beginning of November, 1990 and so I became Acting Consul General until his successor, David Maclennan, arrived a week or so later. This was my first taste of running a real diplomatic post, not counting the two-person post of Antigua.

At this time, there was a domestic British political upheaval caused by the anticipated departure of Margaret Thatcher from the premiership. One of the leading contenders for her position was Michael Heseltine and he had decided just at this time on a fact-finding visit to the Middle East, including Jordan and Jerusalem. I am guessing that he found it advantageous to be out of the UK for a while for reasons connected with his political ambitions.

Having earlier resigned from the cabinet over the Westland helicopter affair, he had no ministerial position at the time and was accompanied solely by his wife. Nevertheless, it was decided that he should have a programme arranged. As Acting Consul General, it fell to me to organise it all: a bit of a responsibility as it was widely considered that he could possibly shortly become Prime Minister.

The Heseltines were coming from the Kingdom of Jordan and crossing the Jordan River to the West Bank by the Allenby Bridge on the 4th of November. At this time, there was no regular crossing arrangement as was introduced later, and we had to liaise with the Embassy in Amman and with the Israeli military authorities. The actual meeting and transfer was like a scene at Checkpoint Charlie from the film 'Funeral in Berlin'. The two vehicles, one each from our Amman Embassy and the Consulate General, backed up to each other in the middle of the bridge, under the watchful eyes of Jordanian and Israeli military, including the baleful oversight of the Israeli machine gunners in the massive concrete watch tower looking straight across the bridge.

After introductions on the bridge, I placed the visitors in the back of the official Range Rover and got in beside the driver for the short trip to the official Israeli entry point. There Mrs Heseltine took the opportunity to inform me that her husband preferred to sit in the front. So we changed places when we got back in after the immigration formalities and Michael Heseltine sat in front beside the driver, while I sat in the back with his wife for the rest of the trip back up the hill to Jerusalem.

Two other events of the Heseltines' visit stick in my mind. The first was a tour of the Dheishe refugee camp on the outskirts of Bethlehem. This was recorded on the front page of the Daily Telegraph by a photo of the Heseltines greeting a crowd of excited Palestinian children. I am visible in the background. During the visit, Heseltine made a statement for the benefit of the accompanying press pack, which included an approving reference to the Balfour Declaration. This had endorsed the establishment of the 'Jewish National Home' in Palestine and, as such, it is generally regarded by the Arab world as evidence of Britain's responsibility for the whole Middle East problem.

When I reported the visit to London, I included a comment to the effect that this was probably the first time that a remark praising Balfour had been made in a Palestinian refugee camp. I was later told that, in the Department, this comment was regarded somewhat askance.

The second event was a short press conference that was held in the American Colony Hotel just after lunch. As part of the programme, I had arranged a meeting with a number of the Palestinian Internal Leadership. At that time, communications were not as easy as they are today and the filing of press stories was more dependent on the limited availability of communication satellites. During the meal, a couple of the hacks interrupted by coming into the dining room to ask if they could hold the conference early in order to take advantage of a satellite position. They got very short shrift from Heseltine, who pointed out with some force that he was having lunch with guests and we later held the conference at the appointed time.

For this, he, his wife and I sat at a table in the courtyard of the hotel, but the cameras were only on him. There were no questions on the Middle East:

they were all about the political succession contest in the UK. I can't remember the details now, but I think his constituency chairman had said something noteworthy. What I do recall clearly is that, below the table, his hands were continually twisting and grasping each other giving the lie to the composed and relaxed appearance he was so successfully projecting for the cameras.

I later received a little note of thanks for the visit in his own hand. His handwriting is atrocious and the signature completely illegible, but helpfully his name was printed at the top of the letter.

Also in late 1990, there was a delegation of female trade unionists who were visiting the area as a gesture of solidarity with their Palestinian sisters. I was still in charge as Acting Consul General during their visit and gave them a briefing about the situation. They had already met a number of Palestinians and were truly indignant at the things that they had been told. When challenged, I confirmed that we knew that these things were happening. Why, I was asked, did we not report the matters to London? I replied that we did; indeed, we sent a regular weekly report, plus reporting on any other events that needed to be covered in the interim. In that case, they demanded, why was there nothing in the British papers about all this? I gently pointed out that although the British Government was aware of the situation, it did not control what appeared in newspapers; perhaps they would like to take the matter up on return? It was quite striking that they had clearly had no background briefing before coming out.

They later wanted to visit a couple of Palestinian women in an Israeli jail and, with the agreement of the Embassy in Tel Aviv, I accompanied them in order to interpret. The Israeli authorities were very correct and the jail, although nothing special, seemed to me to be quite clean and perfectly adequate. The conversation with the one Palestinian woman who would talk to them was fairly uneventful, but they left having managed to tick that particular box.

One of the most interesting aspects of our time in Jerusalem was the opportunity to attend the occasional talks given by the late Father Jerome Murphy-O'Connor one of the leading experts at the Ecole Biblique, a biblical study school in Jerusalem. He was also the cousin of Cardinal Cormac Murphy-O'Connor, the then leader of England's Roman Catholics. These talks were open to all expatriates resident in the area and were mostly attended by UN personnel, although there were also members of the small consular community.

Father Jerry, as he was generally known, had a huge knowledge of biblical archaeology and would take us round a number of the wide variety of sites both in the West Bank and in Israel proper. I have a number of video recordings which I made of these outings. I mentioned to Jerry that he seemed to be very telegenic and might consider appearing on television. At the time he was dismissive, but later he did indeed appear on a number of Biblical and Middle Eastern archaeological TV programmes.

The Israeli rules about who could act as a tourist guide were strict. These allowed only those with Israeli permits or who had been licensed as guides by the Jordanian authorities between 1947 and 1967 to work in this field. However, there was an exception made for religious guides and Father Jerry was one of the few Christian clerics who took advantage of this. The Jordanian licence holders were all retiring, so pretty well all the guides were Jewish and tended to emphasise the Jewish viewpoint.

On one occasion when Jerry was leading us on a tour of Masada, the traditional site of the famous mass Jewish suicide, he got into a heated argument with a Jewish guide there. The events at Masada, where the Jews resisted the Romans to the death, are iconic for Jews and there is no effort to reinterpret them. During the visit Jerry rhetorically asked the sensible question "How do we know what happened if they all killed each other?" and answered it with "Because there was an old lady who hid in the cistern and came out after it was all over." followed by the comment; "There is ALWAYS an old lady hiding in the cistern; this is part of at least eight [I think] stories of Jewish mass suicide." Unsurprisingly, the Jewish guide took strong exception to this.

The Consul-General and I took turns at visiting Gaza from Jerusalem, easily done in a day. Although well known as a huge refugee camp, the displaced Palestinians had been there so long (since 1948) that the individual constituent camps were pretty well indistinguishable from the regular urban settlements.

On one occasion, when I was driving the armoured Range-Rover, I made a visit to the centre of Khan Younis Camp to pick up somebody, I can't remember who or why and was confronted by a somewhat aggressive group of shabbab (which is simply the Arabic for 'youths') who demanded to know who I was and what I was doing. My main objective in this sort of situation was to ensure they believed I wasn't Israeli. I explained my presence in my strained Arabic and had a bright idea to defuse the situation. Would they like me to take their picture? They would indeed, and I have this snap of a collection of Palestinian teenagers, mostly forgetting to look fierce, with our official Range-Rover just in the picture to the left.

We were in Jerusalem during the first Gulf War in 1991, when Saddam Hussein fired a large number of missiles at Israel. Although they were all loaded with conventional explosive, there was widespread concern that he would use gas. As a result, Israeli civil defence precautions assumed a gas attack and gas masks were generally issued and instructions given on how to deal with gas. As the attack became inevitable, and as Westerners were reckoned to be unsafe in Arab areas, I was told to move from our flat in Beit Hanina, an Arab suburb of East Jerusalem, although at the time we felt in no danger. Anyway, just before the fighting started we moved into Notre Dame, the Catholic hostel on the border between East and West Jerusalem. To all intents and purposes it was in fact a 4 or 5 star hotel, but the status of religious hostel gave it considerable tax advantages.

In the run up to the war and during its immediate aftermath, Jerusalem was a strange place. There were no tourists, the lifeblood of the city's economy and all the usual tourist sites were deserted. It made tourism by us remainers very pleasant, but the traders were really suffering economically. On one visit to the Old City during this time we were effectively kidnapped by a shopkeeper into whose emporium we had rashly stepped. He simply attempted to block our way out again unless we bought something. As luck would have it though, while we were arguing with him, another merchant, who we happened to know walked by outside and persuaded his colleague to release us.

It had been decided that, as Tel Aviv would be

the prime target of Saddam Hussein's Scud rockets, families and non-essential staff at the Embassy there should be evacuated to Eilat on the Red Sea, which was out of missile range. Our Embassy colleagues drove up in a convoy to Jerusalem where some of them would be leaving their cars at the Consulate General, doubling up in the remaining transport for the rest of trip. As we all used radios with the same frequency, we could hear them talking to each other as they came within transmission range.

The dependants of staff at the Consulate General were given the option of evacuation, too. These totalled three: the Consul General's wife, Val and Bobby. For my part, I thought about this, but decided that Jerusalem would never be on Saddam's target list and so we stayed. We were later told that the British community in East Jerusalem were watching very carefully to see what we did; had Val and Bobby gone, then they would all have left, too.

Those remaining at both the Embassy and Consulate General were issued by the FCO with NATO standard chemical, nuclear and biological (CNB) protection suits and gas masks. Although we never put on our suits in Jerusalem, staff who remained at the Embassy apparently did so whenever there was an air raid warning. We did, however, put on the gas masks whenever we heard these warnings.

We were in the Notre Dame hostel when the attacks on Baghdad started. At four o'clock in the morning the priest in charge ran round the corridors, knocking on doors and shouting "The war has started. Baghdad has been destroyed and we're under gas attack. Everybody to the chapel." A hell of a wake up call.

The instruction to go to the chapel was not for religious reasons, but because that was the designated gas proof room for the building. As I mentioned, it had been decided by the Israelis that the most likely type of attack would be gas and not high explosive. Therefore, as the expected gas would be heavier than air, sanctuary should be sought above ground level, and the chosen room should be made as airtight as possible. So sheets of plastic and wide sticky tape were generally issued and were to be used to seal all windows and doors. Fortunately this was never put to the test, although the majority of the Jewish population went through the rigmarole at every warning.

The Arab population was schizoid in its reaction. On the one hand, they were supporting Saddam's attacks to the point of going out and cheering the rockets as they flew over, while on the other, they were criticising the Israeli authorities for not providing the same protective measures to Palestinians as they were to their own people.

Eventually, gas masks were made available to Palestinians, but only for adults, not for their children. This led to a number of British wives of Palestinians asking the Consulate General for

273

children's gas masks. Of course, we didn't have any but we did put in a request and eventually managed to get some from a military source in (I think) Germany but on the day they arrived, the fighting and the air raids stopped, so we sent them back without opening the bag they came in. (As an aside, I find it interesting that the armed forces hold stocks of children's gas masks.)

We were also asked by some British citizens to arrange emergency evacuation for them. It was amazing how many Orthodox Jews originally from Britain denied they had ever become Israeli citizens when applying for this. (The rule is, or certainly was then, that if you are British and also hold the citizenship of another country in which you reside, then you can't claim consular protection from the UK.)

Emergency evacuation of British citizens had not been authorised anyway, but we had some difficulty in getting this across to our compatriots. We even had letters from Britain from parents of British wives of Palestinians demanding we arrange the evacuation of their grandchildren from this dangerous situation. One of the most insistent of these came from a Welsh lady to whom I wrote explaining that we didn't think the situation required it and that I, a fellow Welshman, was practising what I preached. I had my family, including a young son, with me and had no intention of sending them home. I received no reply to this.

The first day after the fighting started and after the first night of air raids (they were always at night) I drove to the Consulate General from the Notre Dame through completely deserted streets, even though it was the normal rush hour. A weird sensation. We continued to work normal hours at the Consulate General, although the local staff largely didn't start to come in for several days

After a day or so the food served in the hostel was noticeably decreasing and it became clear that the Notre Dame was running out of supplies. So we removed ourselves to the hostel of St George's Cathedral, the very British-style Protestant centre in East Jerusalem, where we had a very nice room off the courtyard. Gradually a new, if temporary, pattern of life established itself as I could walk to work and we became part of the cathedral community.

The air raid warnings continued, though and the designated refuge for all of us in our new home was the Dean's bathroom. This sounds a bit odd, but it was a very big room on the first floor and had only one window and door to be sealed, so was ideal. The cathedral community got used to congregating there of an evening when the sirens went off, usually around midnight.

On one occasion, though, the Iraqis decided to vary the timing and the alert was sounded early in the evening. We all reacted as usual, even though the timing meant that we were all doing something other than when it usually went off. In the Dean's case this was having a bath. As we all trooped into the bathroom, the water was still running out of the bath and there were wet footprints leading to the bedroom next door. One of the last to eventually join the group before the room was sealed was the rather damp Dean.

During our time in the cathedral, we moved as much of our effects as possible from our Beit Hanina home, including the TV, which was useful for entertaining Bobby. We stayed on in the cathedral hostel after the fighting finished, looking for new accommodation, closer to the centre of Jerusalem than our previous flat. This took some time and at one point the cathedral office gently pointed out that they had bookings from pilgrims over Easter and needed our room. Eventually, we found a flat in the same road as the Consulate General, which was very convenient and we moved in in the spring.

Our personal trips during our time in Jerusalem were to Egypt and to Cyprus. For the Egyptian visit we were able to drive through the border between Israel and Egypt and into the Sinai area. We stayed at a small resort on the Egyptian Red Sea coast for about a week. This was pretty basic, but still represented a good break from the tension of Jerusalem.

At the end of our holiday, when we arrived at the border crossing point, the bank on the Egyptian side was closed as it was a Friday and I wanted to change my Egyptian pounds into Israeli shekels. As we had already passed through the vehicle exit check from Egypt, we could not turn the car around and go back to the nearby hotel where there was a bureau de change.

The Egyptian authorities were very understanding, though, and provided me with an armed guard to accompany me on foot back past the border checkpoint to the hotel to change my money and escort me back again. I think the speculation among the hotel guests must have been that I was in some way under arrest; it certainly looked like that.

I noted that the unfortunate Egyptian soldier detailed to be with me was carrying a long Second World War-style rifle and wearing a First World War-style uniform, buttoned up to the neck and made of a fairly thick material. The poor chap must have been roasting inside.

We also made two visits to Cyprus, one where we stayed in the central mountains and another where we went to the seaside resort of Paphos. On the first occasion we had a tourist taxi to take us around the various sites, including the monastery where Archbishop Makarios had been based. Here, when it was discovered that I was the British Consul in Jerusalem, there was a great fuss and I was placed under the personal care of an English-speaking monk for the whole of the tour, who apologised profusely that the abbot was unable to meet me. All very fine, but we were only there as tourists. However, it did impress the taxi driver considerably to see the somewhat dramatic effect his passengers caused.

Although I had the title of Her Majesty's Consul and a commission from the Queen to prove it, normally I wasn't required to do any actual consular work, although on occasion this was thrust upon me. For instance, in, I think, late December 1992, when the Vice Consul, was on leave, we received notification that a British man had died at a small Palestinian hotel on the Mount of Olives. Apparently, he had originally come to Jerusalem for religious purposes and had decided to remain and spend the rest of his days there.

In this he was certainly successful. He had obtained a job with the hotel owner who, in return for his work, provided him with food and accommodation. The apartment forming his living area was extremely basic: the entrance door gave directly into a snug little room with a bed on one side and a table and chair on the other. There was also a small heater. At the far end of the room was a curtain beyond which, on the left, was a shower and toilet and, on the right, a kitchen sink, a small stove and some cupboards.

I think his meals were normally brought to him from the hotel and, when after a day or so, no reply had been obtained to knocks on his door, it had been opened. It appeared that as he was sitting one evening preparing to drink a cup of coffee, the man had suddenly suffered a heart attack. He had got up in an attempt to get to the toilet and had almost made it when he collapsed and died.

His body was lying towards the toilet to the left with only his feet visible sticking out beyond the curtain. When I got there none of the Palestinians had ventured into the room, even though they could see his feet. Although he had probably been dead for at least a day at this point, it fell to me to confirm this. I was obliged to go in and feel the body and confirmed that at that temperature he was certainly dead.

Then there was the question of reporting the death. The authorities concerned were the Israeli Police and the Palestinians refused to contact them, so the Consulate General had to do this and arrange for the body to be removed. Fortunately by the time formal identification was required, the Vice Consul was back from leave, so I didn't have to have any more to do with the case. This was only the second time I had seen a dead body (the first having been in Antigua) and the first and only time I have touched one.

As my time in Jerusalem drew to a close, I was regarded as ready for promotion to Grade 5 and was considered for a range of jobs at this level. Originally for my next post, the Office had offered me the deputy head of mission (DHM) position in Beirut. I thought about this quite carefully and decided that it would not be safe for somebody who had just served in Jerusalem. Arabs tended to be very suspicious of those who had been in Israeli controlled areas, even when they had been there dealing with Palestinians.

At this time Lebanon was still simmering, all UK-based staff at the Beirut Embassy had full-time armed protection and there were no schools operating that Bobby could attend. Moreover, at the time Beirut airport was not functioning, so that all travel from Britain, including any holiday visits from a boarding school, would have to be to Cyprus and then by hydrofoil to northern Lebanon; all very difficult and with an element of danger. So I turned it down on the grounds of personal safety, even though, somewhat to my continuing surprise, the security evaluation was that there was no danger. My refusal was registered and instead I was offered a similar position in Khartoum, which I accepted.

Before we finally left on transfer, though, I had the sad duty to return to the UK in late January when my mother became seriously ill. The Office authorised a compassionate journey, which I well knew meant that the prognosis was death. The illness was not as sudden as my father's had been and I was able to get back a couple of days before she died on the 1st of February..

While I was there, though, Val's father had a severe stroke and was also not expected to live either. I was informed of this while in the hospital at my mother's side by being called to the nurses' station to take a telephone call from my son, Alun. He told me his grandfather had been admitted to the hospital as an emergency few hours earlier. I then had the considerable shock of turning round from the desk to see my father-in-law's name on the list of patients in the same ward as my mother.

Naturally, Val was also authorised a compassionate journey and, as there was nobody to look after five year-old Bobby, he was allowed to accompany her back. In the event Val's father made a partial recovery, but was never really himself again. However, we were all able to attend my mother's funeral before returning to Jerusalem.

During my final week in Jerusalem, I took my successor on an introductory visit to Gaza in the armoured Range Rover and on the way back there was a repetitive banging noise from the right back wheel. We stopped to look and found that the tyre on that corner had started to shed its tread and this was flailing around on the inside of the wheel arch. There was, of course, a spare wheel so we got this out and the three of us; the driver, my successor and myself managed to jack the four-tonne car up and remove the faulty wheel.

We then got out of the spare wheel, fitted it and

let the jack down. And down and down and down. It soon became obvious that the wheel was insufficiently inflated and the weight of the vehicle had compressed the tyre to the extent that it was not possible to remove the fully retracted jack as some of the weight of the Range Rover was still resting on it.

Eventually, the three of us just managed to lift the vehicle sufficiently to remove the jack at which point of course the under-inflated wheel took the full weight of vehicle. It splayed alarmingly, but held and we managed to drive at a careful crawl to a nearby garage where we topped up the tyre pressure.

On return to the Consulate General, I demanded to know from the driver why this had happened. Oh, I was told, the recommended tyre pressure of fifty pounds per square inch was far too dangerous, so they always inflated to the thirty-odd pounds they used for the Ford estate car!

Over our last few weeks, we had a round of farewell parties as is usual on departure from post, including a quite lavish 'do' arranged by our two lady Vice Consuls in the restaurant of a local hotel in East Jerusalem.

Again, as in previous posts, I had some difficulty in selling my car and pretty well had to accept the price I was offered a day or so before we departed on the 3rd of April, 1993.

CHAPTER 11

KHARTOUM 1993-1997

Before leaving for Khartoum, I had a rather lengthy period of leave and briefing, which included a visit to the headquarters of the Royal Military Police (RMP) in Hampshire. This slightly unusual preparation was because the RMP provided a permanent bodyguard, or close protection team (CPT), for the Ambassador in Khartoum. From time to time, in the absence of the Ambassador, I would be in charge of the Embassy at which point, I would be under the care of the CPT.

On this visit I was accompanied by both Val and Bobby, so we could all familiarise ourselves with weapons and gunfire. Not that we were going to be asked to fight, of course, but, as we were going to be around firearms, it was felt that we should at least know what they looked and sounded like.

We were taken to the base firing range where we were all allowed actually to fire a variety of weapons, both handguns and rifles. I was mightily impressed to discover that my spouse is a fairly good shot with an assault rifle!

After all this, I was off to Khartoum, where I was awarded my final substantive promotion to Grade 5 (senior first secretary) which took effect

283

from my date of arrival, the 2nd of October1993.

Because of family problems, it was decided that our eldest son, David, and his daughters should accompany us to Khartoum. But it wasn't quite as straightforward as that. While I was to go out at the start of October, we decided that Val, David and the girls would not follow until Bobby broke up for the Christmas holidays and then they could all come out together. This decision was largely due to fact that the Office refused to recognise our granddaughters as our dependants. This would mean that hotel accommodation would not be paid for them while we were waiting to move into our permanent accommodation.

During this ten-week period, Val had a horrid time of it. She had the preparations for all the children to make; our young son as well as our two baby granddaughters. This involved selecting hot weather clothing, arranging inoculations as well as the usual 'going away' tasks, compounded by preparations for Christmas. It was a great relief when, on the 15th of December, we could get together and resume our normal double act of married life. David and his daughters stayed living with us until just before the end of the posting.

The Embassy building was a fairly modern, purpose-built structure planned when the staff levels were much higher than when I arrived, so there was plenty of room for the eight UK-based staff. One of its features was a central atrium with wall hangings depicting various aspects of the countryside in the UK. It was really quite impressive, but got very hot in the summer as it had a glass roof and the temperature easily got into the upper 40s centigrade.

The generally high temperatures meant that drinking plenty of liquid was a strong necessity, while the very dry climate meant that perspiration evaporated from your skin immediately and you didn't get 'sticky' as was the case in, say, Abu Dhabi. This had the result that peeing was not often required and on return to the UK on leave we were concerned to note how often this was necessary.

Sudan is huge and, when I was there, it was the largest country in Africa by area, and there are some pretty big countries in Africa. Since then, of course, it has split into two, with the Independence of South Sudan. Although historical Sudan had been linked with Britain for over the half-century or so from 1900, it was never part of the normal imperial set-up as it was nominally an 'Anglo-Egyptian Condominium', the fiction being that it was ruled jointly by Britain and Egypt. On the old imperial maps, it was coloured in stripes of red and green, rather than the solid red of the rest of the Empire. Historically, the Egyptians had always regarded the Sudan as part of their sphere of interest and they still did. The key link, naturally, is the Nile.

Sudan was a connection between sub-Saharan

Africa and the Arab world round the Mediterranean and was made up of two parts geographically, ethnically and, of course, politically. During the Condominium, there had been a number of efforts to devise ways of splitting the country into two to allow for these differences. The overall problem was that, whatever the relationship between the two parts, it would always remain true that the south would effectively remain dependant on the north for access down the Nile and the north would be nervous of whoever controlled the upstream waters of the river. With the discovery of oil in the area, this remains true today, even after the independence of South Sudan

Sudan, as originally constituted, had been granted independence in 1956 as a unified state, but the south was soon in arms and agitating for separate independence. I remember when I had been in Kampala all those years before, we had been visited by a member of the then separatist movement, the Sudan African National Union (SANU), with a request for travel documents. I can't remember now what happened, but I'm pretty sure he went away empty handed.

The insurrection in the south had rumbled on over the years and was still going strong when I was there. SANU had long been consigned to the history books and the main southern protagonist was now the Sudanese People's Liberation Movement (SPLM) and its military wing, the Sudanese

People's Liberation Army (SPLA). Ethnicity and religion were inextricably entwined in the struggle. The south was predominantly Black African and the north was predominantly Muslim. However, not all the southerners were Christian; some were animists. And some were both. While I was there, a local Anglican bishop had been defrocked for practising black magic.

Conversely, not all in the north were Arab; there were southern Muslims living there, too. When I visited the South, I was surprised that the lingua franca there was not English, as I had expected, but a pidgin Arabic.

There were tens of thousands of (mainly Christian) Southerners living around Khartoum as 'internally displaced persons'. That is, they had been driven from their homes by the war and were effectively refugees, but without this status officially as they had not crossed from another state. Their condition was just as bad, though and the Sudanese Government was very poor at taking care of them.

Although the northerners regard themselves as Arabs, their blood line is clearly intermingled with that of the Black Africans and they are very dark, some appearing to be full-blood Negroes. Arabs in other countries tend to refer to all of them disparagingly with the same word that they use for Black Africans; ''abd', which actually means 'slave.'

The regime was generally characterised as

Muslim Fundamentalist and certainly alcohol and gambling and so on were banned, however the fiction was that this was a personal thing for Muslims and didn't apply to non-Muslims. But, to be fair, the strictures applicable to non-Muslims in, say, Saudi Arabia were not found. For a start there was no ban on Christianity: on the contrary there were many churches of various denominations and feasts of both the Western and Eastern branches of Christianity were celebrated. There are not many 'fundamentalist Muslim' countries where you can go openly to Midnight Mass at Christmas. Moreover many women went without head coverings and there was no restriction on them driving cars.

The Ambassador, Peter Streams, was on leave when I arrived and I was greeted by my predecessor, Peter Heigl, who was in charge. During the short period of my handover, Peter Heigl was styled Chargé d'Affaires and I Deputy Head of Mission; slightly odd as we were the same grade, but it seemed a reasonable arrangement in the circumstances. After Peter Heigl left, and before the Ambassador returned, I became Chargé for a week or so.

Peter Heigel took me on the usual round of introductions, including a visit to the Embassy in Cairo, on which we were diplomatic couriers. The local arrangement was that a member of the Embassy's UK-based staff would act as a courier and collect Khartoum's classified diplomatic mail every so often from Cairo where the Queen's Messenger had left it.

After Peter Heigel left and while I was Chargé, Khartoum received a visit from the Orbis aircraft. The Orbis charity runs a small eye hospital in the plane, which is fully equipped and staffed. This continually visits various countries in the Third World providing, not only medical services, but also technology transfer in the form of training for local eye specialists. I was invited to take a tour of the plane and was very impressed by what I saw. I have been a regular supporter of Orbis ever since.

A few days after this, the Ambassador returned from leave. When I met him, I soon realised that Peter Streams made little secret of his dislike for the job he had. After an earlier ambassadorship in a small Latin American capital, this was his 'retirement post' after a career which had brought him up through the ranks via the Inspectorate. He was due to reach the then compulsory retirement age of 60 in April 1995 and meanwhile, as he told me, he looked forward to his retirement dream of buying a large motor caravan in which he intended to tour his twilight years away, while visiting golf courses across Europe.

To this end, he maximised the benefits that came his way as Ambassador. The most notable method of doing this was to avoid the expense of running a car by the simple expedient of declining to own one. Arguing that, as a full time Ambassador, all his activities were representational, he used the official car for everything; shopping, golf, outings - everything. He also reinforced this regime of economy by also, shall we say, minimising his outgoings at every opportunity and living and entertaining frugally.

He also cordially loathed the Sudanese regime and made no bones about letting everybody know it. His German, wife, Margeretta, shared his distaste for the Sudan and was keen to be away from the place as often as she could manage. This openly negative attitude was maybe not the best one for a diplomat to take, and naturally it went down badly with the host government.

But the worst thing from their point of view was that he was also an avowed atheist, and made no secret of that, either. An Arabist would never have admitted to that attitude in a country ruled by an Islamist regime. This combination of political and religious opinions produced a strong personal antipathy towards him within the regime, which eventually resulted in his premature departure and thus my unexpected and lengthy temporary promotion.

He suffered from a bad back and was often short-tempered. I experienced this first on the 12th of November 1993. In response to a negative written comment I had made on the question of hiring a girl as standby receptionist, I was berated and told that I should remember that I was "only a very junior officer." This was hardly true, as I was a senior first secretary, aged 51. I remember the date very well as in exactly two months to the day, on the 12th of January, 1994, I was to take over from him as head of the Embassy for the next 15 months. In general, though, I got on well with him over the short time we were together.

When I arrived, the set up in the Embassy in Khartoum was unusual for an Arab country in that neither the Ambassador, nor the DHM, was an Arabist. Indeed, the Ambassador had never previously served in an Arab, or even a Muslim, country, although Peter Heigl had done a posting in Saudi Arabia. The only Arabist among the UK based staff was the Second Secretary (Political).

While I was waiting for Val to come out, I became a member of the local archaeology society and in mid November, I joined their trip to a site to the south of Khartoum, not far from the Nile. This is a slightly edited extract from the letter I wrote to Val shortly afterwards.

I had set the alarm for 4.30. I got up, got my packed lunch out of the fridge (sandwiches ordered from our cook the previous day from left-over beef. These were neatly cut into fours diagonally and the crust cut off.) I stuffed in some biscuits as well and picked up some bottles of soda water and a can of coke, then walked round to the nearby house of the British Council Director and his wife, organisers of the trip. They gave me a lift to the Greek Club for the pick-up by bus. No bus was there. And only one other person also waiting. 35 minutes later the bus appeared; by now everybody else had also arrived. We departed at 5.45 (All that lost bed time!)

We left Khartoum and headed south. We drove and drove. At about 9.30 we stopped at a wayside stall in a village (one of about a dozen identical ones) for breakfast. This consisted of fried meat, dipped in salt with some beans in oil in a separate dish and the whole lot washed down with a bottle of Coke. If I wanted, I could have had tea. On we went, drive and drive. Stopped by the odd bored policeman or soldier manning checkpoints. The countryside was utterly flat with occasional glimpses of the Nile to one side. We were still in the Arab area, but the people (Black) and the huts (round mud with thatch) looked very African. We skirted a town; Wad Medani. We drove further. At about midday we sighted some hills. We turned off the road across the railway line (no level crossing; we just drove over the rails) and set off across country on a rutted track. The bus had some problems with this, but we never had to get out.

Eventually we reached the village of Jebel Moya; our target for to-day. We all spilled out. The site we wanted was up the side of the hill. Although part of a range, this was literally the nearest hill, in this direction, to Khartoum. We left the bus and the Land Rovers which had accompanied us and climbed the hill. We learned before we went that there was no guide to tell us about the site, although we had found the right place. All that any of us knew was what was written on the one side of the piece of paper we had been issued with when we left Khartoum. At the top of the hill was the skeleton of a stone built house constructed by Henry Solomon Wellcome (he of pharmacy fame), the slightly eccentric gentleman, born American, but later a naturalised Englishman, who first discovered the place before the First World War. We looked at this. The structure was still sound and hardly qualified as an archaeological site. Beyond was a bowl of land, with high ground to the right and a cleft in the rocks to the left. There were two obelisks opposite each other on the rising ground at the edges of either side of the bowl. One was shaped like a traditional British beehive, the other was more elongated and looked more like a huge pine cone. They had obviously been built by Wellcome at the same time as his house and had no obvious function. On investigation they proved to be hollow and to have an entrance hole at ground level. We were none the wiser and, in any case, they still held no archaeological interest.

Meanwhile, back under the desert sun, we walked cross the base of the bowl. It was very hot with no breeze. There were a number of spoil heaps where Wellcome had dug, but all that was left now were some bits of pottery and fragments of stone tools. We collected some of these. Some, in desperation, picked up interesting and shiny stones too. It was still very hot. The children from the village had followed us up the hill. Seeing our interest, they picked shards and stones and tried to sell them to us. One tried his luck with a dried yellow flower. There was no rarity value in their wares and they switched to begging for baksheesh. They were like flies; you shooed them off, but they never went far and always came back. It was still hot and those of us without a drink were very thirsty.

We went back down the hill, surrounded by the children who were still begging. On the way down we met an old woman carrying a teapot. She had come to invite us to tea in her house to meet her daughters. We declined, but she climbed down with us, repeating her invitation. We were very thirsty by the time we got back down to the plain. We looked for the bus, which had our drinks on board. The driver had taken it off out of the sun into the village and fallen asleep., but we didn't know this at the time and we couldn't see it and were extremely hot and thirsty. The children, now including the old woman's daughters, knew a captive audience when they saw one. We stood forlornly in the shade of the village water tower surrounded by importunate black children begging ever more insistently. Three of our number had not came back down the hill. This was noted in an off-hand way. They had gone for an extra walk over the ridge.

The wife of the British Council Director got into their Land Rover and searched out the bus. She found it and it returned and we clambered in gratefully to get some rest and a drink. It was 13.45. We had finished our tour of the archaeological site. The Director's wife drove the Land Rover round behind the bus and simultaneously punctured both back tyres on two stumps of iron fence posts sticking out of the ground. This was quite an achievement, but didn't really count as a disaster as there were two spare wheels available, one from the second Land Rover. The wheels were replaced. This operation had the benefit of providing alternative entertainment for the village children who were otherwise besieging the bus with most of us on board, banging on the windows and still demanding baksheesh.

The errant walkers returned and we got ready to set off. The children, sensing the loss of prey, got bolder and started trying to snatch things through the bus windows. They were repulsed to certain extent by the Indians and Africans amongst us throwing their rubbish at them as they ate their snacks in the bus. One enterprising village girl shied a piece of orange peel back into the bus. As a result some of the windows were shut, but the engine was not running and the air conditioning was not on. It was stifling.

295

There was a commotion at the back of the bus and a local boy ran off into the village. One of our Sudanese colleagues got out and stalked purposefully after him. The boy had actually made a serious attempt at theft through the window. Before we could leave, this had to be corrected. The bus moved a short way and then the village headman and the boy's father brought the boy over to our Sudanese colleague. Apologies were made, the boy was reprimanded, hands were shaken and we all parted on good terms.

Back towards the road we went, but the railway line proved more difficult to cross than when we came. With much advice and manoeuvrings we managed it, again without having to get out, and set off to return north. Many of us however had not eaten our lunches and the British Council Director had a picnic site in mind. It was at Sonnar on the Nile actually on an island beside the dam which feeds the power station there. We disembussed and studiously ignored the motley military personnel posted to the place to protect it from any possible attack. Then we ate. At 4.30 we finished lunch and set off on the last leg, stopping only once more for a cold drink on the way. We returned to our starting point at the Greek Club at 10.15 p.m..

We had spent about 12 hours driving for an hour and a half's archaeology and some interesting experience.

This was the first of many similar outings. As was the case in Syria and Jerusalem, our time in Sudan was made more enjoyable by our ability to visit the huge range of archaeological sites. Most of these were quite remote and involved fairly long journeys into the desert, although we did not visit the more extremely remote ones which involved some three days' drive.

One of the more interesting sites and the more accessible, was Meroe (pronounced 'Mehr-oh-way') to the north of Khartoum. This site consists of a number of pyramids sitting rather forlornly in the desert. Although the inspiration for these presumably came from the more famous Egyptian pyramids far to the north, they are smaller and more pointed than those and in most cases the peaks have been blown off. This was thanks to the efforts in the 19th century of an Italian adventurer, Giuseppe Ferlini, who was convinced that there would be treasure enclosed at the tip of each pyramid and decided to use dynamite in order to take a direct route to recovering it. He found nothing as a result of this vandalism, but his more conventional efforts did recover some artefacts, which he brought back to Europe. Some of these are now in the British Museum.

Conditions in Sudan were pretty uncomfortable compared with many of the other posts we had been in, but there were plenty of positive aspects, too. The

British community was quite small and self-contained and there were not many casual consular cases to deal with. My main title was 'Deputy Head of Mission', but I was also Consul General for the whole of Sudan and, in due course, was issued with a Royal Commission to prove it.

As I have said, when I arrived in Khartoum, there was a 'close protection team' (CPT) from the Royal Military Police to guard the Ambassador or whoever was in charge of the Embassy at the moment. They were later withdrawn and, in my opinion, were never really necessary during my time, although I was the supposed target they were protecting for some six months. From something I read recently, I believe they have since been reintroduced there.

The car we took with us to Khartoum was a Land Rover Discovery. We chose the diesel engine version and found it to be a very suitable car for the area. For the first time we enjoyed driving at about 40 miles an hour across flat open desert, with a dust trail streaming behind. A very pleasant experience.

However the build quality of the machine turned out to be rather poor. One day we noticed that it was difficult to change gear and eventually the car jammed in second gear. If it had to get stuck in any particular gear, second was probably the ratio of choice, as it was still possible to pull away by slipping the clutch, and the car would still move at a reasonable speed through traffic. As it happened, the fault manifested itself in the city area. However, if it had got stuck in reverse while we were in the desert that would have been a completely different story.

Fortunately there was a Land Rover expert resident in Khartoum; an Irish mechanic who was able to strip down the gearbox and fix the fault. What he found was that the retaining grub screw on the selector mechanism had not been properly tightened and had worked loose. Fortunately it had not fallen into the gearbox itself where it would have jammed in the cogs. When I wrote to them, Land Rover paid up the cost of repairs without demur, but appeared unrepentant.

This poor construction record was reflected in a later case where my Italian opposite number had bought a Land Rover Discovery and was puzzled by his inability to get the air conditioning unit to work. Eventually our Embassy engineer had a look under the bonnet for him and discovered that the cover of the compressor unit which circulated the coolant gas had not been bolted down properly at the factory and that all this gas had long since escaped.

Over Christmas 1993, Peter Streams had returned to the UK for the holidays. Almost as soon as he was to return in early January, an official visit by the Archbishop of Canterbury was due to take place. This was part of much wider tour in Africa, including a visit to the south of Sudan. There had been a long drawn-out argument about where the Archbishop should stay in Khartoum. The Anglican community in the country was poor and the official church guest-house was too dilapidated to be used. The two alternatives were that the Sudanese Government should accommodate him, or that he should stay with the Ambassador. The first solution was suggested by the regime, who claimed that this was an official visit and that the Sudanese state was the host and should provide accommodation. The Ambassador took the view that this was a pastoral visit and, as the Anglican Church was the established Church of England, he should be the host.

He certainly felt very strongly about this, but his argument was somewhat undermined from the Sudanese Government's point of view by the fact that he was a declared atheist. In this case, he clearly could not base his attitude on his own religious views and the Sudanese saw it as a purely personal stance antagonistic to the Sudanese regime. They reacted accordingly.

While Peter Streams was away, I was again Chargé d'Affaires and, as such, I was involved with the local Anglican bishops and with Lambeth Palace in the final lead up to the visit. Things did not go well and Dr Carey decided to call off the visit to Khartoum altogether for the time being. (He eventually came in September 1995.)

I had the bishops with me in the Embassy conference room when the call came through from Lambeth Palace and they were able to speak to the Archbishop's secretary themselves. This was on an ordinary outside line and I was aware that the Sudanese security would be listening in. The regime would therefore be well aware that the decision to call the visit off had come from the Archbishop's office and not the Embassy and, in any case, the Ambassador himself was in the UK.

That cut no ice. The Sudanese were furious and claimed to regard the whole thing as a massive snub and purely the result of the Ambassador's attitude. On the 30th of December, I was summoned to the Foreign Ministry and formally told by the Foreign Minister that Peter Streams was personally a hindrance to British/Sudanese relations and was being given 12 days to leave post. A list of his previous perceived unfriendly actions was included in the complaint.

I responded fairly robustly, I like to think, not that it was going to make any difference, and pointed out that the Ambassador was actually out of the country at the time. Were the twelve days to start from the present or from the time of his return? I was told that it was with immediate effect. I was also handed a *note verbale* in Arabic summarising all this. I went back to the Embassy and phoned Peter and the Office and then sent a detailed reporting telegram. Fortunately the Arabic in the note was formal and well within my ability to translate.

At the time nobody could recall another instance where an ambassador had been declared *persona non grata* on purely personal grounds as opposed to the usual political ones. This caused some thought to be applied in the FCO to the proper response. Early in the New Year, a telegram arrived giving the result of these deliberations. As the expulsion was personal to Peter Streams, it had been decided not to appoint a replacement Ambassador until at least the time when Peter would have left post. This would have been on his 60th birthday (at that time the age of compulsory retirement) in April 1995. Meanwhile I would take over as Chargé d'Affaires and draw the pay of a counsellor; one grade higher than my substantive grade and one grade lower than the ambassador's.

There are two occasions when an embassy is headed by a chargé d'affaires; when the accredited ambassador is out of the country, and when there is no ambassador accredited at the time. This can be because diplomatic relations are reduced for political reasons as a gesture of disapproval, or, more usually during an interregnum between the departure of one ambassador and the arrival of the next. These cases are normally for fairly brief periods and so for me to be placed in charge of the Embassy for some fifteen months was very unusual. Personally I like to feel it was quite encouraging, as it seemed to indicate that the Office considered I could do it, even though I had only just been promoted. However, there wasn't much practical alternative and I suspect there would have been a degree of finger crossing about the decision, although there is nothing suggesting this on my file.

I knew that my increased pay would be taken into account in calculating my pension as long as my retirement took place within three years of the end of the last twelve month period of enhanced pay. I had already been toying with the idea of taking early retirement after Khartoum, and a quick calculation now convinced me I should do so. It was just possible I might be promoted substantively to Grade 4 and maybe a small ambassadorship before my 60th birthday, but, in all honesty, it was pretty unlikely. If I didn't, my pension would be based on the lower, Grade 5 salary.

On the 12th of January 1994, after having come back to post to wind up his affairs, Peter Streams left on final departure and I started my acting promotion to Grade 4. The departing Ambassador was seen off by all available fellow Western ambassadors, but his German wife, Margaretta, and adult son, who had both come out after Christmas, stayed on for a few days to tie up personal loose ends.

There was a taste of things to come when Margaretta Streams formally asked me if I could agree to them staying in the Residence and use the official car for these extra days. Naturally, I agreed as it hadn't occurred to me that anything else would be the arrangement. But by this time I, and not her husband, represented my Queen and country in the Republic of Sudan. It was now 'my' Embassy and Residence and Val was the first British lady in the land.

As I have already indicated, among the things I inherited was the full time attention of the Royal Military Police CPT. To start with, I had no intention of moving into the Residence, but the CPT was geared to protect the Residence as well as the person of the head of post and, while I was living in another place, this meant they had to effectively be in two places at once. So after a short telegram from London pointing this out and asking me to make the relocation, we all upped sticks and moved from our house in Khartoum Two to the Residence.

This was a pain. Not only were there now five of us – Val and myself plus David and his two daughters, but we had only just finished unpacking on arrival at post. On top of this, Elsa, the local mongrel bitch we had inherited from the Heigels, had just produced a litter of pups, all of which had to come with us. So everything had to be repacked and the food we had started to buy and store in freezers in the DHM's house carefully and rapidly put into insulated containers, and the whole lot loaded onto a lorry and moved across town.

In spite of all this, and quite unsurprisingly, I liked being Head of Mission very much. We were now in a large Residence, with a private swimming pool, a large garden for the grandchildren, the Union Flag outside the front door and on the official Land Rover, a staff of servants, a team of personal bodyguards and the office just beyond the bottom of the garden.

I also mixed with other Western heads of mission, practically all ambassadors. The main exceptions were the Dutch and the Swiss. A Chargé d'Affaires also headed the Netherlands Embassy, but he had ambassadorial rank within his service. Apparently the Netherlands and Sudan had in the past had a disagreement which had resulted in the withdrawal of the ambassador, but oddly enough nobody seemed to remember any more what this was. The Swiss simply had a low level of local representation, with the accredited ambassador resident (I think) in Cairo.

The Head of the EC Delegation happened to be a Brit while I was Chargé and at the end of one meeting at his office, I felt I should point out that the Union Flag displayed with the other European flags in the centre of the table was upside down. This didn't faze him at all; in fact, to match this, he pointed out that the European flag was also upside down and not one of our colleagues had noticed. (For those who are interested, the twelve stars should have two points down and one up – like little men.) He then turned both flags the right way up.

A special bonus to all this for Val was that the

Residence was blessed with a baby grand piano. This hadn't been much used over the previous couple of years, so we had it tuned and Val found a highly proficient Dutch lady violinist who would come round and accompany her from time to time.

A number of ex-officio duties came with all this, as well. First, I was now on the informal committee of all European Community (as it then was) heads of mission in Khartoum and also had to take my turn, with other Western heads of mission and the Head of the local UN Office, at the joint chairing of the Western Aid committee. This last rotated and every few weeks the meeting was held in the Residence. Other venues were the local UN headquarters building, the European Community Delegation office, the US Ambassador's Residence and so on. I was also required to chair the committee of the local Cheshire Homes charity; something that had become the customary duty of the British Ambassador.

On being appointed Chargé, my instructions from London were to maintain relations with the Sudanese Government without moving closer to them or taking any initiatives. This was a fairly comfortable brief.

Although I was, of course, much busier than when I had been as DHM, some aspects of life were much easier. All my appointments were looked after by my PA, who produced a daily summary of my appointments for me on stiff blue, ambassadorial paper. The ambassadorial driver was there to take me on any official visits I made and, of course, I was accompanied everywhere by a rota of young men wearing blazers in order to conceal their guns. And 'everywhere' meant exactly that; not just official visits, but all private travel within the country, too. Val was with me on many of these visits and characteristically she effectively adopted the guards and simply treated our companion of the day as one of the family.

One of the benefits I really enjoyed was that at the end of an evening cocktail party, when we were ready to go, I would simply nod in the direction of my current minder and he would radio the driver so that the official Land Rover, flag flying, would pull up at the gate of wherever we were just as we walked out. When the CPT were withdrawn, but I was still Chargé, I had to carry my own radio and call up the driver myself – a real chore!

In spite of the presence of the CPT, the only time that there was even a remote risk of personal danger to us was one evening when we were going to a farewell party at the house of the British head of the EC Delegation on the other side of the Nile and had to cross a bridge to get there. There was a security alert and traffic was queuing to be checked at the other side of the bridge.

While we were stuck in the queue, there was clearly a small arms shot from in front of us, presumably from the checkpoint on the far side of the bridge. Our CPT minder asked if I wanted take evasive action. I have never been in a car taking evasive action in this sense, but I think it would have involved driving either forwards or in reverse on the pavement or the wrong side of the road at high speed. (Although local, our driver had been on the appropriate course in England.) I remarked that there had been only the one report, no further or answering fire and no reaction from the traffic in front of us and closer to the event. It seemed to me that, either a soldier had dropped his gun and it had gone off, or a warning shot had been fired. In either case, there appeared to be no obvious risk to us and I declined the offer. So we just went on, although we got to the party a bit late.

My new status was soon underlined by the visit to Khartoum of Bishop Samir Kafity from Jerusalem. As I knew him, I felt I should offer him some entertainment and invited him for lunch. As an Arab Christian he had decided to take the regime's part in their argument with the southern Christians, effectively putting support of his race before that of his religion.

During his visit he had made a statement drawing a parallel between the history of the Palestinians and the Sudanese, blaming all their respective ills on 'imperialism'. He made this point again during our meal and one of the other guests,

Norman Jackson, the head of the local Oxfam office, with his tongue firmly in his cheek, commented that this was "a bit hard on the Ottomans."

One of the things that came with moving into the residence was the care of a small herd of deer that was housed in the garden. Two or three of these animals had been presented to a previous ambassador and he had had a small pen made for them. Over the years they had bred and they now numbered six and I was permitted to claim a fodder allowance for them. They were very nervous animals and, as they had a limited area to run, were often breaking limbs when they reacted to a sudden movement in the garden outside their pen.

Whenever there was a function in the Residence garden, it was necessary to hang coverings over the mesh fence of the pen so that the animals could not see sudden movements: the sound didn't seem to bother them, presumably as it was generally continuous. Once or twice a month, when all was quiet, they were allowed out into the garden where they would run around on the grass. Presumably they enjoyed this; we certainly enjoyed watching them.

On one occasion when one of these animals managed to break its leg in two places, the vet we consulted advised that it was impracticable to set a leg with two breaks and recommended that the animal be put down. So it was duly slaughtered and the meat allocated to the local staff. David claimed the skin and, as far as I know, still has it to this day, although he had a problem curing it.

The Sudanese have a good sense of humour. One of my favourite examples of this was the evening when I was at a party in a Khartoum garden and, in light conversation with a Sudanese, I commented on the fact that that night there was a full moon with a halo round it. "In England," I said, "when we see that, we say that it's going to rain. Do you have any such saying here?" "Oh, yes," he said immediately, "we say the same thing." I was amazed; it was nowhere near the rainy season. "Yes," he continued, "we also say it's going to rain in England."

Early in my posting, and wearing my non-ambassadorial hat, so to speak, I also had one unique duty to perform as Consul General when on 12th March 1964, I married a British couple. This turned out to be the last ever British consular marriage to be performed in Sudan. We had a framed document from the FCO authorising 'The Consul' to perform these ceremonies, but as there was no consul in post, I agreed with the Vice Consul, that I, as Consul General, would do it. When we later sent the required return to London at the end of the year, we received a reprimand. Apparently the authority had been cancelled some time before, but nobody seemed to have told us. They kindly said that this one, last marriage ceremony would be allowed to stand, but the authority was now void and there wouldn't be any more.

And there was also a 'one off' duty as Chargé connected with the award of an OBE to the British Council Director, Adrian Thomas. He had been recommended for the honour before I arrived and the recommendation agreed. The award was to be on the New Year's Honours List for 1995. My task was to check with him that he was happy to accept, which he was, and then announce the award at a small ceremony at the Residence on New Year's Eve 1994.

While in Khartoum, during our first year we decided we would make a trip to Ethiopia where we had the opportunity to stay in a surplus bungalow in the British Embassy compound there. Having made the arrangements, we were very flattered to find that the Ambassador himself had insisted on meeting us on arrival. James Glaze had been First Secretary (Commercial) when I was in Abu Dhabi and generously felt that he should meet us personally at the airport. We certainly hadn't expected this and it was slightly embarrassing when he greeted us with the words "Hello, do you remember me?" and Val looked him straight in the eye said "No". Fortunately I was speaking to him at the same time and I don't think he noticed.

Staying in the Addis Ababa Embassy compound meant that my opposite number (as DHM) felt that he needed to offer some entertainment and also asked if I would mind paying a visit with him to the Ethiopian Foreign Ministry, who had some idea that I would give them indicators of the internal situation in Sudan. Not, I felt, a very ringing endorsement of their Ambassador in Khartoum.

We also managed to go out into the surrounding countryside to see some sites, including what was allegedly the first church in Ethiopia. This seemed to consist of a small cave open on two sides; more of a rock overhang, really. Because of its religious importance there was a monastery nearby, which had been established as a charitable centre with a hospice for those with severe physical problems. The residents of this, having heard that there were two Europeans in the area, decided to approach us for donations. The practical result of this intention was a flood of the deformed and lame hobbling and staggering over the hill, extending hands in supplication. It was reminiscent of a badly directed horror film and I'm afraid that we then re-entered our Mercedes taxi and fled - although we had left a donation in the bowl provided inside the church

We included in our tour of Addis Ababa a visit to the National Museum where we saw the bones of 'Lucy', the early hominid discovered in the country.

I hadn't realised how tiny she was compared with a modern human. We also visited the main cathedral. There, high above us on the inside of the dome, was a series of paintings, mainly of biblical scenes. I was rather taken aback, though, to see included amongst these a depiction of the triumphal entry into Addis Ababa of Orde Wingate when British forces liberated Ethiopia from the Italians and reinstalled Haile Selassie in 1941.

As part of my responsibilities, I occasionally had to visit Nairobi as that was where the southern Sudan rebels based themselves. I would work from the British High Commission and on one occasion, I was taken by one of the first secretaries to a meeting of the local EC representatives with a Kenyan minister on the subject of Kenyan relations with the Sudanese rebels. The meeting was in the ministry conference room round a long table and my companion and I were well down on one side.

The meeting was rather dragging on and I had an appointment with the southern Sudanese a little later, so it became clear to me that I would have to leave before the end. The Kenyan minister had been speaking about the necessity of keeping in touch with the southern representatives when I felt I had to move. I addressed the minister down the table and apologised, explaining I had to leave as I was due to meet the Sudanese, and assured him that I would pass on the sentiments we just discussing.

This clearly surprised a number of those present and rather strained protocol, I think, but produced two results. Rather to my surprise there was laughter round the table. Then Philip Mwanzia, the Kenyan Ambassador to Sudan, who I knew quite well, and who had been sitting out of sight to me next to the Minister, rose and came to speak to me. This gave me the chance to ask him to pass on my apologies again to his Minister. As we left the room, my companion from the High Commission commented to me that it was good to 'leave them laughing'.

There was no badminton game to be had in Khartoum, so our main form of exercise while in Khartoum was the 'Hash'. The Hash was an abbreviation for the Hash House Harriers, a cross-country running and drinking club which had originated among British expats in Malaya in the 1930s. The idea was to gather together at a starting point and follow a trail of scraps of paper set by the volunteers for the day. The trail included signs, false signs and other instructions. There were calls that were shouted as we ran. Usually this was simply 'on, on', but when we found a false trail, the cry was 'back, back' and we had to retrace our steps to the previous sign and follow a different path from there.

Over the months, we often ran over the same territory, and sometimes the locals, having worked out the cause and effect of these calls, would shout 'back, back' as we ran past resulting in some confusion on our part and merriment on theirs.

At the end of the run everyone returned to the starting point, and drove to an agreed house where we took part in what were basically silly games. In the original version in Malaya, this had involved drinking beer, but in Khartoum this was not possible, so we drank soft drinks. Although the runs took place in the late afternoon, the ambient temperature tended to be at least in the mid-thirties, and it was one of the requirements that everyone should take with them two or three litres of water. After a run of some 20 minutes to half an hour in that temperature most people required rehydration on this scale.

Towards the end of our time in Khartoum we also joined the 'Khartoum Crawlers'. This was a fairly small group that went out once a week and ran round a fixed route in the desert a little way outside Khartoum. It was a completely free choice affair, with the younger and fitter participants running for a good five kilometres. This was well beyond our ability, but there were various short cuts we could take to arrive back at the starting point. Also, if we could not run the whole distance, then we would walk fairly briskly. As with the Hash, it was necessary to take a sufficient amount of water to drink at the end of the run. This run tended to be later in the day than the Hash and therefore slightly cooler: but this was only relative, and the temperature would still be in the low thirties.

My first couple of years in Khartoum coincided with that of two world-famous (or maybe it should be world-infamous?) characters; Carlos the Jackal and Osama bin Laden. I never actually met either of them and, to be honest, was not even aware that Carlos had been there until the news of his capture eventually broke. Bin Laden, however, was already very well known locally for the reasons that have since made him so notorious. He was acknowledged to be one of the foremost 'Afghanis', that is those Arabs and other Muslims who had fought against the Soviets in Afghanistan in the 1980s. He was also known to have been disowned by his family in Saudi Arabia and to be very rich, with his money believed to have come from road engineering: his company was alleged to be involved in at least one major road construction project in Sudan. He had a villa and compound on the banks of the Nile just north of Khartoum where, it was rumoured, military training of volunteers took place.

Eventually, under US pressure, bin Laden was thrown out of Sudan in 1995, but while he was still there he was attracting considerable attention. In 1994 the French Ambassador spoke to me claiming the French had evidence that he had recently visited London on a Sudanese diplomatic passport, a claim I have noticed surfacing in the media from time to time since. As all British visas in Sudanese diplomatic passports anywhere in the world were only issued after reference to my Embassy, I ordered a check on all visas issued both by us and referred to us from other posts over the previous six months. We had a picture of the distinctive face of bin Laden from the local press for comparison with the photos submitted with the visa applications, so I was able to assure my French colleague that no such visa had been issued.

June 1994 marked the fifth anniversary of the revolution of 1989 and the Sudanese Government announced there would be a day of national celebration to which all diplomats would be invited. This caused some agitation in EC capitals as the first of January is the official Sudanese National Day and this other commemoration was likely to be an excuse for a military display, not something we wanted to be associated with. After discussions with our various capitals, it was decided that EC heads of mission could attend, but if there was a military aspect to the events, we were to walk out. All EC Embassies were supposed to have had the same instruction, so we were all theoretically singing from the same hymn sheet.

On the day, we all arrived at the parade area and went in to the stand allocated to us. It was reached by an internal staircase giving on to the top of the tiered seating area. We then walked down a terrace to our seats. A little way into the proceedings, it was clear that the celebrations were indeed of a military nature and President Bashir was driving towards us at the head of a convoy of army vehicles. After a quick consultation we decided to make our agreed protest exit. We left our seats and went back up the stand to the door through which we had entered, only to find that the Sudanese had clearly been told what was planned and had blocked the door with a pile of chairs and locked it for good measure.

We milled about, a bit stymied, until my bodyguard of the day told me that there was another way out. (Bodyguards check these things out as a matter of course.) So, we, the EC Diplomatic Corps in Sudan, followed him back down to the bottom of the seating area, clambered over a low brick wall onto the edge of the arena and walked round the stand and back to our cars parked behind. The other guests were slightly bemused. However two of us didn't make it with the main body. Maurizio, the diminutive Italian Ambassador, was stuck beside a large African diplomat and Claude, the French Ambassador, pointedly remained long enough for it to be noticed that he was not with us at this point and left after we were all out of the way.

Was it worth it? Probably not. We all (presumably) duly reported back that we had done as instructed, but apart from those immediately around us, I doubt whether anybody else noticed. The news item broadcast on Sudanese TV that evening was edited to show us all apparently avidly watching the procession and no mention was made of the walk out.

During my time as Chargé I made two visits to the south of the country, which was outside the control of the government in the capital. Before this, my first attempt to travel, in May 1994, was abortive. I had thought that to avoid too much argument with the regime, I would give them notice of what I was about to do. This was taken advantage of by the Sudanese to complain officially in London of my plans. Unfortunately at the time a new Under Secretary had taken over regional responsibility in the FCO and he was wary of my plans and instructed me not to proceed. This irked me and I argued with him in the exchange of three telegrams, pointing out that we were allowing the Sudanese to dictate our movements and that the US Ambassador had made just such a visit a couple of weeks before and the sky hadn't fallen in. This was a waste of effort and simply resulted in a forceful instruction not to proceed. The Department later quietly suggested that I had sent at least one telegram too many.

The first trip I did eventually make was later in the year from the 30th of July to the 6th of August. Direct travel was impossible because of government restrictions and the journey from Khartoum involved a scheduled Kenya Airways flight to Nairobi. I travelled overnight, being fed a Kenya Airways breakfast, before landing at Kenyata International

Airport. From there my journey was by a UN chartered former Soviet troop transport to the UN base at Lokichokio in northern Kenya.

Soviet soldiers clearly did not travel in comfort. Boarding was by clambering up the tail ramp and the seats were simple, uncomfortable, metal-framed canvas slings facing inwards along either side of the fuselage. Some cargo was placed on the floor down the middle of the aircraft, held in place with nets. For civilian use, though, there was an improvement on the stark military arrangement, as toilet facilities had been installed in the form of a sort of portaloo bolted to the floor in the centre of the aircraft.

As the windows in the fuselage were small and behind the passenger seats, this formed an irresistible focus of attention during the hour or so of the flight and also seemed to exert a strange physical attraction for some as it was in fairly constant use.

On arrival at Lokichokio I was placed in the care of a pleasant Canadian lady from the World Food Program (WFP). This UN agency was responsible for running the Operation Lifeline Sudan (OLS) food distribution scheme.

Although I had travelled overnight and not had any sleep to speak of, as soon as I got to the base, my lady guide asked if I wanted to go up and see a food drop. A big C130 Hercules of the Belgian Air Force was sitting on the runway, the final stages of loading food supplies having just been completed. It seemed to me to be a good idea and, in spite of my tiredness, I said I would indeed like to go. My minder went over to the crew, who didn't look over-enthusiastic. It was probably against all sorts of Belgian, NATO and international rules to carry civilians on the flight and heaven knows what my life insurance would have said, but, partly because my minder was an attractive woman, I expect, they said yes.

My suspicions about the reason for their agreement were strengthened when I was consigned to the depths of the hold, along with several tonnes of bagged food and a number of bored and sweaty Belgian airmen, while my female companion was ushered up to the flight deck some 12 feet above me. I was told I would be allowed to sit up there on the way back.

The food was delivered, not by parachute, but by free-fall and so was triple bagged. This, it was explained to me, ensured that well over 90% of the bags survived the fall. These bags were lashed to strong wooden pallets which allowed them to be transported easily as far as the hold of the plane. The drop was carefully calculated; the height was minimal and the speed was as slow as could be safely managed so the impact on the ground was as slight as possible. The pallets were sacrificed as they fell with the bags and the harness in the plane snapped the bands holding the bags to the pallets ensuring that the bags fell free.

The pallets also fell free, of course, and, being

made of good stout wood, usually survived and were highly prized. Much use was made of them and the furniture in many tukels and the doors and door frames, as well other parts of various structures, were to be seen sporting sundry excerpts of the WFP and OLS logos.

I noted that NATO and Warsaw Pact countries had a similar attitude towards military comfort as the seat I had in the Hercules was very like that in the ex-Soviet plane from Nairobi. I had been sitting uncomfortably on this webbing/steel frame seat for about half an hour when there was activity. The crew came to life and started checking the load. Webbing harnesses connecting the pallets to the plane were checked for tension; the bands securing the food bags to the pallets were inspected; the rollers on the floor were checked for a clear run of the pallets to the ramp at the back of the plane; and the load-master went to check the intercom with the pilot. I was motioned to move aft as well and then was fitted with a harness and hitched to a line which was securely tethered to the right hand rear bulkhead.

There were no windows in the fuselage and I could see nothing of the outside, but the motion of the plane suggested that we were on a more or less even keel, coming in over the drop zone. True the engine notes were varying, but that was no doubt explained by the fact that the plane was jockeying for height as it lined up with the ground target markings. Just then, though, the tail door hydraulics started to slowly drop the tailgate of the plane and the resulting view, which gradually expanded as the gap widened, contradicted this reassuring impression. Where I should have been looking at a portion of sky, I was looking at the ground. The scenery consisted of flat grassland with scattered clumps of smallish trees. This was fine: what was not so fine was that it all appeared to be rushing past a hundred feet below us at about 45 degrees to the horizontal. The plane was by no means on an even keel; it had made one pass over the site and was actually now banking steeply as it circled tightly for the approach to the actual drop. What I had assumed was gravity was actually centrifugal force.

My eyes and brain accepted the situation, but my stomach was not at all happy with this revelation and the Kenya Airways breakfast stirred. There was enough action going on, however, to divert attention from the immediacy of the contradiction of motion and visual signals. The load-master, on the intercom to the pilot, was holding up four, three, two and then one fingers to the crew. At the end of the countdown, all 12 tonnes of food, complete with their wooden pallets rolled smoothly off the end of the extended ramp and dropped, parachuteless, into the African countryside. The plane lurched upwards as the load left it, then immediately banked sharply round again to allow the crew to check the accuracy of the drop. The extra motion didn't help my personal comfort one bit.

The tail ramp remained open at this point. My minder had come down from the flight deck for the operation with her camera and was now also tethered to a bulkhead, but standing out on the ramp itself. She was gazing down. "Look", she said, excitedly, "Elephants! Down there."

I looked half-heartedly, but could see no wildlife and as the tail ramp was raised again into position, I unhitched myself and staggered back to my seat. I noted there was no offer to allow me to sit upstairs. This was just as well, as on the way back, I had to ask a crewman for the necessary waterproof container for the temporary reception of the Kenya Airways breakfast, which had now firmly decided that it wished to leave me. I sat for the return journey in embarrassed discomfort, clutching the container holding my erstwhile breakfast. When we got back to the camp at Lokichokio, I grabbed the chance of a short nap in my allocated tukel.

A tukel is the common traditional structure in the Horn of Africa, the building and the word is used in south Sudan, Ethiopia and northern Kenya and Somalia too, I think. There are various types, all circular and those I saw were about 12 feet in diameter and surrounded by a wattle and daub wall of about 5 feet in height and topped with a conical thatch adding another 5 feet at its point. This is a good size for a bedroom and, although most people need to stoop to get through the entrance door, inside it is high enough to seem quite airy. The lower, inner side of the thatch was lined with recycled woven plastic food sacks. This was to shield the sleeper from the various bugs that were attracted to the thatch and tended to fall through during the night. Overall, the structure is simple and effective, as you would expect of a building design with a long tradition.

In my accommodation on this occasion, there was only a little furniture; just a bed and a chair. Both were made from the wood of recycled food pallets previously dropped by the World Food Program. As I have commented, the legend 'WFP' was a recurring motif.

The next day there was to be a flight to the rebel occupied area of southern Sudan with an overnight stop. Our destination was, like so many other places there, flat and featureless, except for the odd river or old river bed meandering through the plain. The place was shown as a town on maps, in fact, it was considered a regional centre.

Reality was otherwise. From the air we could see it consisted of a number of disparate tukels, scattered about the countryside, but tending to accrete towards a centre, where there were the remains of brick-built structures. A medical centre was under construction. Nothing was higher than about 20 feet. Also in the centre and, presumably the reason for the settlement being where it was, was a well with a number of local inhabitants obtaining their daily supply of water. The airstrip, a levelled (mostly) area of ground cleared of vegetation by the passage of arriving and departing aircraft, was a few hundred yards away from the centre.

The pilot of our Cessna Caravan made a faultless landing on the level, but rough surface. After we had taxied back to the reception committee and swung sharply round to face back up the strip ready for take-off, the engine was switched off and unloading went ahead. The cargo consisted of basic supplies for the small expatriate compounds there. These essentials included Kenyan beer in crates, the empties being taken on board for return via Lokichokio.

Watching us alight were members of the reception committee; the "civilian" representative of the rebel group in command of the area at the time; the expatriate staff of the three or so NGOs based there; and a cluster of children and general bystanders. Six months later another group captured the place, burning it to ground in the process.

We were gathered into a Toyota pick-up, along with the supplies, and bounced off across the dirt track that was the main thoroughfare of the town to the UN compound. This had not been noticeable from the air as it was built in the local style; a group of tukels of various sizes, some run together to provide the main living quarters.

The arrangement of the camp was basic, but quite acceptable. Across from the sleeping tukels, which were grouped together on one side of the compound there were three showers and two toilets. These structures were not tukels, but cubicles formed of a wooden frame with corrugated iron sides on a cement base and were open to the sky. The showers themselves consisted of a canvass bag slung from a wooden beam over the middle of the cubicle. A simple tap operated by a short chain allowed the water to fall on the bather. The water bags had to be filled from above with buckets.

There was no water supply to the toilets, which were described as the 'VIP' type. This sounds very grand, but the acronym is extremely misleading. It does not indicate, as might be assumed, any great and unlikely luxury in the African fastnesses. In fact, it stands for 'Ventilated Improved Pit', which gives you more of the flavour, so to speak. All it actually means is that the hole provided is of a depth and design so that the arrangement does not smell too much and is too deep to attract insects, particularly mosquitoes. Apparently, they won't go beyond a certain distance from the open air.

The two toilet cubicles catered for the African and European traditions respectively. The first was an unadorned hole in a concrete slab over the pit, the other was blessed with the benefit of a raised concrete rim with a wooden batten to sit on. They were not labelled as for being for the use of any particular group, however, and there was evidence of some cross-cultural misunderstanding. In the seated toilet cubicle, the following request was written with a felt-tip pen in large, indignant letters on a piece of card pinned to the inside of door:

IF YOU MUST STAND ON THE SEAT,
PLEASE TAKE OFF YOUR SHOES FIRST

Our hosts in the UN compound were young volunteers from Canada and Australia. As dusk drew in, I was talking with one of the men who told me about an animal they often saw in the compound, which he thought must be a hedgehog, although he had never seen one before. They had none where he came from, but he was familiar with their appearance from books.

I assured him in what I'm afraid was a slightly condescending manner that I didn't think it could be a hedgehog. They lived in Europe and are temperate climate animals. They hibernate; how could they do that in a place like this? I would ask around when I got back to Khartoum about animals in this part of Sudan. My didactic flow was brought to a halt. A movement about ten feet away on the ground at the edge of the tukel in front of us caught my eye.

"There it is now", said my host. I looked down in surprise that turned to acute embarrassment. A small, but undeniable and definitely non-hibernating, hedgehog waddled urgently past in the African dusk, hugging the wall of the tukel.

I hastily revised my ruling on the geographical range of the genus Erinaceus and confirmed that yes, it was certainly a hedgehog. It was a bit smaller than the ones in England, though, I added as if this had anything to do with it. The hedgehog scurried on its way to our left, eventually hiding under some scrub bushes that grew in that corner of the compound. They were very nice about it and didn't laugh at me, at least not to my face.

Later that evening, we had a very acceptable meal, accompanied by a number of bottles of wine brought round from the next compound by the French doctors of *Medicins sans Frontieres*. (MSF). These also presumably had been brought as essential supplies on the flight from Kenya.

The hedgehog re-emerged during the evening and joined us at the foot of the table (or at the foot of one of the legs of the table, to be exact). It also dined well, crunching its way through a steady supply of lightly cooked moths and beetles which fell to the ground in front of it after flying into the hurricane lamp on the corner of the table above, the generator having been turned off for the night.

Before the evening meal, I had had a shower. The makeshift system worked well and I happily washed off the dust and sweat of the day. In the evening the shower water, which had been warmed by the day's heat, was pleasantly luke-warm. I had asked whether there was any problem with water supply as I didn't want to run the establishment short if I had another shower in the morning, although I didn't actually say that that was the reason for asking. "No problem", I was assured.

The following morning, I was up in good time and found that I had been joined during the night by a bat which was now, as the light increased, trying to find a dark corner. I managed to get a photo of it, hanging upside down in the approved manner after it came to rest. Although I slept quite well, considering that I usually have difficulty dropping off in a strange bed, the tukel was not very well ventilated and I felt the need for another shower, so I got up and went over to the shower cubicles before most of the camp was up.

As before, I positioned myself under the toggle-operated tap and pulled, expecting a refreshing stream of the tepid water. A douche of what felt like an icy stream took my breath away. The African night had allowed the water to cool considerably, probably helped by evaporation through the canvass skin of the bag. Anyway, having got this far, I was wet enough to continue and went on to soap myself cursorily. I then pulled the chain again, braced for another wakening splash. This time there was a problem of another nature. A feeble trickle of cold water reached the crown of my head. The water had run out. It was now clear that the water bags were topped up later in the morning.

A moment of introspection came over me. Here

I was, the Head of the British Embassy in the largest country in Africa, naked, wet and quite cold, standing on a cement slab in a structure made of ill-fitting corrugated iron sheets, open to the sky and with a door secured by a rusty bent nail. And all as part of my duties. Oh, so different from the endless round of cocktail parties that cartoonists portray diplomats enjoying.

In the end, I reached up and manoeuvred the canvass bag, squeezing the last drops of water out and made do, leaving the shower cubicle with a slightly slippery skin and a very soapy towel.

I had asked to see around the area, thinking in terms of social or developmental aspects. However, there was very little we hadn't already seen and our host took this as a request for a general tour and took us to the one tourist spot. This was a shrine about two or three miles away where a holy hermit had once lived.

Off we went in the one serviceable Toyota pick-up that was to spare. I had never before been in a place where there was simply no road (or track, that I could see) to where we were going. We simply drove out into Africa. The land, as I had seen from the air, was level, but that did not mean that it was smooth, and we lurched across tuffety grass, past tukels with small gardens around them and some stands of trees. I kept instinctively wondering when we were coming to the road, which, of course, was never. The area being flat, there were no obvious landmarks and I assumed that our guide was navigating by his memory of trees and huts.

After a short and uncomfortable time, we arrived in sight of a distinctive clump of vegetation surrounded by more agriculture than we had seen elsewhere in the area. In fact, the crops were so dense, that we agreed to leave the truck a distance from the trees and walk the rest of the way through a field of maize. There were still no convenient paths (or, at least, no obvious ones), and we literally pushed ahead through the field.

Our destination proved to be a small lake next to a hillock and surrounded by a few trees. The hillock had been masked by the trees from the distance. There was quite a community in the area and we were soon surrounded by the usual crowd of inquisitive, friendly children. One old man was visible in the distance and there were some women washing (clothes and themselves) in the lake. Also in the lake, but some distance away, were a couple of reptiles that didn't seem to bother anybody although they appeared to be over a metre in length. I later reckoned they were monitor lizards.

The hillock was a little distance from the lake. It was not clear to me whether it was natural or not. It was no more than 20 feet high and was bounded on the side near the lake by a thin sort of palisade of elephant tusks, planted with the points curving in towards the centre. I gathered from our guide that the hillock was a place of sacrifice of bulls, but I could not grasp why, or whether the practice still continued. I did understand him to say that the level of the ground had been increased because of the blood of the sacrifices. It was clearly quite old, as it was many years since elephants had ranged this far north.

Nearby, under the trees, was a small hut. It had a wooden door, but unlike the traditional tukels it was square in plan and was very low; no more than 5 feet high. We were told that this was the hermit's house. I asked when he had lived there and was told that it had been "hundreds of years ago".

Our guide gestured to a tall, thin old man in a worn greatcoat who was herding a small flock of goats and told us that he was the great great-grandson of the holy hermit. I asked if he was also holy. No, I was told, but he was respected by the people. Also, he was a sub-chief. We looked suitably impressed. I took it the old coat was a badge of status: it was certainly of very little use, and not much ornament.

The holy man's descendant came over and spoke to our guide/interpreter. We had not told him of our coming, so he had not made the proper reception for us. I asked that the sub-chief be told we were sorry he had no news of our coming. The next time we came we would send news first.

His goats were foraging more widely and tending to move off and he would have to go after them soon. I felt I should bring the conversation to an end and give him a chance to follow his goats without losing face, so I turned to the guide and asked him to make our excuses. This was translated and the old man mumbled what I took to be a valedictory, and wandered off after his goats.

After we got back in the afternoon, we heard that the local commander had returned from a regional conference and would be happy to see us. This would be the military commander of the local rebel militia. We went to a small brick-built building a little way from the centre of the settlement. I don't know its original purpose, but it was furnished with a desk at one end and chairs around the walls. There were not one, but six commanders present, the others being on their way back to their territories from the same conference. The local commander took precedence. The meeting was rather formal, but opened in a familiar way.

After the preliminary introductions were over, the commander wanted to know what we had brought for them. I explained that I was there to familiarise myself with the situation in the South. As for giving anything, the British Government was supplying aid to the South through the UN agencies such as the World Food Programme. Cue for my minder to chip in about the relief programme.

They were clearly not expecting a great deal and so were not that disappointed. But they had something for me. It had been agreed that in my honour, all the babies born on this day in the area would be named after me. Very flattering, I thought, but a bit tough on the girls.

To help run the place, the organisers had hired the services of a local woman and I had a very short chat with her before I left the camp. This was in pidgin Arabic as she knew no English, which should have given me some warning. Anyway, I told her I came from England. There was no response. In Europe, I explained. Still nothing; she had never heard of either place. At last I said I was from the north. "Oh", she said, "from Khartoum". I think this was the first time I had come across anybody who had never heard of England. And to think we had ruled the place for over half a century.

While we were on leave in August and September 1994, it was decided to withdraw the RMP bodyguards and they were gone when we came back. So, for the last seven months of my chargeship, we had the Residence to ourselves.

They had left, but their weapons lingered on and, although the (NATO standard) ammunition was transferred to the US Embassy who still had armed guards, the guns themselves had to be returned to the UK. Now some countries, I suppose, would simply stick them in the diplomatic bag and send them off, but this would be against international convention and we don't do that. So they had to be properly declared with all the paperwork in order.

It seemed to me that there was scope for mischief or embarrassment here, so I called on the Foreign Minister and formally advised him of the situation. During our meeting I also emphasised that we would both have to be careful about this. He looked slightly puzzled. The trade statistics, I pointed out, would show that Sudan was now exporting arms to the UK. He found this greatly amusing.

This should have been an end to any possible difficulties and it was as far as we were concerned, but apparently after the consignment left us there were problems. There were no direct flights to the UK from Sudan and so the guns were consigned to travel by Lufthansa via Frankfurt. On arrival in Frankfurt it was pointed out by the German authorities that no permit had been granted to import weapons from Sudan and the whole shipment was held up for several weeks. Very ironic.

I later made a second trip to the south from the 19th to the 23rd of November 1994 to accompany a visitor from the Overseas Development Administration (ODA). We travelled down to Lokichokio as before and overnighted at the camp there.

The following morning we left on the next plane doing a round of the area. On the way back to Lokichokio we first stopped briefly at a village to drop off a couple of the MSF doctors, but there was no time to do more than shake the hands and have a few words with the inevitable officials at the airstrip before we left again.

In addition to the usual empty beer bottles for return to Kenya, we were also taking with us an official from one of the local factions who had hitched a lift back to Lokichokio. Strictly this shouldn't have been allowed, and was to have unfortunate repercussions. We had one more visit to make, though. There was a food distribution due at the next stop and we should be able to see that in progress.

From the air, the land looked more interesting than the place of our last visit; we were further south now and coming to an area of hills on the Sudan/Kenya border. As we flew in I could see evidence of motorised use of tracks, with bridges over stream beds; the land undulated, and had some large rocks, but was mainly green and tree-strewn. The village we were approaching lay scattered around a large rocky outcrop. We landed on a larger airstrip than before, and there was much more activity obvious on the ground.

Leaving our unofficial hitch-hiker and Ian, our New Zealand pilot, on aboard, we got out of the plane. We could see two groups of several hundred people each sitting in the sun to one side of the airstrip. It was early afternoon and they had, I was told, been there for several hours. At the end of the

337

airstrip was a large pile of white food sacks which had been delivered that morning by cargo plane. The groups were being head counted before the food was to be shared out. They consisted mainly of women and children and were amazingly patient, both with the delay in obtaining their food allocation, and with the white strangers who were now walking among them taking close-up shots of small children and 'interesting' faces among the old women. I found this a distasteful obsession and took my snaps from a distance.

I asked one of the receiving officials why there were two groups. The one, he told me, was from the local area, the others were 'internally displaced' from elsewhere in the country. It seemed that the food allocation for the fixed population was calculated on a different basis from that for the displaced. In addition to that, there were more displaced coming into the area all the time, as we were to see for ourselves very shortly.

In due course, the ubiquitous Toyota pick-up arrived and we were taken off to see the area. As honoured visitors we were not allowed to sit with some decent elbowroom in the back, but all had to cram into the cab. We were taken to a Norwegian Church Aid medical project established there before the fighting. Although there were no Norwegian staff any longer, there were still some medical facilities, although in an uncertain condition.

As we rounded the hillock which seemed to lie

in the centre of the sprawling village, there, on one side, were the ruins of a brick building. That had been the church, I was told, but nobody had bothered to renovate it. There seemed to be armed men everywhere, a goatherd was even keeping watch over his flock while holding a Kalashnikov. We passed a line of roofless brick buildings on the right; these had been part of the Norwegian medical establishment.

We drove on to a spot outside the village, or rather a point where the village appeared to have petered out and parked under a tree. An irregular, but steady stream of armed men and boys, many in bits of uniform, but for the most part barefoot, trudged in line from the bush in front of us towards the centre of the settlement. They were not so much accompanied by, as walking in the same general direction as, a number of women and children and one or two old men. I asked our driver who they were and he told me they were coming from a place where there had been a battle some three months previously. In other words, they had been walking for three months.

I thought about it. From the purely logistical point of view, that was probably rather a long time for them to walk the more than hundred miles, but they were unlikely to have had an easy passage and would almost certainly have had to make detours. Another aspect struck me; there were comparatively very few women. That, it was explained to me, was because the women allowed the men to take most of the food, so not all the women would make it to the end of the journey. The men had to be fit and able to protect the group in order for the maximum number to survive.

In front of us was another semi-ruined building, but this one was in use. This, we were told, was the area clinic. We were met by the senior person present. He was local man, a paramedic and his wearing of a white coat indicated his status, although I noticed he had no shoes. He was clearly dedicated, operating in, what would be regarded in other places as, impossible circumstances. He administered not only pills and treatment for ailments such as the ulcer eating through to the bone of a man that we saw, but also (presumably) the minor surgery that had resulted in the amputation of the toe of an old man in the clinic. I say presumably as there was no mention of any visiting doctor, but the toe had certainly gone.

We were taken into the building, where there were a number of sick men (I remember no women), some of whom were walking, but many were lying on the concrete floor. One was motionless. I asked what was wrong with him. The medic was consulted and the pidgin Arabic reply included a word I knew - 'mawt'. The patient was dead. It had only recently happened; we were hastily assured he would soon be moved outside.

I wondered where they buried the dead and was

told that burial was not possible and the bodies were left outside. I looked out. There was an open area behind the clinic before the African scrub started about 100 yards away. Off to the left was the track into the village along which I could see the long line of the displaced still passing on their way to the village. I felt the explanation given lacked something, and asked what happened to the bodies. "The wild animals take them in the night" was the reply.

The fact that these people were unaffected by the missionary activities of the Norwegians many years before, to the extent of not bothering to bury dead bodies, paled somewhat beside the revelation that there was still enough wildlife in the area presumably to make it very dangerous to go out too far. All our awareness had been of the human dangers posed by the rebel groups and the possible danger of an air accident. This realisation that we were in a very basic part of the world was unexpected. However, the human danger remained the most urgent as we were to be reminded.

Word now came to us that the local military commander would see us at his headquarters. Apart from the fact that we were quite keen to see him, it was probably an invitation that we could not refuse. The commander was in his compound in the village. We could have walked the short distance, but protocol and image suggested that we should arrive in a vehicle. So back to the squash into the cab of the truck. There was also a message that there had been some sort of trouble with our hitch-hiker on the plane, but the details were unclear and anyway that would have to wait.

The truck lurched back towards the centre of the village, stopping at a traditional African compound, which consisted of a roughly woven fence of vegetation round a group of tukels. There were a number of armed and uniformed men around the entrance. These were not like the ones we had seen coming in from the bush; they all had complete uniforms, including boots, and the look of bullies and were apparently suspicious of us.

We went into the compound. The commander was seated to the right of the entrance on a chair flanked by armed men - the traditional position of an African leader formally receiving visitors. We were also offered chairs, which we took, after shaking hands all round. The commander was called Taban Deng and spoke perfect standard English; he must have been educated in Britain. I see he later became a Vice President of South Sudan. The conversation was pretty inane and I can remember hardly any of it and after a while we took our leave.

The hitch-hiker whom we had left in the plane was now in the back of the Toyota pick-up which had been waiting outside. He looked very sorry for himself. He had a swollen mouth, a large, pink sticking plaster on his left elbow and, when we all got out at the airstrip, we could see that he now walked with a limp. Rather pointedly, nobody asked what had happened.

The drive back to the airstrip was a little tense. When we got there, I noticed that Ian had fitted his captain's four gilt bars to the epaulettes of his pilot's bush shirt. I asked him why he had done this. "Sometimes it's necessary for these things to go on", he commented rather cryptically. The food distribution still had not started and the women and children continued to sit in the sun, waiting. We took no pictures this time.

Our leaving was not prolonged; we said good-bye to the accompanying local group and I, for one, was very relieved when we were in the air again. As we turned for Lokichokio, I asked our battered companion what had happened, but he was uncommunicative.

Later, when we had got back I pieced together the story. After we left the airstrip, the hitch-hiker had foolishly got out of the plane and was recognised by a member of an opposing rebel group. He had got back into the plane as a sort of sanctuary, but although Ian had objected and tried to protect him, the guns of the local security men were an overwhelming argument. They had taken him away and interrogated him (in other words, beaten him up), but apparently without checking with the commander. Taban Deng had realised that taking a man by force from a UN plane and beating him up while there were visitors around would be poor PR for his cause. So he had arranged for us to be delayed by inviting us to visit him, while the unfortunate man was patched up and put in our truck. I say unfortunate, but if he hadn't been travelling in a UN plane, I'm pretty sure it would have been much worse for him.

Our pilot, Ian's, part in this was unhappy; not only had he been unable to save the man from being taken, but he was at fault for having him on the plane in the first place. The OLS rules were very strict - no lifts to unmanifested passengers. The reasons for this rule were now only too clear, although the benefit to a passenger of a half-hour plane flight compared to a week's hike often caused the pilots to turn a blind eye to it.

We visited a number of other places in the south, mostly only for a few hours. I found that whenever we were in a community, the small children tended to come over and hold our hands as we walked about. The females of the party were always very taken with this habit. I asked about it and was told that as all the doctors the locals saw were white, it was generally assumed that all whites had medical ability and the children took this further to the extent of believing that touching a white person ensured health. I have never been quite sure whether I am happy with this.

One of the recurring WFP projects in Sudan was the provision of "tools and seeds" to the South to allow the people there to grow their own food rather than have it provided. This was an extension of the old adage of give a man a fish and feed him for a day, but give him a fishing line and feed him for life. However this always assumes that the recipients are moral and honest people who would not dream of manipulating the system for their own ends. The two parts of this particular scheme were, of course, a supply of millet seed and traditional hoes, which had metal heads and wooden handles.

On my two trips to the south, I had noticed a number of places where the metal heads of the hoes were lying around on the ground in the middle of villages, apparently discarded. The wooden hafts had obviously been used for something else and, although hopefully the seeds had been planted and not eaten, no thought had been given to retaining the metal part of the hoe for future use. It was rightly assumed that more tools would be provided in the fullness of time. I found this particularly interesting as metal was not widely available in the area and no attempt had been made to use the hoe head for any other purpose. I assume that smithing was beyond the local technical ability.

There were a couple of other instances of money being provided by the well-meaning not being used to its best advantage. First there was the group of American Christians, who were determined to fight against slavery in the Sudan.

This slavery freedom project had identified an area between the north and south where there was slave trading, northerners habitually raiding their southern neighbours and capturing them. A slave trader was approached by the Americans in order to free those southerners that he held. He announced that the price was $50 a head and, having collected a considerable amount from the good folks at home, the visitors were able to pay this and the slaves from the south were duly freed.

Following this, two things happened. First, the Americans returned home rejoicing and full of tales of their good deeds. And second, the slave trader having made an extremely good sale, proceeded to replenish his stocks in the usual way by raiding the southerners – possibly the same individuals who had been briefly freed. So, at the end of the affair, money had been transferred from America to the slave trade, the Americans felt good, the slave trader felt rich and the southerners were no better off.

On another occasion, a Rotary club in Canada had been impressed by tales from one of their number, who had visited Khartoum, of the need and suffering of the displaced southerners living in camps around the capital. They had collected a considerable amount of money in order to buy and ship to Sudan a container of clothing and gifts for these people. At the time, I was a member of the Khartoum Rotary Club and the container was delivered to our care. So I was present when it was opened and found to contain such well-intentioned, but slightly useless items such as knitted winter woollies and cans of iced tea. The cost of transporting the container from Canada to Sudan had been C$5,000 and presumably the contents had cost considerably more. It was difficult for the Khartoum Rotarians to try and explain to their Canadian brothers that the money would have been much more use if it had been sent to Sudan and spent there.

We were delighted when Alun and Stephanie were able to come out for Christmas 1994. We were still in the Residence and, as the bodyguards had left, there were bedrooms for all. So on Christmas Day that year, the whole family was together, including the two grandchildren. Val was in her element. It turned out to be the last time (to date) that the family was to be all together at Christmas.

In mid-March 1995, Val was persuaded to play the piano for 'The Dream Maker', a production by the local international Unity School. She was duly rewarded with a fulsome letter from the teacher in charge and a huge card signed by all the children taking part. It was rather endearingly addressed to 'Mrs Val'.

There had been discussion in London about what to do about British diplomatic representation in

Sudan in the longer term in the wake of the expulsion of Peter Streams. Various possibilities were considered, including closing the Embassy completely, leaving it without an ambassador, downgrading the post of ambassador or replacing Peter Streams as originally scheduled. Leaving the place without an ambassador would have meant my staying on as chargé d'affaires for the rest of my time, while downgrading the ambassador's post might (just) have given me the chance of filling that position on promotion. In the event, it was decided that there would be a return to the *status quo ante* on the date Peter Streams would have left; i.e. his 60th birthday and, in due course that Alan Goulty, currently DHM in Cairo would take over.

As soon as we knew this, but before it was announced, Val and I took the opportunity to go down to Cairo in December 1994 to introduce ourselves. Or, rather, reintroduce ourselves, as we had known Alan at MECAS when he had been married to his first wife. The chance arose for me to have my fare paid as I put myself down as the casual courier for the diplomatic bag. Val's fare I paid for, of course. During a meal with Alan and Lilian at their home in Cairo I took the opportunity to mention that I had decided to take early retirement at the end of my posting. This produced a response that should have alerted me to dangers ahead. Alan's immediate, and, as far as I recall, only, comment was to the effect that this meant I would be immune

348

to any pressure over my career prospects.

Of course, the reinstatement of relations at ambassadorial level meant that we had to reverse the transfer process from the ambassadorial Residence to my original house in Khartoum Two. The extended family, all our personal possessions, the food in the freezers and the dog had to be moved back. And this time there were no helpful RMP bodyguards to assist, as there had been in January 1994. At least there were no puppies this time.

On the 23rd of March 1995, after attending the Pakistan National Day reception, I went to the airport with the Management Officer to formally greet the new Ambassador and his wife. I had discussed with him the level of representation from the Embassy he would like at the airport on his arrival. The new French Ambassador had arrived shortly before and on that occasion, my French opposite number had instructed the whole of his embassy staff to attend. Alan Goulty did not want this level of attendance; as long as we weren't outnumbered by the official Sudanese delegation, that would be fine. The official Sudanese delegation consisted of just the Head of Protocol from the Foreign Ministry, so I decided there would be just the two of us. I rather think Alan had expected more Sudanese.

In the first week of September 1995, the Archbishop of Canterbury, Dr. Carey and his wife paid their much-delayed visit to Khartoum. Since the events that led to the expulsion of Peter Streams, the local Anglican community had refurbished their guest-house and the Archbishop stayed there. That argument having gone away, there was no objection to the Ambassador giving a reception in the Residence garden in the Archbishop's honour. Neither of the Careys seemed to remember Val and me from Jerusalem and I saw little point in reminding them.

In September I had a fairly basic performance report covering my fifteen months in charge of the Embassy. I had had no reporting officer during this period, so it was compiled in London by the political department in consultation with various other departments. They were generous and awarded me a 'Box 1', the top grading. As I subsequently saw on my file, there was also discussion about whether I should be 'put up' for an OBE. However, this was felt to be '*de trop*' in view of the subsistence pay I had been getting, and it was decided to wait and see what the new ambassador thought.

These thoughts were made clear in December when, based on his experience of me over the previous eight months, the Ambassador awarded me a 'Box 5', the bottom grading. Or, as he generously reconsidered, a 'Box 4' because of my family circumstances. In his written comment he alleged that my continued presence was "a brake on the efficiency and productivity of the mission" and, in a later letter about staffing, in speaking about me, he wrote "So he will have to go".

But I didn't. There was discussion about this situation in London, but nothing of substance came of it. In contrast, though, there were remarks recorded in a minute to the effect that a number of the negative comments in the report were "not supported by the Department's views" and that the criticisms aimed at me "appeared to be unjustified."

The letter which was sent to the Ambassador in response to this report simply pointed out that there was an inspection coming up, which would look at the staffing levels of the Embassy and that to take any action before the subsequent report would not be wise. Of course, after the inspection report, my departure time would be so close as to make any change before that pointless.

Before this, and in anticipation of a different outcome, the Ambassador's wife was putting out the word in Khartoum society that I was to be transferred before Christmas 1995. I contradicted this, at that point anonymous, allegation at a Rotary lunch and announced very firmly that I was leaving in January 1997, which is exactly what I did.

Well before this, in the summer of 1995, while we were on leave in the UK, the Ambassador had seen fit to sack Val from the part-time secretarial job she had done in the Embassy since our arrival. He informed her of this by letter to our UK address, and

351

later resisted claims for compensation for lack of notice, until she wrote to the Office complaining and he was told to pay up. 'Pay her off' he wrote on the letter from London giving this decision when he passed it to the Management Officer.

Late in 1995 we were informed that the 'Fantasea II' had been intercepted off the Sudanese coast and taken to Port Sudan. This luxury dive vessel was either operating out of, or based in, Eilat in Israel and had strayed into Sudanese waters. I suspect it habitually did this, but had the bad luck to have been spotted this time. There were British and Commonwealth citizens on board, and they were being detained, so, in view of my 'Israeli connection' and, as the Vice Consul was away, the Ambassador decided that, as Consul General, I should go down and arrange their release. There was no scheduled commercial flight at the time, so we chartered a small UN plane for a day trip. Our senior local staff member claimed to have contacts in Port Sudan whom he would advise of my impending arrival.

However, as in Syria when paying visits outside the capital, when I did arrive, it was clear that whatever message he may have sent, it hadn't reached the authorities at the airport. The plane landed at the Port Sudan International Airport and parked a short distance from the control tower. It was not a busy airport and nothing else was moving as I disembarked in the hot Red Sea sun and walked

352

across the scorching tarmac to the airport buildings.

I went in and eventually found an official who noted my story and took me into the VIP lounge. Very nice, except that it was full of VIPs. In chairs round the room were a dozen or more senior Sudanese military officers, both army and navy. I made a circuit of the room, shaking hands and explaining who I was and why I was there. I don't know whether they were coming or going, but they were still there when I left about a quarter of an hour later after some small talk.

My departure from the airport was thanks to the arrival of an army colonel who had clearly been dispatched from Port Sudan town, a little way along the coast. Whether or not he had previously known I was coming, by the time I met him he seemed to have been briefed on the reason for my visit and drove me back to town.

This was one of the more frightening experiences of my life. The colonel was accompanied by a private, who, I assumed, was his batman and their transport was, inevitably, a Toyota pick-up truck. The batman was banished to the back, I got in the passenger seat and the colonel drove. To say his driving was furious is not to convey the sensation at all. He simply put his foot down as far as it would go and pointed the vehicle down the road towards Port Sudan.

The road was fairly quiet and mercifully straight, but worryingly potholed. In fact it ran alongside the coast and it must have been a pleasant drive in more relaxed circumstances. On this occasion, however, my circumstances were not relaxed. The truck was not new; it had no safety belts and the seats were smooth plastic. The jolting of the potholes caused me to slide about and I wedged myself in my seat as best I could with my feet pressed hard against the floor and my hand grasping the door grab handle. I tried to look as composed as I could while the truck bucked and bounced along at breakneck speed. The batman, poor fellow, was even worse off, standing up in the back and hanging on for dear life.

Eventually, we reached the town and had to slow down. I was deposited at an hotel while the colonel went off to make arrangements for my reception by the port authorities A while later I was taken to see the Port Manager who had with him the captain of the boat and another westerner, who must have been the tour manager or something similar. The Port Manager expanded on the seriousness of the transgression committed by the good ship Fantasea II and, after making his importance manifest for a time, pronounced that the whole thing could be settled for a fine of $5,000.

This was deemed acceptable and we all went off to the harbour to see and visit the ship itself. The fine was taken out of the ship's safe in cash and handed over, we all had a cold drink and that was that. I had the impression that there had probably been some tension before I arrived and, although, while the Sudanese were out of the way, I asked if there was anything that anybody wanted tell me, nothing was said.

Later I was driven back to the airport (I don't specifically recall this trip, so presumably the driving was unmemorable), got back in the UN plane and was back in Khartoum in time for the weekly session at the Embassy social club, The Pickwick Club, in the late afternoon. By the time I got back, the Fantasea II had already sailed and radioed a report of its release. This had been passed back to the Embassy from London along with a report, based on radio monitoring, that the Sudanese had probably been impressed by the fact that I had been dispatched to deal with the matter and this had helped things along. Ah, the 'Spy School' again.

When I duly reported my side of the events to Consular Department in London, I suggested that Mr Rosenstein, the owner of the boat, should be charged the $3,000 it had cost the Embassy to hire the plane in order to obtain the release of his boat. This idea was dismissed out of hand.

In 1996 I was instructed to get out a bit more and make a couple of presentations of aid in Wau and Dongola. Wau is some way to the south-west of Khartoum and now lies in the South Sudan, although at that time it was held by Sudanese government forces. There was a railway link, but trains ran only once or twice a year and the normal method of getting there was by air.

I flew in a scheduled flight which ran a former Soviet transport plane. This was smaller than the one I had flown in from Nairobi to Lokichokio and only took a few passengers as well as quite bit of cargo. I was honoured with the only first class seat, which seemed to have been originally the navigator's as it was right behind the flight deck. It had a most complex web belt, which was no doubt very safe, but which I couldn't fathom. It also had its own window - a Perspex bubble into the side of the aircraft which allowed me to look up, down and fore or aft.

Once more, unfortunately, word of my visit did not seem to have arrived before me. Nevertheless, it was insisted that I be taken to meet the local Governor. Doubly unfortunately, this gentleman was at the time presenting awards to the current batch of graduates of the Sudan prison service. I was ushered into the hall where this ceremony was taking place and had to sit on the dais beside the Governor while the process was completed.

Courteously, the Governor, after we had finished our business, insisted on presenting me with a local walking stick as a present. This was carved from wood and had an interesting motif of a fish swallowing its own tail worked into the handle. Later at the airport, after I had performed the handover formalities and as I was about to depart, my escort for the day felt he should also offer me a gift and insisted on presenting me with another of these walking sticks. I don't know what I was supposed to do with two of them, but I still have them both.

My visit to Dongola was different. Dongola is on the Nile north from Khartoum and was on the regular Sudan Airways route to Saudi Arabia, so this time I travelled in an Airbus. Much more comfortable and real first class, too. A pity that they forgot to serve the obligatory coffee until the plane was in the process of landing, though.

This time, the message about my arrival had got through and I was welcomed at the foot of the aircraft steps and taken to meet the local Governor, who was not at all as welcoming as his counterpart in Wau. In spite of the fact that I was there to formally hand over some hospital equipment, he treated me with considerable suspicion bordering on hostility. He was the only person to act like this, though. The others I met were all typically welcoming.

I was then taken to meet the head of one of the prominent local families, who lived on the other side of the river. Today there is a four-lane highway carried on a nice new bridge. At that time, there was an overworked and rather ancient ferry to get me to the other side. While on this, I was interviewed for Sudanese television, but I never saw the item broadcast.

When we got to the other bank we were transported by the inevitable Toyota pick-up. The whole area was desert, of course and I was very interested in the driving technique used to get through the soft sand. Normally in sand and snow, the trick was to keep the vehicle moving. However once when it got stuck, the technique was not to engage four-wheel drive, which was available, but to remain in rear wheel drive while rapidly turning the steering wheel alternatively left and right. I don't know how, but it worked.

On my departure, again it was necessary that I be presented with a gift. This time it was a bag of sorghum, which is a staple food crop in the area. However it was no use to me and on return to Khartoum, I gave it to the Embassy driver.

In July 1996 we had a post inspection. As DHM, it fell to me to co-ordinate the reports from the various parts of the Embassy. On the whole, it went well, even if one of the recommendations was that the DHM post should be downgraded further. It had been Grade 4, then brought down to 5 and was now to be further lowered to 6. But this didn't bother me as I was off in few months anyway.

One point I recall from the report was that concern was being expressed in London about morale at post and two of the questions all staff had to answer were; who did they regard as responsible for maintaining morale at post, and how happy were they with the situation. The answers were anonymous. One person said the Ambassador was responsible, one the Management Officer and one said everybody. I assume the Ambassador and Management Officer 'voted' for themselves. Everybody else said it was the DHM, i.e. me. And the satisfaction score was 80 percent. So I saw that as a pat on the back.

In August 1996, I was to make another visit, this time to Juba, the capital of the south of Sudan. Although Juba was government-controlled, there was no commercial flight between there and Khartoum, as this would cross the area being contested on the ground, so I arranged to be taken down on an ICRC (Red Cross) flight which went about once a week. I arrived at the domestic section of Khartoum Airport, found the man with the Red Cross passenger manifest, on which I saw my name had been written in at the bottom in Arabic and reported my presence.

I then sat and waited. And waited. And waited. Eventually, I went over to the security departure desk and asked when the Red Cross flight would be boarding. I was told I should sit and wait. There was no doubt that everybody knew I was there; not only had I checked in as far as possible, but I was, for the whole of my time there, the only white face in the place, so I could hardly have been overlooked. In the end somebody kindly told me the Red Cross flight had left. So I went back to the Embassy.

There was never any satisfactory explanation about this. A Red Cross official I later spoke to said they thought that I had been busy at work because of the hijacking of a Sudanese Airways plane to London which happened that day. But, in retrospect, it seems to me that the Sudanese security for some reason did not want me to travel to Juba at that time and not allowing me to catch the flight was the best way of ensuring that. They did, after all, regard me as an accomplished spy.

We had three breaks during my last year in Khartoum: in March/April, August and November. In March Val went home over two weeks in advance of me to be with her father who had been going steadily downhill for a number of months. I followed on the 28th of March, but on the 17th of April, the day before we were due to return to post, he died in the night. Although this came as no great surprise, the timing was a bit awkward. We managed to cancel all our travel plans and delayed our return to Khartoum for a week in order to make the funeral arrangements. We eventually got back to Khartoum on the 24th of April, a delay about which the Ambassador expressed some irritation; I promised him it wouldn't happen again.

In August, while Bobby was out on holiday we went to Kenya for a week's safari trip arranged through a travel agent in Khartoum. We had a good week, with our own allocated vehicle and driver, and managed to include a hot air balloon trip, as well as visits to two game parks, where we saw pretty well the whole range of African wildlife.

Nairobi is pretty well on the equator and Khartoum was very hot at that time, but in Kenya, it was cooler than we had expected. In fact, both Val and Bobby bought pullovers when we arrived in Nairobi. The Asian shop we patronised was almost exactly the same as those I remembered from Kampala all those years earlier, with the owner or family member representing him, sitting at the cash desk near the door and the lesser jobs being done by African staff.

Both pullovers were of dark blue wool, with cloth reinforcements at elbow and shoulder, very similar to the style worn by the local police. So similar, in fact that Val was actually asked by a local person if she was in the Kenya Police. This struck me as being rather fanciful, as I don't how long it had been since that body had employed a middle-aged white woman in their uniformed branch, if ever.

The trip back home in November had no specific purpose, but, as I was entitled to one last journey at public expense, we took it.

Bobby was with us for our last Christmas in Khartoum and we invited round a number of friends.

Among them was my opposite number from the Russian Embassy who was a Muslim Cossack. He seemed to enjoy himself and entertained us after lunch with the singing of the Russian song that we know as 'Midnight in Moscow'. It was a pleasant and relaxed affair, which was only slightly marred, if that is the correct word, by my inability to explain the symbolism of the blazing Christmas pudding. This was quite embarrassing, as the whole purpose of inviting my Russian friend was to show him how a traditional British Christmas dinner was presented.

Before we left post finally on 12th of January, 1997, we had a number of the usual farewell parties, but none from my colleagues in the Embassy, except for a small reception given by the Ambassador, which lumped together the presentation of an MBE to Oxfam's Norman Jackson and a welcome for my successor with my own farewell.

Selling the car this time was comparatively easy. Our merchant friend, Zuhair Sa'eed, was keen to have it and I was satisfied with the price, which was a few million Sudanese pounds, but represented only a small profit over the purchase price for us.

Our departure from this, our final, post was lower key than any other in our career and we were not seen off at the airport apart from the local Embassy 'fixer' who always oversaw these matters. Even though Sa'eed Sa'aad, the Head of Protocol in the Sudanese Foreign Ministry, with whom I got on very well, had said he might be there, he wasn't; I would guess this was under instruction from his masters. But I did make the point of going through the VIP lounge one last time.

A few days after returning to England, I made a last visit to the FCO as a career diplomat. I had a final debriefing meeting with my grade officer, at which I signed off from the Official Secrets Act. This had the effect of binding me to the commitment I had made on joining Government service in 1962 to keep any secrets I may have been privy to and informing me that I would not be entrusted with any more of them.

I formally left Her Majesty's Diplomatic Service on the 23rd of January 1997 and duly received the usual 'thank you letter' from the Office.

And now I am in the process of what I hope to be a long and restful retirement – after a fairly long and very interesting career.

Printed in Poland
by Amazon Fulfillment
Poland Sp. z o.o., Wrocław